MW00477142

# SCHLOSS IN
# BADEN-WÜRTTEMBERG

## THE FASCINATING ROYAL
## HISTORY OF GERMAN CASTLES

### SUSAN SYMONS

Published by Roseland Books
The Old Rectory, St Just-in-Roseland, Truro, Cornwall, TR2 5JD
www.susansymons.com

Copyright ©2019 Susan Symons

The moral right of Susan Symons to be identified as the author of this
work has been asserted in accordance with the Copyright, Designs,
and Patents Act 1988.

All rights reserved. No part of this publication may be reproduced,
stored in a retrieval system, or transmitted in any form or by any
means electronic, mechanical, photocopying, recording, or otherwise,
without the prior permission of the publishers.

ISBN: 978-0-9928014-9-6

To my dear niece Jo, for her bravery and fighting spirit.
www.bebrave-bebald.com

# CONTENTS

# 1

# INTRODUCTION

The federal state of Baden-Württemberg is the most fascinating part of Germany for royal history I have visited so far. I think of it as the land of vanished kingdoms. In the middle-ages, the area was part of the vast duchy of Swabia ruled by the important Hohenstaufen (or Staufer) family that provided Holy Roman emperors and German kings (see Hohenstaufen and Kloster Lorch in chapter 4). But after the execution of the last Hohenstaufen duke in 1268, the duchy of Swabia collapsed and over time its territory shattered into many small pieces. On the eve of the French Revolution, what is now the federal state of Baden-Württemberg in south-west Germany was made-up of dozens of royal duchies and sovereign territories as members of the Holy Roman Empire. Twenty years later, after Napoleon had cut a swathe through these small German courts, there were just four.

Napoleon had no time for the Holy Roman Empire. In place of the patchwork of small states in south-west Germany, the French emperor created the two large client or vassal states of Württemberg and Baden as a buffer between France and Austria. (The same process took place in south-east Germany to create the kingdom of Bavaria – see *Schloss in Bavaria*.) The Hohenzollern principalities in south-west Germany also survived Napoleon's cull due to a close personal relationship between a runaway Hohenzollern princess and Empress Josephine (see Sigmaringen in chapter 5). The royal states swept away by Napoleon had long and riveting histories – the Palatinate, Hohenlohe, a host of little territories around Lake Constance ... Those that survived saw an increase in territory and an elevation in rank – Württemberg became a kingdom and Baden a grand duchy. Their alliance with France was cemented by marriage into Napoleon's family. Enforced conscription meant there was a worse price to pay. More than twenty thousand men from Württemberg and Baden marched to Moscow with Napoleon's army – only a few hundred came back.

Schloss is the German word for castle or palace and the plural is schlösser. The thrilling royal history and vanished kingdoms of southwest Germany have left behind a cornucopia of beautiful schlösser. Schloss in Baden-Württemberg visits twenty-five castles and palaces in this federal state and tells the colourful stories of the historical royal families connected with them. Seeing the places where events happened adds a new dimension to history and helps bring it to life; knowing about the personalities and their stories always adds to the enjoyment of visiting a historic site. As I stood on the lake shore at Schloss Monrepos at Ludwigsburg near Stuttgart (see Monrepos in chapter 4), I could imagine the excitement of the state visit of Tsar Alexander I here in 1814. To entertain the tsar, King Friedrich of Württemberg had the back wall of the schloss opera house taken down so the audience could watch hundreds of Württemberg soldiers taking part in the opera battle scene.

A hand-drawn map of the federal state of Baden-Württemberg in south-west Germany is included at appendix A at the back of this book, showing some of the main cities and the approximate location of the twenty-five schlösser we visit. The state only came into existence in 1952 on the merger of what were, before World War I, the kingdom of Württemberg with its capital in Stuttgart, the grand duchy of Baden with its capital in Karlsruhe, and the Prussian province of Hohenzollern in the Swabian mountains. Some local people told me they still identify more with the pre-merged territories than with the present-day state. To the south, Baden-Württemberg is bordered by Switzerland and Lake Constance; to the west, by the Black Forest and France across the river Rhine. To the east it shares a long boundary with Bavaria and has much of the same topography. A refrain I heard many times was 'Baden-Württemberg is just as beautiful as Bavaria so why do so many British tourists go there and not come here?'. A good question.

*The price of survival.*
*The marriages arranged by Napoleon between his extended family and the royal families of the surviving south German states.*

**Baden** – *Karl (grandson and heir of Grand Duke Karl Friedrich of Baden) married Stephanie de Beauharnais (cousin of Empress Josephine's first husband) on 8 April 1806. Stephanie was adopted by Napoleon just prior to her marriage. See Barockschloss Mannheim in chapter 2.*
**Württemberg** – *Katharina (daughter of King Friedrich of Württemberg) married Jérôme Bonaparte (Napoleon's youngest brother and at that time, King of Westphalia) on 22 August 1807. See Schloss Monrepos in chapter 4.*
**Hohenzollern-Sigmaringen** – *Karl (son of ruling Prince Anton Aloys) married Antoinette Murat (niece of Joachim Murat, Napoleon's marshal and brother-in-law) on 4 February 1808. See Schloss Sigmaringen in chapter 5.*
**Bavaria** – *Auguste Amalie (daughter of King Maximilian I of Bavaria) married Eugene de Beauharnais (son of Empress Josephine) on 14 January 1806. Eugene was adopted by Napoleon just prior to his marriage. See 'Schloss in Bavaria'.*

This book includes schlösser from the royal states in south-west Germany that survived the end of the Holy Roman Empire and from some that were dissolved. It uses the words *schloss* and *schlösser* in a wide definition to denote any type of royal residence – from a fortified castle, to a grand state palace, to a summer villa. It is organised by royal family with different chapters for each historic royal state (or regional group of states) and within each chapter a separate section for each schloss. We start at the iconic castle of Heidelberg (in the north-west of Baden-Württemberg) in what was once the electorate of the Palatinate ruled by the Wittelsbach royal family. Our tour of schlösser then goes clockwise around the state through the principality of Hohenlohe, the kingdom of Württemberg, the Hohenzollern south German territories, the small courts of Lake Constance, and the grand duchy of Baden. It ends in the magnificent baroque palace of the prince-bishops of Speyer at Bruchsal.

With so many beautiful schlösser in Baden-Württemberg to choose from it was hard to restrict my selection to twenty-five. This is why a further fifteen are also mentioned more briefly in the narrative or in text boxes. I have tried to include a cross section of schlösser from different royal states and families and also some that are less well-known. Heidelberg castle is one of Germany's top tourist sites and was crammed with visitors of all nationalities. But other schlösser in this book rarely see an English-speaking visitor. One reason for writing my books is to encourage more overseas visitors, particularly from the UK and USA, to go and see these wonderful places.

Another reason for writing the books is to share my view that history seen through the stories of royal lives is informative, fascinating, and fun. Appendix B includes charts and family trees to illustrate the royal stories; they are referred to at appropriate points in the text. Monarchy as a system of government depended on perpetuating the royal family line, but a theme that crops up again and again is the failure of so many sovereigns to produce a son and heir. We discover the prince without a son who tried to engineer the future genetically through the marriages of his granddaughters (Mannheim in chapter 2); the baby heir who was allegedly snatched from his cradle so another line could take the throne (Karlsruhe in chapter 7); and how a series of non-dynastic marriages debarred the descendants of eight royal sons leaving a single eligible heir (Bebenhausen in chapter 4).

## The Holy Roman Empire and Baden-Württemberg

*The Holy Roman Empire of the German Nation was a loose alliance of states under the leadership of an elected emperor. It was called 'Roman' because it was considered to be the successor to the Roman empire of the West; and 'Holy' reflected that early emperors were crowned by the Pope. There is a famous quote by the French philosopher and writer Voltaire that, despite its name, the Empire was 'neither holy, nor Roman, nor an empire.'*

*The Holy Roman Empire was made up of independent sovereign territories that were each subject directly to the emperor and the imperial institutions, such as the diet (parliament) and the courts. The members ranged enormously in size from large and powerful states ruled by prince-electors (such as the Palatinate in chapter 2) to small territories centred on a single schloss (Neckarbischofsheim, also in chapter 2). As well as secular states, the members included ecclesiastical (church) states ruled by the bishop of a diocese or abbot of a monastery (Meersburg and Salem in chapter 6).*

*A crowning moment in its history was when the combined imperial army defeated the Turks at the Battle of Vienna in 1683 and stopped further encroachment by the Ottoman Empire into Europe. Schloss Rastatt in chapter 7 commemorates the victories against the Turks of Margrave Ludwig Wilhelm of Baden-Baden, known in history as Türkenlouis (Turkish Louis).*

*When French Revolutionary troops occupied the territory of the German princes on the left bank of the Rhine in 1794, it was the beginning of the end. The emperor was forced to agree to compensate them with lands from elsewhere in the empire. Starting in 1803, under a process called secularisation and mediatisation, hundreds of ecclesiastic and smaller secular states lost sovereignty and their lands were parcelled out in a spectacular land-grab. As one example in south-west Germany, the prince-bishopric of Speyer became part of Baden (see Bruchsal in chapter 7).*

*The final demise of the empire came in 1806 as member states seceded to join Napoleon's new grouping, called the Confederation of the Rhine. The last Holy Roman emperor, Francis II, recognised that it had become untenable. He resigned and dissolved the empire in 1806.*

Women were generally ineligible for the throne but could rule as regent for their underage sons (Rastatt Favorite in chapter 7). Their marriages also played a key role in securing succession rights – at Heidelberg (chapter 2) we meet Elizabeth Stuart whose German husband gambled everything for a kingdom and lost, but whose grandson became King George I of Great Britain.

This is my fifth book about the fascinating royal history of German schlösser. I have always been intrigued at how, through a restricted marriage market where royals had to marry someone of equal 'blood', Europe's royal families were bound together in a tight network of family relationships. This means there are many connections between the personalities and the schlösser in my books. Elizabeth Stuart came to Heidelberg as a bride; her daughter (mother of George I) married a duke of Brunswick-Lüneburg and her story is told at Herrenhausen in my first book (*Schloss*). Clemens August of Bavaria is responsible for the state apartments at Mergentheim (chapter 3); he also built Augustusburg (*Schloss III*) and his father built Schleissheim (*Schloss in Bavaria*). Where appropriate I have cross referenced to the other four books, shortening the titles for ease to *Schloss, Schloss II, Schloss III* and *Schloss in Bavaria (IV)*. More details of these are shown at the end of this book, *Schloss in Baden-Württemberg (V)*.

I started to write about schlösser when my husband and I began to spend time in Germany each year. We drive around the countryside, finding some out-of-the-way places, and everywhere visiting the local schlösser. This book looks at the schlösser from two perspectives. The first perspective comes from my observations and impressions when visiting each schloss as part of researching the book. My comments are from the viewpoint of an overseas visitor who does not speak German. They are entirely personal; another visitor at another time could have a different experience. I never want to be negative and I always try to find the positive in my visits. I know how hard it is to give each visitor a good experience and that anyone can have a bad day. However, part of the format for these books is to share my personal experience.

The second perspective is given by extracts and stories from the royal history connected with each schloss. The sources I have consulted for this historical information are shown in the notes section and the bibliography. The book is illustrated throughout with a mixture of present-day photographs, old postcards, and royal portraits. I stress that this is not a comprehensive history or a detailed travel guide. Opening hours and other information for visitors is usually available on the schlösser websites.

Because of its colourful royal history with a plethora of sovereign territories, Baden-Württemberg has a rich legacy of wonderful schlösser. I discovered royal families I had not heard of while researching this book. They include the counts of Montfort who ruled a small state of the same name near Lake Constance. Like other eighteenth-century rulers of small German courts, the counts of Montfort aspired to grandeur and competed to display their high status through the magnificence of their schlösser. In pursuit of this obsessive building dream, three generations of counts of Montfort bankrupted their state to create a grand new schloss at Tettnang. When the mortgage on this schloss fell in, Count Franz Xaver was forced to abdicate and sell his state to Austria in 1779. Franz Xaver died soon after his abdication and the long line of counts of Montfort, once one of the most important noble families in the region, came to an end. But their new schloss survives and we visit this in chapter 6. (For more about Count Franz Xaver's story, see Tettnang Neues Schloss.)

# 2

# THE ELECTORATE OF THE PALATINATE

The north-west of Baden-Württemberg was part of an independent state in the Holy Roman Empire called the electorate of the Palatinate (Kurpfalz in German)[1]. From 1214, until it was dissolved in 1803 during the break-up of the Empire, the Palatinate was ruled by the Wittelsbach royal family who, through another branch, were also dukes of Bavaria. As one of only seven sovereigns with the right to elect the Holy Roman emperor, the Wittelsbach elector (kurfürst) of the Palatinate was one of the most high-ranking and important princes in Germany.

In this chapter we visit the iconic ancestral castle that saw their glory days before all was lost following one elector's fateful decision; the grand palace where another tried to manipulate the future and secure the family line through the marriages of his granddaughters; and the gracious summer palace where the tragic story of an unhappy marriage was played out. A recurring problem for this dynasty was the failure of so many electors across the centuries to produce a son and heir.

### Heidelberg

Schloss Heidelberg is one of the top tourist sights in Germany. Its red sandstone ruins sit on the hillside above the old university town like a golden crown. This was once the magnificent residence of the Wittelsbach electors of the Palatinate and the enthralling story of their rise and fall is embodied in its ruins. The schloss was badly damaged in the Thirty Years War (1618-1648) and destroyed by French troops in the War of the Palatinate Succession (1688-1697). At the turn of the twentieth century there was a move to reconstruct it, but fortunately another view prevailed. The romantic ruins need nothing to enhance them and fire the imagination of one million tourists every year.

1. The red sandstone ruins of the schloss
are like a golden crown above Heidelberg.

With so many visitors, Schloss Heidelberg was by far the busiest place in this book. My tip is to get there early, take a self-guided tour with an English audio-guide, and go straight into the schloss courtyard.

By mid-morning this will be choked with groups and tour guides holding up numbered paddles. Around the courtyard are a number of dramatic and distinct-looking buildings, built by different Wittelsbach electors and each with its own story. I thoroughly enjoyed drifting through this space before the crowds arrived, listening to their fascinating history.

The Ruprecht Building, on the west side of the courtyard, is the oldest surviving part of the schloss and was built by Elector Ruprecht III (1352-1410). Ruprecht tried to depose the Holy Roman emperor and was elected German king (the emperor-in-waiting)[2]. But he failed to impose his authority and was never crowned as emperor. Diagonally across the courtyard, in the north-east corner, is the Hall of Mirrors Building built by Ruprecht's great-great-grandson, Elector Friedrich II (1482-1556). This is named after its banqueting hall, once decorated with expensive Venetian mirrors. After the French Revolution this building became home to a French émigré aristocrat called Count Charles de Graimberg. He campaigned tirelessly to preserve the deteriorating ruins and is credited with single-handedly saving Schloss Heidelberg from further destruction.

On the east side of the courtyard is the Ottheinrich Building, described as the most important early renaissance building in Germany[3]. Built by Friedrich II's nephew and successor, Elector Ottheinrich (1501-1559), its splendid and ornate exterior is decorated with allegorical statues of princely power and virtues, such as Hercules, Jupiter, Faith and Justice. High over the magnificent portal is a medallion bust of Ottheinrich himself, carved in stone. He took over the Palatinate late in life and reigned for only three years but was hugely influential. Ottheinrich introduced the Protestant Reformation, transformed the old Heidelberg Castle into a sumptuous palace, patronised the arts and science, and formed a famous collection of books called the Bibliotheca Palatina (Palatine Library). This elector became so fat he could not walk and he died in the unfinished Ottheinrich building, aged fifty-seven. (For more of Ottheinrich's story as duke of Palatine-Neuburg, before he became elector Palatinate, see Neuburg in *Schloss in Bavaria*).

Elector Friedrich IV (1574 to 1610) built the Friedrich Building on the north side of the courtyard as a celebration of his right to royal power. The facade displays a gallery of statues of his ancestors, starting with Charlemagne and ending with Friedrich himself. The Friedrich Building is the only part of Schloss Heidelberg to have been restored, causing an outcry when it was reconstructed in historicist style (an imagined version of the past) around 1900. This led to a debate about the best way to preserve historic sites and subsequent restoration work at Heidelberg has left the ruins largely unchanged.

Religion was the motivating force of Friedrich IV's life and in 1608 he became the leader of the new Protestant Union of German princes to defend their faith against the Catholic Holy Roman emperor. Unfortunately drinking was another of his main interests and his diary entries refer to being 'totally drunk'[4]. The Barrel Building was built during his time to house the Great Barrel for tithes (taxes in kind) of Palatinate wine. The current barrel dates from 1750 and has a capacity of fifty-eight thousand gallons (two hundred and twenty thousand litres). It is so big there is a dance floor on the top! By the entrance to the barrel is a memorial to the court dwarf Clemens Perkeo, jester to Elector Karl Philipp (1661-1742). The story goes that Perkeo could down the barrel at a gulp and died from the shock of drinking a glass of water, prescribed by his doctor! The pleasures (and perils) of alcohol are something of a theme at this schloss. As we left the courtyard one tour guide was giving a lively rendition of the drinking song from an operetta, The Student Prince, set in old Heidelberg. You can hear the marvellous Mario Lanza singing this on YouTube.

Heidelberg is the romantic setting for the story of Elector Friedrich V (1596-1632) and his wife, Elizabeth Stuart (1596-1662). Friedrich was the son of Friedrich IV and, due to his father's early death at thirty-six from alcoholism, came to the throne in 1610 while still a minor. On Valentine's Day (February 14) 1613, the sixteen-year-old elector married Elizabeth Stuart, only daughter of King James I of England and VI of Scotland, in London. Many at her parents' court, (including

2. The courtyard of Heidelberg with (left to right) the Friedrich Building, Hall of Mirrors Building, and Ottheinrich Building.

her mother) thought Friedrich was not good enough for Elizabeth and she ought to marry the son of a king. But James I had decided on a protestant bridegroom to maintain the European balance of power (he hoped for a catholic bride for his son). Like his father, Friedrich was leader of the Protestant Union. The couple took an instant liking to each other and their arranged marriage would turn out a love match.

The new electress made her ceremonial entrance into Heidelberg on 7 June 1613 amid extravagant celebrations. Elizabeth wore a dress of cloth of gold and rode through triumphal arches in a velvet-lined carriage pulled by six horses. In the courtyard of the schloss, her new husband was waiting under the biggest arch of all, nearly sixty-five feet (twenty metres) high. The celebrations went on for days and their wedding is still celebrated in Heidelberg with firework displays each summer. Friedrich was small, slight and dark whereas Elizabeth was fairer, taller, and well built. Her build was seen as an advantage as it was thought she would be able to bear many sons[5]. The new bride was pregnant before she left her home country and the couple would have thirteen children in nineteen years.

Their first years together at Heidelberg were the halcyon days of their marriage. Friedrich had built the English Building to the west of the courtyard in contemplation of his marriage; for Elizabeth's nineteenth birthday he added the Elizabeth Gate in front of this. Legend has it the gate was built in a single night as a surprise birthday present. Between 1616 and 1619, Friedrich also laid out a new garden to the east of the schloss with terraces, grottoes, water features, statuary, mazes, geometric flower beds, and exotic planting. Dynamiting and landfilling the hillside to create terraces was a massive feat of engineering. This famous garden was never finished and soon fell into decay, so that we know it only from contemporary paintings and drawings. But even as it was being created, the Hortus Palatinus (Palatine Garden) was referred to as *The Eighth Wonder of the World*. Today the site is a surprisingly peaceful place to walk as the tour groups do not venture this far. The best views of the schloss and the town of Heidelberg are from the terrace at the far end of the garden.

In 1619 their Heidelberg years came to an end when Friedrich V accepted election as king of Bohemia and moved with Elizabeth to his new capital of Prague. It has often been alleged that Elizabeth pushed her husband to take this throne saying 'she would rather eat sauerkraut at a king's table than feast on luxuries in an elector's house'[6]. But it seems more likely she simply supported what her husband wanted to do. It proved a disastrous decision – Friedrich had set himself up in direct opposition to the Catholic Holy Roman emperor and his Protestant allies (including his father-in-law) deserted him. The centuries-old rivalry between the two sides of the house of Wittelsbach also reached a peak when the Catholic Duke Maximilian of Bavaria joined forces with the emperor against Friedrich.

In November 1620, Friedrich's army suffered a crushing defeat at the Battle of the White Mountain near Prague and he and Elizabeth were forced to flee in ignominy. They were given the derisory name of *The Winter King and Queen* because their reign in Bohemia had lasted for only one winter. The emperor placed Friedrich under the Imperial

Ban and stripped him of his lands and titles. His rank of elector and part of the Palatinate were given to Duke Maximilian as a reward. Heidelberg was occupied by catholic troops and the famed Bibliotheca Palatina shipped off as a gift to the Pope in Rome[7].

The Battle of the White Mountain was the first battle in the terrible Thirty Years War (1618-1648) that desolated Germany as competing armies marched repeatedly to and fro bringing destruction, famine, pestilence and death. The population of the Palatinate was reduced by two thirds[8]. In the peace treaty that followed the war, Friedrich and Elizabeth's son was restored to a reduced inheritance[9], but Elector Karl I Ludwig (1617-1680) lacked the resources to fully rebuild the destroyed schloss and his weakened territory was now vulnerable from the west to the expansionist plans of King Louis XIV of France. One of the great surprises of royal history is how Karl I Ludwig's sister Sophia, the twelfth child of Friedrich and Elizabeth, was named as heir to Queen Anne in the 1701 Act of Succession. Sophia (1630-1714) died eight weeks before Queen Anne and her son became King George I of Great Britain. (For Sophia's amazing life story see Herrenhausen in *Schloss*.)

The troops of Louis XIV invaded the Palatinate in the War of the Palatinate Succession (1688-1697)[10]. Their commanders followed a scorched earth policy causing great devastation and loss of life. Schloss Heidelberg was captured twice (in 1688 and in 1693), when it was blown-up and set on fire making it uninhabitable. One curiosity for tourists today is the Exploded Tower, whose thick walls burst apart and part fell into the moat.

3. Liselotte of the Palatinate remained resolutely German throughout fifty years at the French court.

*Liselotte of the Palatinate*

*Elisabeth Charlotte of the Palatinate (1652-1722) was the only daughter of Elector Karl I Ludwig. Liselotte, as she was called from childhood, was born and brought up at Heidelberg until she was sent to live with her Aunt Sophia to get her away from her parents' poisonous marriage. Karl I Ludwig had more or less openly taken a mistress and there was an uncomfortable ménage a trois in Heidelberg. Her aunt was Electress Sophia of Hannover, daughter of the Winter King and Queen and mother of George I. Liselotte always said her years in Hannover were the happiest of her life.*

*In 1671, Liselotte made a great dynastic marriage to Philippe D'Orléans (whose title was 'Monsieur'), the only brother of Louis XIV. It was a complete misalliance – Monsieur was an effeminate fop who showered favours on his male favourites; Liselotte remained resolutely German and never adapted to life at the sophisticated French Court. Perhaps in compensation for her unhappy marriage, Liselotte became a prolific letter-writer.*

*Many of Liselotte's letters are to her beloved Aunt Sophia in Hannover. They are down-to-earth, frank, indiscreet, and often hilarious. In one letter Liselotte has a cold and tells her aunt that, dressed up in diamonds for a court occasion, she expects to look like 'a shat upon carrot'![11]*

*Liselotte's father must have hoped her marriage would help protect his country against the greedy eyes of Louis XIV. But after Liselotte's childless brother, Karl II (1651-1685), died the French king claimed Liselotte's rights of inheritance on behalf of his brother Monsieur. French troops occupied and laid waste to the Palatinate. Liselotte's letters show her despair*

> *I am so filled with horror at all the destruction there that every night, as I fall asleep, I seem to find myself in Mannheim or Heidelberg gazing at all the devastation. ... I can't get out of my mind what it used to be like in my day, what has become of it, what indeed has become of me, and this makes me weep bitterly[12].*

*She never saw her homeland again.*

Louis XIV celebrated the destruction of Heidelberg by minting a special medal with the motto *Heildelberga deleta* – literally Heidelberg deleted! The schloss would never regain its previous importance as the magnificent residence of the electors. A bolt of lightning caused a further large fire in 1764 destroying much of what had been rebuilt. Instead, with its romantic ruins, picturesque views, and fascinating history Schloss Heidelberg would in later centuries become a world-famous tourist site.

### Barockschloss Mannheim

On 12 April 1720, Elector Karl Philipp (1661-1742) abruptly changed the capital of the Palatinate from Heidelberg to Mannheim. He had intended to keep Heidelberg as the elector's residence and looked at options for revamping the old castle or building on a brand-new site. But religious differences got in the way – his attempts to reintroduce Catholicism met resistance in the staunchly Protestant town of Heidelberg. So, Karl Philipp moved to Mannheim and relegated Heidelberg to provincial status.

4. Barockschloss Mannheim was built by Elector Karl Philipp.

In Mannheim Karl Philipp built a magnificent new schloss to befit his high rank and divinely ordained status as an eighteenth-century ruler. The foundation stone was laid on 2 July 1720 and the elector moved there in November 1731. It was the fashion for German princes of his time to model their courts on the absolute style of monarchy of King Louis XIV of France. Versions of Versailles sprang-up everywhere – neighbouring Margraves Ludwig Wilhelm of Baden-Baden and Karl Wilhelm of Baden-Durlach built theirs at Rastatt and Karlsruhe respectively (see chapter 7). With a frontage of over four hundred metres and one thousand rooms, Mannheim was the largest of them all, second in size only to Versailles itself. The schloss was in contemporary baroque style. In front was a new city built on a rectangular street-plan; behind, the gardens swept down to embankments on the river. Mannheim was called *the Palatinate Florence* and *Athens of the river Neckar*[13]. The decoration of the belétage (the state rooms on the first floor of the main wing) was among the most opulent in Europe.

Barockschloss Mannheim was badly damaged by bombing in World War II. Photographs taken in 1945 show it as a roofless and broken shell. The rebuilt schloss is now part of the University of Mannheim and is hemmed in by railway lines and busy roads. It was difficult to find anywhere to park! Only a single room survived the bombing. The Cabinet Library of Electress Elisabeth Auguste (granddaughter of Karl Philipp) on the ground floor was part of the Garden Apartment which opened directly onto the gardens and was used in summer. Decorated in delightful rococo style in the 1750s, it is (rightly) treated as a precious jewel and displayed to visitors behind a glass wall.

The final phase of rebuilding Barockschloss Mannheim was completed in 2007 when the reconstructed rooms of the belétage opened as a museum of courtly art and culture. In the centre is the huge Rittersaal (Knight's Hall) with marble pilasters, ancestral portraits, and glittering chandeliers. On either side are a matching set of rooms – for the elector on one side and state guests on the other. It would be more usual in a baroque palace for the second set of apartments to be for the

*The problem of the Palatinate succession*

*One of the perceived advantages of monarchy as a form of government was the orderly transition of power from father to son. Yet such are the vagaries of human reproduction that several electors failed to have a son giving rise to problems with the succession as well as personal sadness. Charts 1 and 2 are a simplified family tree for the electors of the Palatinate from 1398 until 1803. They show how the line of succession died out four times so that the role of elector passed sideways across five branches of the house of Wittelsbach.*

*When Elector Ruprecht III died in 1410, his inheritance was divided between his sons. The original* **Old Heidelberg branch** *(1), descended from Ruprecht's elder son, died out with Elector Ottheinrich in 1559. All subsequent electors were descended from a younger son. When the* **Simmern branch** *(2) became extinct on the death of the childless Elector Karl II in 1685, the succession was challenged (unsuccessfully) by King Louis XIV of France citing the rights of his sister-in-law, Liselotte of the Palatinate (see Heidelberg). The* **Neuburg branch** *(3) then held the role for two generations until the death in 1742 of Elector Karl Philipp. He tried to engineer the future genetically through the marriages of his granddaughters (see Mannheim). The next elector was Karl Theodor from the* **Sulzbach branch** *(4). He endured two unhappy marriages in the quest for a son but he died without a male heir in 1799 (see Schwetzingen).*

*The last elector of the Palatinate was Maximilian IV Joseph of* **Zweibrücken-Birkenfeld** *(5) and he did have a son. His line has proved more enduring and is the only branch of the house of Wittelsbach to survive today. (For more on the Zweibrücken-Birkenfeld branch, who became kings of Bavaria in 1806, please see chapter 6 of 'Schloss in Bavaria').*

electress, but Elector Karl Philipp was a widower twice over. He would marry for a third time, but this was morganatic and in secret so his third wife did not become the electress. These rooms have not been reconstructed to an exact replica of the original but only to give an impression of what they once were. No matter – it is the stories from this schloss that stay in my mind rather than the magnificence of the rooms. Here the house of Wittelsbach reached the high point of its prestige with the celebration of a double marriage and the election of a Wittelsbach Holy Roman emperor in 1742.

5. Barockschloss Mannheim before it was destroyed
by bombing in World War II.

When Karl Philipp succeeded his elder brother as elector in 1716, he was fifty-five years old[14]. His dynastic problem was that he had no son – Karl Philipp's only surviving child was a daughter called Elisabeth Auguste. He had already witnessed one destructive war of succession over a daughter's rights of inheritance[15] and to put matters beyond doubt this time, Karl Philipp arranged for Elisabeth Auguste to marry the heir to the Palatinate, Joseph Karl of Sulzbach, in 1717. It should have secured the future line of succession but (like Karl Philipp's own two dynastic marriages) it failed to produce a son. Elisabeth Auguste endured eight pregnancies but when she died in childbirth in 1728, following an agonising still-birth, both her young sons had already predeceased her[16]. Her husband (Karl Philipp's heir) died the following year. The elector was left with three small granddaughters – Elisabeth Auguste (named after her mother) aged eight, Maria Anna (seven), and Franziska Dorothea (five). Karl Philipp must have been fond of the little girls as he had them painted as three rococo demons in the ceiling painting over the grand staircase at Mannheim[17]. He also tried to engineer the future succession in the house of Wittelsbach through their marriages.

On 17 January 1742, the eyes of the Empire were on Barockschloss Mannheim. In a repeat of her mother's marriage a quarter of a century before, Elisabeth Auguste (eldest granddaughter of Karl Philipp) wed his new heir to the Palatinate, Karl Theodor of Sulzbach, on her twenty-first birthday. At the same time, the second granddaughter, Maria Anna, was married to Clemens Franz, a potential future heir to Bavaria. Yet a third Wittelsbach wedding was also agreed – of the youngest granddaughter, Franziska Dorothea, to Friedrich Michael of Zweibrücken-Birkenfeld. (See chart 3 for the marriages of Karl Philipp's granddaughters.) The splendid double wedding celebrations showcased the house of Wittelsbach at its zenith. The elector of Bavaria (shortly to be elected as Holy Roman emperor) occupied the state guest apartments; his brother (the archbishop-elector of Cologne) married the two couples. A month later the archbishop would crown his brother as Emperor Karl VII in Frankfurt cathedral.

For Karl Philipp the wedding of his favourite granddaughter and his successor was the culmination of a plan laid since they were children. He danced at their wedding in his wheelchair[18]. He might have liked to live to see the birth of a great-grandson, but on 31 December the eighty-one-year-old elector died at Barockschloss Mannheim. Less than a year after their marriage the young couple were elector and electress. We take up the story again at Schwetzingen.

The Palatinate became part of the grand duchy of Baden on the breakup of the Holy Roman Empire[19]. On 19 July 1806, Stephanie de Beauharnais made her first visit to Mannheim as a new Baden bride. The city gave her an enthusiastic welcome. She would always feel more at home in Catholic Mannheim, where she was popular, than in the Baden capital of Karlsruhe, which was Protestant and where she was rejected by her mother-in-law as an unwanted parvenu. Stephanie has

6. The distinctive face of Stephanie de Beauharnais, grand duchess of Baden.

a distinctive face and is instantly recognisable in her portraits; she is a figure from royal history that has always interested me.

Stephanie's father was first cousin to Empress Josephine's first husband, Alexandre de Beauharnais[20]. She was an orphan at boarding school when Emperor Napoleon decided to bring her to Paris and adopt her as his daughter. He was short of Bonaparte princesses to implement his marriage strategy. On 8 April 1806, to cement the diplomatic alliance between France and the Grand Duchy of Baden, sixteen-year-old Stephanie was married to the heir to Baden, Karl. The young couple were given Barockschloss Mannheim as their residence and this would become Stephanie's preferred home. Her aggrieved mother-in-law (dowager countess Amalie of Baden), who had not wanted the marriage, retired to her widow's residence at Bruchsal (see chapter 7).

Becoming a princess at first went to Stephanie's head, earning a reprimand from Empress Josephine. Neither bride nor groom was enthusiastic about the marriage. Karl had been engaged to someone else until Napoleon broke it off. Stephanie did not like her husband and spent the wedding night with a girlfriend rather than sleep with him[21]! From the start Stephanie lived mostly at Mannheim while Karl stayed in Karlsruhe. It was only after Napoleon personally nudged Karl to be nicer to his wife that matters improved[22] and they fulfilled their dynastic duty. Five children were born between 1811 and 1817 –

three girls and two boys. (Chart 18 shows the children of Stephanie and Karl.) Napoleon's changing fortunes can be charted in the children's godparents. The French emperor himself stood godfather to the eldest child, a daughter born in 1811, but by the time the younger son was born in 1816, his godfather was the man who had defeated Napoleon, Tsar Alexander I. Karl's family urged him to repudiate his wife after Napoleon's fall, but he loyally stuck with Stephanie and she was the only Bonaparte to keep her status as a ruling royal.

Karl and Stephanie became grand duke and duchess of Baden when Karl succeeded his grandfather days after the birth of their first child in 1811. Unfortunately, both their sons died as infants so that Baden (like the Palatinate) faced a succession crisis (see Karlsruhe in chapter 7). This fostered later rumours of skulduggery and claims that a mysterious youth called Kaspar Hauser was in fact the elder of the two sons and had been snatched as a new-born, to take him out of the succession, with a sickly baby substituted who died soon after. (For more about Kaspar Hauser, see Schloss Ansbach in *Schloss in Bavaria*).

Karl died in 1818, aged thirty-two, from dropsy. This is an old-fashioned name for water retention (oedema) and the underlying causes are heart disease or kidney failure. Dowager Grand Duchess Stephanie retired to Mannheim and concentrated on bringing up and marrying off her daughters. The eldest daughter, Luise, married Prince Gustav Vasa (son and heir of the deposed king of Sweden); the middle daughter, Josephine, married Karl Anton of Hohenzollern-Sigmaringen and was the ancestress of the royal houses of Romania, Yugoslavia and Belgium (see Sigmaringen in chapter 5); the youngest, Marie, married the duke of Hamilton and their daughter became a princess of Monaco and the great-grandmother of Prince Rainier (see Lichtenstein in chapter 4). Grand Duchess Stephanie was elegant, artistic, a fashion trendsetter and ambassador of taste. You can see some of her rooms made-over from baroque into the new-classical style. Grand Duchess Stephanie of Baden had lived at Barockschloss Mannheim for fifty years when she died in 1860.

## Schwetzingen

The courtyard at the front of Schloss Schwetzingen looks quite modest (see illustration 7) but walk through the entrance passageway and you will find a masterpiece of garden art – a unique fusion of a circular formal parterre merging into a flowing landscape park. This garden marvel is a cornucopia of flower beds, topiary, bosquets (groves of pruned trees), pergolas, arcades, statues, water features, garden structures, follies, and much more. You must allow plenty of time to explore it. There is an excellent plan available in the ticket office.

7. Schwetzingen was the summer palace of
the electors of the Palatinate.

Schwetzingen was the glorious summer residence of Elector Karl Theodor of the Palatinate. His main residence was in Mannheim but every May he moved to Schwetzingen, with his family and an entourage of up to fifteen hundred courtiers and servants, and stayed (weather permitting) until October[23]. The schloss dates to the fourteenth century and was used by previous electors. This is where Karl Philipp mostly lived while he was building Barockschloss Mannheim. But a new era began for Schwetzingen when Karl Theodor succeeded to the Palatinate in 1742 at the age of just eighteen. Over the course of his long reign of fifty-seven years he extended and enhanced the schloss with its gardens as the centrepiece.

Elector Karl Theodor was intelligent and well-educated, interested in science and a lover of arts and music. During his reign he would sponsor new Palatine academies of science and painting and set up the Mannheim National Theatre. The music at his court would attract Mozart, Gluck, and other famous musicians, in what later became known as the Mannheim School of Music. Karl Theodor was a polyglot who spoke five languages fluently (German, English, French, Italian and Latin) and read Shakespeare in the original English. His favourite language was in fact English which he spoke a great deal better than his contemporary, King George II of Great Britain[24]!

Karl Theodor began at Schwetzingen by building two long curving pavilions, one to either side of the garden front, containing orangeries and party rooms. Together with the main building they formed a semicircle and this gave the court gardener an inspired idea. He completed the circle with two long curving trellised walks (to match the pavilions) and created a circular baroque parterre inside. This formal style of symmetrical, structured garden was the fashion at the time and is still the focal point of the garden today. To my mind it beautifully complements the schloss. We sat on a bench at the edge of the circular parterre underneath the tallest topiary I have ever seen – lime trees sculptured into arches around thirty feet (nine metres) high.

Beyond the circular parterre the formal gardens merge into an English landscape park. As the craze for this new style of gardening swept the German courts, Karl Theodor sent a young gardener to England for several years in the 1770s to study its principles[25]. Everywhere the gardens are studded with surprises and unusual structures. I liked the open-air theatre used for summer plays and concerts, with a gracious Temple of Apollo providing the backcloth and statues of Sphinxes guarding the entrance. The most unusual building in the garden is undoubtedly the Mosque with dome, minarets, and a huge rectangular colonnade of pointed arches. Mosques were a popular feature of eighteenth-century gardens, reflecting another contemporary craze for the oriental. That built at Schwetzingen was the largest and is the sole surviving in Germany[26]. An intriguing reference on the plan took us to my favourite part of the garden. What on earth could be *The End of the World Illusion*? It turned out to be a trompe l'oeil painting of an endless perspective at the end of a long pergola. I felt that if I walked down this narrow tunnel, I might indeed walk off the end of the world! The Illusion is part of a garden within the gardens created by Karl Theodor for his private use. Here, shrouded by hedges, he could entertain guests in a small but opulent building called The Bathhouse (named after a marble bath inside). In front of this, through an arch dripping with wisteria, is an aviary of real birds and a water feature called *The Fountain of the Water-spouting Birds*. From the top of a trellis, artificial birds spout water down onto an eagle-owl sitting in an oval basin. I thought it a pretty scene until I read that the birds are pouring scorn on the eagle-owl because it is the only bird that kills others of its kind[27].

Most visitors to Schwetzingen come to see the gardens and there were only four of us on the guided tour of the interior. Because this was a summer residence the style of décor was simpler and more relaxed than in the ceremonial palace at Mannheim. But it is well worth making time for the tour because it tells the spellbinding story of the elector's marriage. On 17 January 1742, seventeen-year-old Karl Theodor married Elisabeth Auguste of Sulzbach, granddaughter of his predecessor (Elector Karl Philipp). The couple were first cousins (their fathers were brothers) and they had been brought up together at the court in Mannheim after first Elisabeth's father, and then Karl Theodor's father, died when they were children. Elisabeth Auguste was four years older and as children this age difference would have mattered; perhaps it set the tone of their relationship[28]. Elisabeth Auguste had to wait for her fiancé to grow up and when they married, she was twenty-one and by the far the more mature.

8. *The Fountain of the Water-spouting Birds* in Karl Theodor's private part of the gardens.

Elisabeth Auguste was dominant in the relationship and usually got her own way. She was an extrovert who was full of life and revelled in in the fun of court entertainments. She enjoyed the company of handsome men and is known to have had an affair with her sister's husband, Clemens Franz of Bavaria. She wrote him intimate letters about assignations in the Schwetzingen gardens[29]. Karl Theodor on the other hand was more reserved and diffident. He was not a strong ruler because he had no staying power and disliked confrontation[30]. Elisabeth Auguste interfered in politics and demanded key appointments for her favourites. Faced with his wife's determination and temper tantrums, Karl Theodor would give way – anything for a quiet life[31]!

The marriage came to crisis at Schwetzingen in the summer of 1761. After nineteen years of childless marriage, forty-year-old Elisabeth Auguste was pregnant. Imagine the elector's feelings – would he at last have a son, or would he, like so many of his predecessors, be

9. In 1777 Karl Theodor of the Palatinate also inherited Bavaria.

doomed to have no heir. In June that year Elisabeth Auguste gave birth to a son in the electress's bedroom at Schwetzingen. It was a difficult forceps delivery and the baby boy died the following day as a result[32]. It was disastrous for their relationship – Elisabeth Auguste's influence over her husband was at an end and the marriage was over. From now on husband and wife lived separately except for official occasions, and Karl Theodor turned to other women. He had a series of mistresses who bore him several illegitimate children, including one son – Karl August von Bretzenheim, born in 1769 (see Zwingenberg on the next page).

In 1777 Karl Theodor also inherited Bavaria after the Bavarian line of the house of Wittelsbach became extinct. He had little attachment to his new lands and toyed with a suggestion from the Hapsburg emperor of swapping Bavaria for somewhere nearer to the Palatinate (see *The Bavarian Swap* under Nymphenburg in *Schloss in Bavaria*). Naturally this made him very unpopular with Bavarians. When Elisabeth Auguste died in 1794, the elector, now seventy, made a quick second marriage in a last-ditch attempt to produce an heir. It was a bad decision and his eighteen-year-old new wife, Maria Leopoldina of Austria-Este, refused to sleep with him. Karl Theodor's rule in Bavaria is overshadowed by that of his successor who became the first king of Bavaria in 1806. King Maximilian I was the son of Franziska Dorothea of Sulzbach (Elisabeth Auguste's little sister) whose marriage was also arranged by Karl Philipp (see Barockschloss Mannheim). So, the old elector's dynastic planning did work out after all!

## Zwingenberg

*Schloss Zwingenberg was not on my list to research but when we saw it in the distance, we just had to make a detour. The schloss has a spectacular location on the forested bank of the river Neckar. Zwingenberg dates to the thirteenth century and the original owners were robber barons called the lords of Zwingenberg who extorted customs duty from the river traffic. In the eighteenth century the schloss became part of the Palatinate and in 1778 Elector Karl Theodor endowed it on his natural (illegitimate) son, Graf (Count) Karl August von Bretzenheim.*

*One reason why Karl Theodor was interested in exchanging Bavaria for more readily realisable assets was to provide for his family of illegitimate children. After the birth and death of his only (legitimate) son in 1761, Karl Theodor turned away from his marriage and took mistresses. Karl August's mother was on the stage before the elector noticed her at the opera following the death of the first of these. She was ennobled as Gräfin (Countess) Josepha von Heydeck and bore several children – first a daughter, and then a son (Karl August in 1769), before dying following the birth of twin daughters in 1771. She is buried in the chapel at Zwingenberg where visitors can see her memorial.*

*When the Palatinate was dissolved, Zwingenberg was purchased by the grand duke of Baden and remains a private home for the family. Guided tours are only by prior arrangement but by serendipity we were invited in and shown around. The schloss is also open for the summer music festival and a garden show in autumn. The princess is a keen gardener and her lovely garden enhances the schloss with climbing plants and flower beds in every corner. There are wonderful views of the Neckar river valley.*

## Altes Schloss Neckarbischofsheim

The Altes (Old) Schloss at Neckarbischofsheim was the centre of one of the smallest states in the Holy Roman Empire. The territory of Bischofsheim was surrounded by the Palatinate but was ruled by its own lords, who were subject directly to the emperor. From the thirteenth century the ritter (knights) von Helmstatt were the equivalent of kings in Bischofsheim and held the power of life and death. Their executioner's sword from 1678 is on display in the museum at the schloss and is grim evidence of this. Engraved on the blade is the blindfold figure of justice and the words (roughly translated from the old German) 'The lords dispense justice and I carry it out'. When the Holy Roman Empire was disbanded in 1806 the von Helmstatt lost their ruling rights and Bischofsheim became part of the grand duchy of Baden. To distinguish it from two other places with similar names (Tauberbischofsheim and Rheinbischofsheim), it was renamed Neckarbischofsheim even though it is more than ten kilometres from the river Neckar.

10. The Altes Schloss was built by the first von Helmstatt in Neckarbischofsheim.

My visit to Neckarbischofsheim was one of the most enjoyable research trips for this book. This was largely due to a warm welcome from volunteers of the Heimatverein Neckarbischofsheim (the local association who run the museum and look after the schloss) who made my visit memorable. They kindly gave me a tour of the schloss in English and shared their knowledge of its history. Thanks to their generosity and enthusiasm I learned about the family who had such a big impact on this town. The last von Helmstatt died in 1935 and the Altes Schloss now belongs to the community. But their long story is told in the museum and many of the exhibits were gifts from the family.

The first documentary mention of a von Helmstatt in Bischofsheim is of Dieter von Helmstatt in 1274. He probably built the original moated castle on the marshy site. Later generations of the family would adapt and remodel his schloss to meet the changing needs and fashions of their own day. Wiprecht I von Helmstatt made major extensions in the late fourteenth century to reflect his important status as a councillor and trusted adviser to Elector Ruprecht III of the Palatinate. (Ruprecht made a bid to become the Holy Roman emperor – see Heidelberg.) In the sixteenth century the family were very wealthy and Johann von Helmstatt renovated the old schloss in the newly fashionable renaissance style. The money came from the marriage of his father-in-law, Philipp von Helmstatt, to an heiress called Margarete von Neipperg. Their combined coat of arms is carved in stone over the entrance to the schloss.

One fascinating thing about the Altes Schloss is how the building today is so clearly the rump and legacy of all the previous changes. There was a top (fourth) floor made of wood but this was destroyed in the big fire of 1859 that devastated the city. Walled-up doors (like the one you can see on the first floor in illustration 10) show where passages or walkways used to lead through to parts of the building that no longer exist. The oriel window and the staircase tower date from the renaissance make-over in the 1540s. But the covered balcony (called the Altane) on the second floor is built into a wall so thick (two and a half metres) that it must be much older – probably part of the original fortified tower. From the Altane there is a good view of a second schloss just a few metres away. In 1829 Ludwig Nepomuk von Helmstatt demolished a fourteenth-century supplementary building to replace it with the Neues (New) Schloss. This is now a schloss hotel but I was delighted to find references to the von Helmstatt family here too. On the floor at the entrance is a mosaic picture of their heraldic badge – a raven (rabe in German).

The most famous of the family was Raban von Helmstatt (1362-1439). He was the son of Wiprecht I and one of the first students at the new Heidelberg University (founded by Wiprecht's patron, Elector Palatinate Ruprecht III). Raban was chancellor of the Palatinate and then in 1396 he became prince-bishop of Speyer. This was an important position – the prince-bishop was not only the spiritual head of a religious diocese, he was also the sovereign ruler of an independent church state in the Holy Roman Empire. The role was elected (unlike the ruler of a secular state it was not hereditary) but due to Raban's influence further family members would follow him (see chart 4 for their family tree). In the museum at the Altes Schloss there are portraits of Raban, who was prince-bishop from 1396 to 1438; Reinhard, who followed him from 1438 until his death in 1456; and Ulrich, who was elected when Reinhard died. Ulrich chose not to take up the position[33] and there is a question mark over whether his portrait is really him at all (all three portraits were painted centuries after their

11. Raban von Helmstatt was prince-bishop of Speyer and archbishop-elector of Trier.

12. The renaissance Knights' Hall is a popular wedding venue.

subjects' death). But in 1478 his younger half-brother, Ludwig, became the last von Helmstatt prince-bishop of Speyer.

In 1430 Prince-bishop of Speyer Raban von Helmstatt became one of the most important men in the Holy Roman Empire when he was also made archbishop-elector of Trier. It was not uncommon for the sons of noble families to hold more than one church appointment simultaneously. Raban was now one of only seven electors entitled to vote in the election for a new emperor; within the empire they were second in status only to the emperor himself[34]. This was the zenith of the family history. Von Helmstatts continued to hold high positions at the Palatinate court until the Thirty Years' War (1618-1648) when they fell in importance and never regained their previous eminence. This is why the name von Helmstatt is virtually unknown outside of Neckarbischofsheim. The last notable member of the family was Bleickard von Helmstatt (died 1636) who was a commander in the Thirty Years' War.

The last in the male line of the family was Viktor (1851-1935). He married and had several children but both his sons died before their father – one from a childhood illness as a toddler; the other in an accident as a student[35]. The town of Neckarbischofsheim bought the Altes Schloss in 1975 and gradually began renovation. Among the treasures this uncovered were the renaissance wall paintings in the Knights' Hall. Today the schloss is home to the local history museum and is open on advertised days, for special events, and by prior arrangement with the Heimatverein (see heimat-nbh.weebly.com). The Knights' Hall is a popular wedding venue with many couples choosing to have their wedding reception in the next-door Neues Schloss.

A final highlight in Neckarbischofsheim was a visit to the atmospheric parish church of St John the Baptist (known to locals as the Totenkirche). This dates back to 950 and is the burial place of the von Helmstatt family. Their carved stone grave memorials line the walls and have been beautifully restored by the Heimatverein. Here is Wiprecht (1344-1408), councillor to Elector Ruprecht III, depicted in his armour with two small animals at his feet – the lion of power and dog of loyalty. Also, Philipp (1496-1561), shown with his wealthy wife Margarete von Neipperg; and next to them a sad reminder of the high infant mortality in a memorial to their dead babies and small children. The remains of Bleickard von Helmstatt, who died in France in 1636 were brought back here thirty years later (in 1663). And there are many more von Helmstatts commemorated in the church. Every year, the carol service in the Totenkirche on 26 December is full, even though there is no heating in the church. It is another reminder of how much this town owes to one family.

# 3

# HOHENLOHE

From the Palatinate we travel east, to the beautiful pastoral region of Hohenlohe in north-east Baden-Württemberg. With its wooded hills and verdant river valleys, this is one of Germany's hidden delights. The principality of Hohenlohe was small and was further divided many times to provide even smaller sub-states for each son. This makes their family tree convoluted and difficult to follow; chart 8 is my attempt at a simplified version showing the different branches. The Hohenlohe lost sovereignty in the process called mediatisation when the Holy Roman Empire was dissolved. But the family kept their royal status and eligibility to marry into Europe's sovereign houses.

Two famous tourist routes pass through Hohenlohe, linking historic towns and magnificent churches, as well as fascinating schlösser. We visit the Hohenlohe family museum at Schloss Neuenstein on *The Castle Road*; and the time warp schloss at Weikersheim on *The Romantic Road*; where little changed after this branch of the Hohenlohe family died out in 1756. But first to Langenburg to see how three marriages have connected this schloss with the British royal family.

## Langenburg

During the guided tour at Langenburg, one of the other visitors suddenly turned to me to translate from the German and ask a question. 'The guide says this is a portrait of Queen Victoria's sister' she told me 'but surely that can't be right, because wasn't Queen Victoria an only child?'. Victoria did indeed have an elder sister (or more correctly a half-sister) called Feodora, to whom she was very close. Feodora (1807-1872) was the first person to greet the teenaged Victoria on the morning of her coronation; and after Albert's death it was Feodora that Victoria wanted to come to live with her. Feodora had married Prince Ernst I of Hohenlohe-Langenburg and left home to become the chatelaine of Schloss Langenburg when Victoria was a just a child of eight. But the two sisters wrote affectionate letters to each other for the rest of Feodora's life.

13. Schloss Langenburg commands superb views
of the surrounding countryside.

Queen Victoria and Feodora of Hohenlohe-Langenburg shared the same mother. Victoria (born 24 May 1819) was the only child of Princess Victoire of Saxe-Coburg-Saalfeld by her second husband, Edward Duke of Kent (the fourth son of King George III). The duchess was a widow when she married the duke of Kent and would be widowed for a second time only months after Victoria's birth. There were two children (half-siblings to Victoria) from the duchess's first marriage to Prince Emich Karl of Leiningen – Karl, born 12 September 1804 and Feodora born 7 December 1807.

14. Feodora of Hohenlohe-Langenburg was the half-sister of Queen Victoria.

When Feodora married and came to Langenburg in 1828, it would be the first of three marriages to connect the schloss with Victoria and the British royal family (see chart 6). The second was in 1896, when Feodora's grandson, Ernst II of Hohenlohe-Langenburg, married Victoria's granddaughter, Alexandra of Saxe-Coburg and Gotha[1]. The third brought the connection right up to the present-day when Feodora's great-grandson, Gottfried of Hohenlohe-Langenburg, married Queen Victoria's great-great-granddaughter, Margarita of Greece and Denmark in 1931. Margarita was a sister of Prince Philip, Duke of Edinburgh, husband of Queen Elizabeth II. The current prince of Hohenlohe-Langenburg, born in 1970 and called Philipp like his great-uncle, is Margarita's grandson.

The schloss dates back to the thirteenth century and takes its name from the natural feature on which it is built – the langenberg or long mountain. In her first letter to her little sister from her new home in Langenburg, Feodora wrote

I live in a very old castle on the top of a mountain from which there is a fine view ...[2]

In the early seventeenth century the old castle was converted into a renaissance residence by Graf (count) Philipp Ernst (1584-1628). This is commemorated by an inscription running around the eaves in the courtyard that says 'Philipp Ernst, Count of Hohenlohe, Ruler of Langenburg ... completed the whole work, which started in 1610 and was finished in 1616 ....' Philipp Ernst also built the renaissance chapel in the south tower, consecrated in 1621. This chapel is unlike any other I have seen because it is circular in shape with two tiers of circular galleries painted with biblical scenes.

The guided tour begins outside the imposing east wing (to the right in illustration 13). This was remodelled in grand style as the main entrance by Fürst (prince) Ludwig of Hohenlohe-Langenburg (1696-1765) after he was promoted from count to prince in 1764. The tour ends out through a door from an upper floor in the west wing (far left in illustration 13) onto the top of the Lindenstamm Bastion. Feodora used this as an outdoor terrace and liked to sit here in fine weather. In between there is so much to see and to my delight, we were permitted to take photographs. Too many schlösser have a policy of no photography! Langenburg is very friendly to its visitors and my only complaint is that the tour was not long enough (forty-five minutes) and the English handout left me thirsting for more.

From the courtyard we climbed a spiral staircase painted with a historical timeline (but no chance to stop and look at this) into the Baroque Hall on the second floor of the west wing. This is the largest room in the schloss and used for concerts and special occasions. There was a reception here for Queen Elizabeth II and Prince Philip when they visited Langenburg in 1965. On display in the hall were two large and very interesting banners (but not enough time to look at them in detail), one showing the various branches of the house of Hohenlohe since 1551 and the other a family tree for the Hohenlohe-Langenburg branch. Then quickly off to the Bretterner Gang (Wooden Gallery) in the south wing with display cases of fascinating family memorabilia. This was originally an outside gallery but covered in to create exhibition space when the schloss was opened to the public in 1960. On display was the christening dress with tiny lace jacket and bonnet thought to have been a present from Victoria to her sister on the birth of one of Feodora's children. Family photos show the dress being used at the christening of subsequent heirs to Langenburg including Fürst Philipp's son, Max Leopold, born in 2005.

15. The Feodora Library in the gothic-style west wing.

My favourite rooms were in the west wing, remodelled in the eighteen-twenties in gothic style[3]. The Feodora Bibliothek (Feodora Library) and Lindenstammzimmer (Lime Tree Room) are crammed with family portraits, photographs, statuettes, and other keepsakes. Some of Queen Victoria's biographers have suggested that Ernst I of Hohenlohe-Langenburg was a poor match for Feodora and that she was married off by her mother for ulterior motives. One suggestion is that King George IV was showing romantic interest in her, raising fears that he might marry Feodora and father an heir to displace Victoria.

*Stetten*

Our route by road to Langenburg took us directly past another dramatic hilltop castle called Schloss Stetten. At first sight we thought it might be Langenburg but soon realised our mistake. Stetten has been owned and lived in by the same family for more than eight hundred years but for the last thirty-five has also had another, most unusual, use. What you cannot see from a distance is that the grounds are the location of a retirement village offering assisted living for the over seventies! I am always intrigued by the different ways in which schlösser are put to a commercial use today – but Stetten must be unique in this respect.

The family of Freiherr (Barons) von Stetten was first documented in the Hohenlohe region in 1098. They built Stetten around 1200 and have

lived there ever since. In the twentieth century (like so many other schlösser) Stetten struggled to be financially viable and was home to various enterprises including a turkey farm, hotel, and riding stables. The current Freiherr, Professor Doctor Wolfgang von Stetten, turned things around when, in 1983, he decided that the best way to preserve and renovate the schloss was to develop it as a retirement village.

We decided to take a detour and drop in at Stetten where we received a friendly welcome from the receptionist in the clubhouse. We also bumped into an English resident who lives here with her (German) husband and told us what a nice place it is to live. The schloss itself is still a private home but, if you want to visit, they have theatrical performances each July and August in the moat.

The queen herself was certainly aware of this story in later life. Another is that the duchess of Kent wanted no influence over her younger daughter except her own and so packed off Feodora to a distant German schloss[4]. But, despite their mediatised status, the Hohenlohe were of equal royal rank and Ernst, as the first cousin of Queen Adelaide (wife of William IV), was well connected with the British court[5]. There are portraits of William and Adelaide in the Lime Tree Room.

16. When Queen Elizabeth II and Prince Philip visited Langenburg in 1965, there was a reception in the Baroque Hall.

Feodora and Ernst had six children – three boys and three girls (see chart 7). Their eldest son was a disappointment; shortly after his father's death, Karl renounced his rights and married a grocer's daughter from Weikersheim village. So the succession passed to the middle son, called Hermann. The youngest son, Viktor, was somewhat accident prone and, following a schoolboy escapade, his Aunt Victoria suggested he join the British navy as a cadet. Viktor followed a career in the Royal Navy until forced to retire due to ill health, when he became a sculptor with a studio in Kensington Palace Gardens. Viktor also renounced his titles after his father's death to marry Laura Seymour, a British admiral's daughter[6]. Count Gleichen, as he was then known, made his home in Britain, eventually becoming a naturalised Briton.

Two of Feodora's daughters died before her; the eldest, Eliza (Elise), from tuberculosis in 1851; and the youngest, Feo (Feodora), from scarlet fever in 1872[7]. In the Feodora Library there is a charming 1840 portrait of Feodora with her middle daughter, Ada (Adelheid), born in 1835. Ada married the duke of Schleswig-Holstein-Sonderburg-Augustenburg and was the mother of Empress Auguste Viktoria of Germany, wife of Kaiser Wilhelm II. Through Ada's marriage, Langenburg is also linked with the Hohenzollern royal family.

After Albert died in 1861, Victoria proposed that Feodora (widowed the year before) should make her home with her. But Feodora valued her independence and found it hard to deal with Victoria's extreme grief. She wisely but tactfully declined, suggesting instead that she could make lengthy visits[8]. Feodora never recovered from the blow of her younger daughter's death and died herself a few months later on 23 September 1872. In her last portrait, by Winterhalter in 1871, she looks a lot like her sister, Queen Victoria. For some reason I have never fully understood, Feodora's important place in her sister's life has been largely overlooked and she is a shadowy figure in the history books. Reading their letters, she impressed me as a grounded and sensible woman and one of the few who could disagree with the imperious Victoria.

Disaster struck Langenburg on the freezing cold night of 23 January 1963 when fire broke out in the north and east wings. Firefighters were helpless to fight the blaze as the water mains were frozen and the water in the river froze when they tried to pump it up the hill. Photographs on display in the schloss show the devastation caused by the fire. Feodora's possessions went up in smoke, including such treasured mementoes as the bridesmaid's dress her little sister Victoria wore at her wedding. The Hohenlohe family crest is the phoenix and their motto is 'Ex flammis orior' (We rise from the flames). True to this pledge, the gutted wings of Schloss Langenburg had been rebuilt by 1968. The family financed the work by selling our next schloss to the state of Baden-Württemberg.

## Villa Hohenlohe

*After her husband died, Feodora left Langenburg and retired to the spa town of Baden-Baden at the edge of the Black Forest in western Baden-Württemberg.* Her new home resembled a Swiss chalet and was called the Villa Friesenberg. Queen Victoria came to visit her ill sister here in spring 1872. When Feodora died in September 1872, she left the Villa Friesenberg to her sister.

Victoria renamed the house Villa Hohenlohe and stayed there when she visited Feodora's grave in the cemetery at Baden-Baden. On her visit in March 1876, Victoria wrote 'With what sad and mixed feelings did I drive up ...to my beloved Feodore's dear little house on the Friesenberg, which I call Villa Hohenlohe, & which now belongs to me'[9].The next day she visited the grave and wrote, 'I felt heart-sick and upset as I approached the grave. Victor's monument, which I had seen in clay, is very pretty, & the grave beautifully decorated with wreaths of fresh flowers, & flowers planted all round, but the enclosure is alas! very small.'[10]

The Villa Hohenlohe was demolished fifty years ago but we were able to visit Feodora's grave in the Baden-Baden cemetery. This was very much as Victoria described it, with a steep climb up from the town and wonderful views. The kind cemetery manager showed us the small plot marked by a beautiful memorial of an angel in flowing draperies seated on a cross. She looks out across the valley to where the Villa Friesenberg used to stand[11]. The memorial was sculpted by Feodora's son (and Victoria's nephew,) Count Viktor Gleichen, and on the base is a list of the family members who contributed to it. It includes all Feodora's surviving children and is headed by her sister – Queen Victoria.

## Weikersheim

In 1586, following one of the frequent divisions and reorganisations of family lands, Graf (count) Wolfgang II (1546-1610) moved to Weikersheim and founded this sub-branch of the house of Hohenlohe. He decided that the old moated castle at Weikersheim was not good enough for his needs and engaged a Dutch architect called Georg Robin to transform it into a residence befitting a great renaissance prince. Robin came up with a unique design for the new schloss with three wings in the shape of an equilateral triangle[12]. Rooms in the old moated castle were restored as temporary accommodation for Wolfgang II while the new schloss was being constructed. But in fact only one wing of the plan was ever built (the South or Hall Wing) and the temporary accommodation still stands. The floor plan of Weikersheim has ended up, not as a perfect equilateral triangle, but as an uneven, wonky, and broken-sided triangle. The separate line of Hohenlohe-Weikersheim died out in 1756 with Wolfgang's great-grandson and the schloss went into a time warp. Amazingly, Wolfgang II's South Wing has survived untouched and is regarded as one of the greatest examples of renaissance architecture in Germany.

The new South Wing, completed in 1603, contained government offices, the chapel, and the huge and stunning Knights' Hall for use on state occasions. Wolfgang II was married to Gräfin (countess) Magdalena of Nassau-Katzenelnbogen (a sister of Willem the Silent, the first prince of Orange and founder of the Dutch royal house). They were prolific breeders producing fourteen children, all of whom survived to adulthood[13]. An intricate carved chimney piece on the far end wall of the Knights' Hall displays the heraldic coats-of-arms of Wolfgang and his wife. To either side of this are the most extraordinary sculpture-relief portraits of the couple – Wolfgang to the left and Magdalena to the right. From their full-length reclining figures sprout their family trees, each going back five generations and demonstrating impeccable lineage through sixty-four noble quarterings.

17. Wolfgang II's renaissance wing at Weikersheim;
the unusual shaped gables reflect the architect's plan
to build the schloss as an equilateral triangle.

Hunting was a major preoccupation for renaissance princes and the other theme of decoration in the Knights' Hall is a celebration of the chase. Scenes of hunting for game of all sorts (elk, heron, boar and even lions) are painted on the ceiling and lifelike statues of deer spring out of the upper part of the walls. These are made of chalk and animal hair topped off with real antlers and must have seemed astonishingly real in the days before taxidermy[14]. The leaping figures start at the entrance with smaller deer, grouped in twos and threes, and then progress down the long (forty metres) room to bigger animals, including a growling bear. The culmination at the far end of the room (next to the reclining figure of Gräfin Magdalena), is an elephant with long protruding tusks! There are impressive festive halls in other schlösser in this book but the Knights' Hall at Weikersheim is surely the most unusual.

Wolfgang II was succeeded by his eldest son, Georg Friedrich (1569-1645). The figure of St George slaying the dragon over the great portal (doorway) in the Knights' Hall is an allusion to Georg Friedrich's service in the army of the Holy Roman Empire fighting against the Turks[15]. But he fell out with the Catholic emperor through his firm adherence to

45

the Protestant side in the Thirty Years' War. Weikersheim was invaded and looted by imperial troops in 1634 and Georg Friedrich outlawed by the emperor. He was forced to cede his tiny state to the Order of Teutonic Knights (who had their headquarters just a few miles away in Mergentheim – see later in this chapter)[16]. Georg Friedrich died before the war was over, and left behind no son, so when Weikersheim was restored in the peace treaty it went to his brother's son. (See chart 8 for a family tree for the counts of Hohenlohe-Weikersheim). Siegfried (1619-1684) started on a new wing (the East or Langenburg Wing) but died while this was still a builders' shell. He was childless and it was his nephew, Karl Ludwig (1674-1756), who fitted this out and finally provided Weikersheim with the grand residential rooms it lacked.

18. The Knights' Hall is a celebration of the chase.

Karl Ludwig was one of four brothers and under the house of Hohenlohe family law they all had equal rights to rule. But one brother died young and another was mentally incapacitated. Karl Ludwig and his remaining healthy brother, Johann Friedrich II, decided to split their inheritance – but who should get Neuenstein-Öhringen (inherited from their father Johann Friedrich I) and who Weikersheim (from their uncle Siegfried)? Weikersheim was the least attractive of the two and the schloss had been neglected since Siegfried's death. On 30 May 1708, the two brothers drew lots to decide their fate. The lottery tickets they used resemble playing cards and still survive today[17]. Karl Ludwig drew the short straw; he made his official entrance to take up residence at Weikersheim on 6 January 1709.

### The House of Hohenlohe

*The house of Hohenlohe dates to the twelfth century and takes its name from Burg Hohenloch (Hohenlohe) near Uffenheim (now just on the Bavarian side of the border with Baden-Württemberg). The first family member to use the name was Heinrich of Hohenloch (died 1215). In the thirteenth century the family was granted lands in present-day Baden-Württemberg and around 1450 became sovereign counts. The house did not follow the practice of primogeniture (inheritance by the eldest son) and there were divisions and reorganisations of the family lands across the centuries, in order to split ruling rights between brothers. It is notable that seven different sub-branches survive today.*

*In 1551 there was an important division when Ludwig Kasimir founded the Protestant branch of Hohenlohe-Neuenstein and his brother, Eberhard, founded the Catholic branch of Hohenlohe-Waldenburg. Both were elevated to the rank of prince during the eighteenth century - Neuenstein in 1764 and Waldenburg in 1744. Following the 1551 split, each branch went through later subdivisions and chart 5 shows these in simplified form. The seven Hohenlohe sub-branches existing today are Langenburg, Öhringen, Bartenstein, Jagstberg, Waldenburg, Ratibor and Schillingsfürst. This book includes schlösser from the Neuenstein branch – Hohenlohe-Langenburg (current head Fürst Philipp, born 1970), Hohenlohe-Öhringen (Fürst Kraft, born 1933), and Hohenlohe-Weikersheim (extinct 1756).*

*Hohenlohe ceased to be a sovereign territory in 1806. Most of the region was then merged into the new kingdom of Württemberg, except for the eastern side which became part of the new kingdom of Bavaria.*

In the Langenburg Wing, Karl Ludwig created suites of state apartments, each for one person and consisting of three rooms – antechamber, audience room and bedchamber. In the time of his great-grandfather, Wolfgang II, royalty had held their audiences in huge, impressive, rooms such as the Knights' Hall. But now, in the time of the baroque, the fashion had changed to use smaller, more intimate, spaces.

In 1713, Karl Ludwig married Princess Elisabeth Friederike Sophie of Oettingen-Oettingen and her dowry enabled him to furnish these apartments in the richest style. As a princess she was a great catch for Karl Ludwig since he was only a count and she outranked him[18]. The princess's state bed is an extravaganza of embroidered silk and gilded carving, with lion-head feet, cupid finials, and a carved phoenix (emblem of the Hohenlohe) on each side of the canopy. Beside it stands the cradle made for Karl Ludwig and Elisabeth Friederike's only son,

19. Entrance to the schloss from Weikersheim village;
Karl Ludwig redesigned the market square as the palace forecourt.

Albrecht Ludwig, born in 1716. He died before his father following a heavy fall from a horse and the Hohenlohe-Weikersheim branch came to an end with the death of Karl Ludwig in 1756. Weikersheim was rarely used after that and these exquisite apartments still have their original décor and furnishings.

Over a reign of nearly fifty years Karl Ludwig overspent lavishly, and impoverished his treasury, to aggrandize this schloss. Perhaps he wanted to live up to his wife's high rank. He knocked down a chunk of the village outside the gates in order to create an elegant new market square to act as a forecourt. And to the south of the schloss, from the terrace in front of Wolfgang II's renaissance wing, he laid out a beautiful baroque garden parterre. It still stretches down, in formal patterns of paths, ponds, and planting, to twin orangeries at the far end, across the entire width of the garden, and views out into the countryside beyond. I liked it that these orangeries are still in use by the gardeners and home to potting shed paraphernalia as well as orange and lemon trees. There was once a gilded statue of Karl Ludwig on horseback standing in the space between them. My favourite garden feature at Weikersheim was the mischievous Zwergengalerie on the balustrade of the terrace. This is a series of eight contorted statues of dwarves (zwergen); caricatures of figures at Karl Ludwig's court.

The reason Weikersheim is fascinating is because so much from the time of Wolfgang II and Karl Ludwig has survived in the original. When Karl Ludwig died in 1756, the schloss reverted to his brother, Johann Friedrich II and, after his line died out in turn, to the Hohenlohe-Langenburg branch. Weikersheim was used only occasionally as a secondary residence and little was altered. This means that visitors can step back in time and see how the nobility lived. In 1967, Prince Kraft of Hohenlohe-Langenburg sold Weikersheim to the federal state of Baden-Württemberg to finance the rebuilding of Langenburg after the great fire. I think this was a win-win for today's visitors as it meant that both schlösser were preserved as museums to the history of this interesting house.

Unfortunately our visit to Weikersheim was somewhat marred by a grumpy tour guide. We were sent by the ticket office to join the tour just after it had started and for some reason she did not want to add us on to her group, even though there were only two other people. Her efforts to eject us were stymied when even more visitors turned up late, also sent by the lady in the ticket office. The guide was not welcoming and it left a sour taste although her negative attitude was fortunately counterbalanced by many positives at this wonderful schloss.

## Neuenstein

Neuenstein came into the possession of the house of Hohenlohe around 1250, when Konrad IV (German king and duke of Swabia – see chart 14), granted lands to Gottfried of Hohenlohe (died 1254) in return for his support in a local war. The schloss is built in the middle of a small lake and you get the best views of the building by walking around the lake. Neuenstein is still the family home of the fürst (prince) of Hohenlohe-Öhringen. It is also home to the house of Hohenlohe museum, the eclectic contents of which make for a most interesting guided tour. Our tour was busy, and all the other visitors were German, but the young guide still took the trouble to point out particular contents and give a brief translation for our benefit. He could not have been more welcoming and friendly.

The Hohenlohe became one of the most important families in southern Germany. The wife of Kraft VI (1475-1503) was a relative of Holy Roman Emperor Maximilian I and the emperor visited Neuenstein in 1495 on his way home from the imperial diet (or parliament) at Worms. Fifty years later (in 1547) the emperor's grandson, Emperor Karl V, also stayed at the schloss with a large retinue as the guest of Kraft's son, Albrecht III (1478-1551). The Emperor's Hall on the ground floor is named to commemorate these great events and now displays a collection of arms. Hanging from the ceiling is a phoenix in the flames – the first of many references here to the Hohenlohe heraldic badge.

20. Schloss Neuenstein houses the museum and archives
of the house of Hohenlohe.

Also contemporary to the emperors' visits is the fifteenth-century
kitchen, the oldest room in the schloss and still pretty much in its
original condition. We were able to wander around this kitchen, amid
the gothic stone arches, while the guide demonstrated various kitchen
implements and described their use. A nice thing about this museum
is that visitors are close to and can experience the exhibits. It was cold
inside the schloss but fortunately I had been warned in the ticket office
and had a coat. The temperature went up once the tour reached the
south wing. This is where the prince of Hohenlohe-Öhringen has his
home, on the third floor.

Neuenstein took on its present rectangular shape under Graf
Ludwig Kasimir (1517-1568). He was the founder of the Neuenstein
branch when the house of Hohenlohe split in 1551 (see chart 5).
Ludwig Kasimir spent large sums rebuilding Neuenstein and we waited
for the tour to begin in the beautiful internal courtyard he created,
with renaissance gables, picturesque staircase towers, and intricate

carved doorways[19]. Ludwig Kasimir's younger son Philipp (1550-1606) made further building alterations but he lived most of his time abroad. Philipp was an important commander for the Dutch Republic in their war of independence against the Spanish and married a daughter of Willem the Silent (founder of the Dutch royal house). His elder brother was Wolfgang II who built the renaissance wing with the Knights' Hall at Weikersheim (see above) and married Willem the Silent's sister. Neuenstein also has an impressive Knights' Hall with seventeenth-century ceiling paintings illustrating the history of the house of Hohenlohe, books from the schloss's important library, family portraits, and many other interesting contents. Whimsical carvings of phoenix sit on the balustrade of the gallery. There is a lot to see in this room and I would have liked to spend much more time here. The Knights' Hall was restored thirty years ago (in more simplified form than the original) having previously been divided up into several rooms and damaged when the ceiling collapsed.

21. The Knights' Hall with seventeenth-century ceiling paintings illustrating the history of the house of Hohenlohe.

A highlight of the guided tour at Neuenstein was the Kunst und Wunderkammer (Art and Miracle Cabinet) – a diverse collection of curios that dates to the fifteenth century. Such cabinets were often collected by princes, but most have long since been broken up and their contents dispersed to museums. Neuenstein may be unique as the only one never to be disbanded[20]. The contents range from precious artefacts, like the *Bowl of Breda* presented to Graf Philipp when he drove the Spanish from the town of Breda, to downright oddities such as the world's largest bladder stone dating from 1637. The story about this goes that the poor sufferer agreed to have the bladder stone removed but died during the procedure. His wife then claimed

22. Christian Kraft of Hohenlohe-Öhringen carried out a major restoration just before World War I.

it as a macabre memento of her husband and carried the stone around with her in an ornamented box (also on display)![21] Also in the Art and Miracle Cabinet is a cupboard decorated with ships. It seemed perfectly normal until we were asked to look underneath this with the help of a long-handled mirror and found pictures of naked ladies! This caused many giggles on the tour. Other unusual items I remember were the single shoe of Empress Catherine the Great of Russia, born a German princess, and the battered hat of King Gustav II Adolf of Sweden, who campaigned in Germany in support of the Protestant cause during the Thirty Years' War. Graf Kraft of Neuenstein (1582-1641) was also forced to flee during this war and the schloss was looted by Catholic troops in 1634. (He was the brother of Georg Friedrich who lost Weikersheim during the same war – see above).

During the eighteenth century the main residence moved to Öhringen (see page 55) and Neuenstein went into a long period of neglect and structural decay. It became an orphanage and workhouse for the poor and later also housed a weaving mill and cloth factory. The schloss was saved by Fürst Hugo of Hohenlohe-Öhringen (1816-1897) and his son, Prince Christian Kraft (1848-1926), who carried out extensive renovations from 1870 and 1906 respectively. There is a model made as part of the planning for the 1906 work in the Knights' Hall. The Hohenlohe-Öhringen branch was immensely wealthy from their landholdings and mining interests in Eastern Europe. Like many princes, Christian Kraft was an avid hunter and one room is given over to his hunting trophies and the stuffed animals he killed. World War I halted his renovation before the interior was fully completed but Christian Kraft restored Neuenstein to its former glory.

The museum was founded after World War II with exhibits collected from several family schlösser. They include many more interesting items than I have written about here. I might also have mentioned, for example, the renaissance rooms in the south wing, the collection of baroque sleighs, or the sacred regalia of Cardinal Gustaph Adolph of Hohenlohe-Schillingsfürst (from the Catholic Waldenburg side of the family) who died in Rome in 1896. I understand that only a fraction of the contents of this museum are out on display[22] and do wonder what other fascinating treasures are hidden away.

23. Prince Hugo of Hohenlohe-Öhringen and his wife Pauline.

## Schloss Öhringen

*I went to see Schloss Öhringen without high expectations. The town of Öhringen bought the schloss from the Hohenlohe family in 1961 and since 1977 it has been government offices. The schloss is not a museum and I thought there might not be much to see. But I was pleasantly surprised. We asked at the tourist information office (housed in the schloss) and they took us to see the historic rooms. The*  *Blauer Saal (Blue Room), Speisesaal (Dining Room), and Weisser Saal (White Room) were renovated in the 1840s by Prince Hugo of Hohenlohe-Öhringen and his wife Princess Pauline. They are now used for events.*

*Schloss Öhringen was built between 1611 and 1616 as a widow's residence for Gräfin Magdalena (wife of Wolfgang II of Hohenlohe-Weikersheim). Magdalena's grandson, Johann Friedrich I (see chart 8), extended the schloss in the late sixteen hundreds. His son, Johann Friedrich II, bought up the land behind the schloss in the early seventeen hundreds and laid out a court garden in the formal French style. But when his son, Ludwig Friedrich Karl, died in 1805, the Neuenstein-Öhringen branch became extinct in the male line and the schloss passed (through Ludwig's nephew – his sister's son) to the princes of Hohenlohe-Öhringen. The last major phase of building was in the early nineteenth century when Prince August of Hohenlohe-Öhringen (1784-1853) built the Prince's Wing.*

*The schloss fronts directly onto the market square so that we came upon it suddenly. Be sure to walk through the arch which leads to a broad terrace at the rear and a modern staircase down into the court garden. This was renovated just a few years ago for a major garden event. The garden is well worth exploring and there are marvellous views up to the court theatre built by Johann Friedrich II in 1743.*

## Mergentheim

In 2019, Schloss Mergentheim celebrated eight hundred years of association with the German Order (Deutscher Orden) – a religious order of warrior monks better known in English as the Teutonic Knights. The Order recruited trained knights from Germany to serve in the Holy Land. They were often the younger sons of noble families who made significant donations as a sort of entry fee.

24. Mergentheim was the headquarters of the German Order (the Teutonic Knights).

On 16 December 1219 Andreas von Hohenlohe joined the German Order and donated the schloss and other property at Mergentheim. A week later his brothers, Heinrich and Friedrich, also joined and gifted further family property. Heinrich went on to be elected as grand master (chief officer of the Order) in 1244. Schloss Mergentheim was first a regional centre (called a commandery) and later the headquarters and residence of the grand master. Since 1961 the schloss has housed a special museum documenting the eight-hundred-year history of the German Order.

Entrance to Schloss Mergentheim is across the moat and through the entrance tower (to the left in picture 24). The importance of this schloss is immediately apparent from a plaque just inside the entrance showing a list of the Holy Roman emperors who stayed here as guests of the German Order. Over the centuries these included (as examples) Ludwig the Bavarian (Wittelsbach) in 1343 and 1346; Friedrich III (Hapsburg) in 1475 and 1485; Ferdinand I (Hapsburg) 1540, 1545 and 1558; Karl VII (Wittelsbach) in 1742; and the last Holy Roman emperor, Franz II (Hapsburg), in 1792 and 1802. Their visits evidence the close links between the emperors and the Order; their family names illustrate the struggle between two great families for supremacy within the Empire. Both families provided grand masters for the German Order.

The museum in Mergentheim extends over two floors all the way round the four connecting wings. Everything is very well displayed with models, illustrations, and storyboards, a limited amount of which is translated into English. We concentrated on the section about the German Order but even so it took us two and a half hours. Other sections of the museum cover the history of the city of Bad Mergentheim; display the Adelsheim collection of antiquities (gifted in 1864 by a local collector to start the museum); and show a collection of dollhouses (put together by another local collector after World War II).

On our return to the ticket office, the friendly attendant suggested that we really ought to talk to their local expert on the history of the German Order. It was nearly closing time, but nevertheless she telephoned, and he kindly came to meet us. This charming gentleman has spent a lifetime studying the Order after becoming interested as a schoolboy. He gave us a riveting second tour with the benefit of his huge knowledge and sharp insights. It went well past closing time but the museum obligingly stayed open. A not-to-be-forgotten visit!

## The Teutonic Knights

The Order of the Hospital of St Mary of the Germans in Jerusalem (the German Order) was founded in 1190 during the Third Crusade. It is better known in English as the Teutonic Knights. It was the last of the three great religious orders established in the Holy Land during the time of the Crusades; the other two were the Knights Hospitallers (Knights of St John) and the Knights Templar. The German Order was originally set up as a hospital brotherhood to look after sick Germans in the crusading army. But in 1198 it was transformed into a religious-military order of warrior monks to help protect the fragile Christian Kingdom of Jerusalem against the infidel.

The knights wore a white mantle bearing a black cross and took an oath on entering: 'I promise the chastity of my body, and poverty, and obedience to God, Holy Mary, and You, to the master of the Teutonic Order, and your successors, according to the rules and practices of the Order, obedience unto death.'

From early on (1230), the German Order was also active in crusading against pagans in the Baltic region of Eastern Europe. When the Kingdom of Jerusalem fell in 1291, their focus shifted to Europe and (in 1308) the grand master moved his residence to the fortress of Marienburg in Prussia (now Malbork Castle near Gdansk in Poland.) The Order conquered large areas of Prussia and set up their own state, bringing in German settlers and farmers and building castles to defend them. They also took over lands further round the Baltic in Livonia (now parts of Estonia and Latvia).The Teutonic Knights have been accused of creating the Prussian military ethos that later dominated Germany and as being forerunners of the Nazi ideology of 'Drang nach Osten' (Push to the East) because of their colonisation of these lands.

As the Baltic pagans converted to Christianity the German Order became less effective in its crusading role. A crushing defeat by Polish-Lithuanian forces at the Battle of Tannnenberg in 1410 was the beginning of a century-long decline. The history of the Order state in Prussia came to an end in 1525 when the grand master secularised their remaining territory and became the first duke of Prussia.

On 10 April 1525, Grand Master of the German Order Albrecht von Hohenzollern-Ansbach paid homage to the Polish king in the marketplace at Cracow and became the first duke of a secularised Prussia. This was a pivotal moment in the history of the Order and his actions have polarised opinion ever since. For some, the dissolution of the Order in Prussia was the principled decision of a pious prince in response to an impossible situation (the Order had so shrunk in Prussia that the grand master had neither enough knights to defend it nor the money to pay mercenaries to do so). For others it was high treason and a gross betrayal for personal gain. Albrecht (1490-1568) was a big-name recruit to the Order when he joined in 1511. He came from the noble and well-connected Hohenzollern family: his father was margrave of Brandenburg-Ansbach and his cousin the elector of Brandenburg. Through his mother, he was nephew to the king of Poland and to the king of Bohemia and Hungary. The Order hoped these relationships could save them from extermination in Prussia. Albrecht was head-hunted for the role of grandmaster and was installed in the position on the same day as he joined[23].

As a young man, Albrecht was not ready to embrace an ecclesiastical life. He had to be assured that the provisions of the traditional oath did not apply to him as grand master; otherwise he would never have joined. Officials of the Order helpfully reinterpreted the pledge to celibacy as meaning that the grand master could not marry, rather than he must refrain from having sex (chastity)[24]. In his early days as grand master Albrecht caroused around his capital of Königsberg[25], but as he grew older and more battered by adversity he settled down and became pious. In 1522 Albrecht travelled to the imperial diet at Nuremberg (parliament of the Holy Roman Empire) to plead for money to fight the Poles. He pleaded in vain and instead came under the influence of the Reformation and the ideas of Martin Luther. Albrecht was an early and high-profile convert to Lutheranism and his new duchy of Prussia was the first state to be Protestant as the official religion. Many of Albrecht's knights originated from Germany and were also sympathetic to the new ideas to reform the church. From the time of the Reformation membership of the Order was open to all religious denominations although the grand master was always Catholic. After he became duke of Prussia, Albrecht married and had a family. Through marriage to Albrecht's granddaughter, Anna of Prussia (1576-1625), who was heiress to the duchy, Elector John Sigismund of Brandenburg (1572-1619) became duke of Prussia in 1618 and ruled the two in a personal union. His descendant, Friedrich I (1657-1713), was elevated to king in Prussia and crowned in Königsberg (where the young Albrecht had junketed) in 1701. The use of Prussia (rather than Brandenburg) in the title was a ruse to get around the convention that there could be no kings within the Holy Roman Empire (it might upset the prerogative of the emperor). Brandenburg was part of the Empire but Prussia was outside its boundaries. And Friedrich I's descendant, Wilhelm I (1797-1888) was further elevated to be German emperor in 1871. So you could say that Albrecht's actions in 1525 were the foundation of the Hohenzollern family's future dominance in Germany.

25. Grand Master Clemens August, brother of the Holy Roman emperor.

The loss of Prussia meant a restructuring of the Order. This was somewhat eased because, as a means of raising money, Grand Master Albrecht had already sold the German and Livonian organisations to their local chief officers in 1523[26]. Emperor Karl V (Hapsburg) confirmed the German master as the new grand master and the headquarters moved to Mergentheim in 1525. The German Order was now firmly fixed in the Holy Roman Empire and aligned with the emperors' policies. It relived some of its earlier crusading glory when Teutonic Knights fought with the imperial armies in their campaigns against the Turks. The Order also adjusted its mission to include providing 'an adequate lifestyle' for the younger sons of the Empire's nobility[27]. The assets and revenues were still significant, making the lucrative role of grand master attractive. The list of grand masters from the seventeenth and eighteenth centuries is littered with the younger sons and younger brothers of Holy Roman emperors.

This star-studded list includes Clemens August (grand master from 1732 to 1761), who was a brother of Holy Roman Emperor Karl VII (Wittelsbach). Clemens August was a serial church office holder. It was not uncommon for princes to hold more than one senior church appointment simultaneously, but Clemens August took it to extremes. In addition to grand master of the German Order he held five prince-bishoprics, earning him the nickname of *Prince of Five Churches*[28]. (For more about him see Augustusburg in *Schloss II*.) Clemens August furbished a new set of prince's apartments in the south wing of Mergentheim, modelling the layout (antechamber, audience room, throne room, and bedroom) on the court ceremonies at Versailles[29]. The original furniture was dispersed when the Order was disbanded by Napoleon but you can still see Clemens August's desk, emblazoned with the black cross of the German Order, in his bedroom. He also completed the stunning rococo schloss church using two of south Germany's most famous court architects – Francois Cuvilliés and Balthasar Neumann. The suggested route round the museum goes through the church gallery with a great view of the exuberant interior.

Clemens August was motivated by rivalry and 'to show that Wittelsbach is at least as good as Hapsburg'[30] but after him all the grand masters were Hapsburg up to the end of the monarchy. Grand Master Maximilian Franz of Hapsburg-Lorraine (1780 to 1801) was the youngest son of Emperor Franz I and Empress Maria Theresa of Austria. He carried out the last major upgrading of the schloss and created the stately Chapter Hall (Kapitelsaal). His portrait hangs in this room opposite that of his uncle (the brother of Emperor Franz I) Grand Master Alexander of Lorraine (1761 to 1780).

The Napoleonic Wars brought the end of Mergentheim as the headquarters of the German Order. In 1809, Napoleon abolished the Order in the territories he controlled and Mergentheim became part of the kingdom of Württemberg. The German Order relocated its headquarters to Vienna in Austria and shifted its focus to spiritual and welfare work. The Hapsburgs continued to be grand masters for another hundred years until Archduke Eugen (grandson of Emperor Leopold II) resigned in 1923 so that the Order should not be identified with the fallen Austrian monarchy. All subsequent grand masters have been priests. Today Schloss Mergentheim houses the most important museum anywhere on the history of the German Order. Theirs is a fascinating eight-hundred-year story with many royal links. The German Order still exists today.

26. The stately Chapter Hall created by
Grand Master Maximilian Franz.

# 4

# THE KINGDOM OF
# WÜRTTEMBERG

The royal house of Württemberg takes its name from their ancestral
castle near Stuttgart built by Graf (count) Konrad I, founder of
the dynasty, around 1080. Württemberg was a county until 1495 when
Graf (count) Eberhard V of Württemberg (known as *the Bearded*)
was elevated to duke. It became a kingdom on 1 January 1806 when
Duke Friedrich II proclaimed himself a king during the Napoleonic
Wars by courtesy of the French emperor, Napoleon. The last king of
Württemberg was Wilhelm II who stole quietly away in November 1918,
after revolutionaries raised the red flag over his palace in Stuttgart.

In this chapter we meet three colourful eighteenth-century dukes
of Württemberg – Eberhard Ludwig, who built Ludwigsburg for his
mistress; Karl Eugen who built Hohenheim for his; and Friedrich II
(later King Friedrich) who turned Mon Repos into a party schloss to
showcase his high-born wife. We also visit the dramatic mock-medieval
castle of a nineteenth-century duke, who was debarred from the throne
by his parents' unequal marriage; and the converted monastery home
of the last king of Württemberg after his abdication.

## Ludwigsburg

Württemberg was not a particularly wealthy or important duchy but Duke Eberhard Ludwig (1676-1733) had aspirations to greater glory. He set his heart on an elector's crown and was disappointed when this went instead to Hannover[1]. The duke did not succeed in elevating his rank or significantly increasing his territory; he did however build one

27. The garden front of the New Corps de Logis with the curved Marble Hall in the centre.

of the largest palaces of the age to symbolise his power and prestige. He must have felt this could rival anything built by Elector Maximilian II Emanuel of Bavaria at Nymphenburg and Schleissheim (see *Schloss in Bavaria*), or by Margrave Karl Wilhelm of Baden-Durlach (the brother of his hated wife) at Karlsruhe (see chapter 7). This would be the Württemberg Versailles! Eberhard Ludwig chose the site of an old hunting lodge ten miles (fifteen kilometres) north of Stuttgart and laid the cornerstone in 1704. He called his new schloss after himself – Ludwigsburg (Ludwig's castle).

All too soon it became clear that the first plans were not on a grand enough scale and over the next thirty years the new schloss grew as more and more buildings were added to form a long courtyard. I think of it as doing a jigsaw puzzle or building Lego on a board. First the Old Corp de Logis (main building) and then, stretching down in front of it in matching pairs, the Order Wing and Giants' Wing; the Chapel of the Order and Chapel of the Court; the East and West Cavalier Wings; and the long galleries (the Gallery of Paintings and the Ancestral Gallery) connecting to a much bigger New Corp de Logis at the far end. It was all complete when Eberhard Ludwig died in 1733. There were problems with the sloping site and with the schloss design. The entrance had to be rerouted to go through a side wing and it is only inside the courtyard that you see the front of the schloss and appreciate its huge size. The guided tour of Ludwigsburg goes through seventy rooms!

From 1711 Eberhard Ludwig lived at Ludwigsburg with his mistress, Wilhelmine von Grävenitz, whom some writers have called the German Pompadour[2]. They met when Wilhelmine was trailed in front of the duke by a coterie of courtiers seeking to increase their influence or further alienate him from his wife, Johanna Elisabeth of Baden-Durlach. Eberhard Ludwig had little affection for his wife and is said only to have married her to bring her attractive lady-in-waiting to his court[3]. Johanna Elisabeth was a spiky character and she refused to turn a blind eye. She lived in the schloss at Stuttgart while Wilhelmine played the role of senior lady at Ludwigsburg. In 1718, Eberhard Ludwig officially moved the capital of his duchy from Stuttgart to Ludwigsburg.

For twenty years Wilhelmine enjoyed a privileged position as the duke's acknowledged favourite. A grand house was built for her just a few yards from the schloss gates[4]. She also occupied apartments in the schloss and frolicked in the gorgeous little pleasure palace of Favorite that Eberhard Ludwig built in the gardens. Wilhelmine influenced the duke politically and was the only woman in his cabinet of ministers[5]. She became hated by his subjects who blamed her for all their misfortunes. Wilhelmine has gone down in history as the epitome of an avaricious and scheming mistress, although I can't think she was worse than many other (including male) courtiers.

### The German Pompadour

*Eberhard Ludwig fell for Wilhelmine von Grävenitz in a big way and married her in secret in 1707. The duke was not troubled by committing bigamy as he considered himself an absolute ruler and above the law. He succeeded his father at less than one-year-old and had a full-blown idea of his own importance. 'I am the pontiff in my own country and in consequence quite in order with the Good Lord!⁶'*

*When his second marriage became known however, his wife, the Württemberg parliament, and ultimately the Holy Roman emperor, disagreed. Eberhard Ludwig was forced to divorce Wilhelmine and exile her from Württemberg. But this was more than just a passing infatuation. When the scandal had died down and the political climate changed⁷, Eberhard Ludwig arranged a marriage of convenience for Wilhelmine to a bankrupt aristocrat. As Countess von Würben she was given a senior position at his court and returned in triumph to Württemberg. Her husband (in name only) was effectively paid to keep away and not exercise his marital rights.*

*His relationship with Wilhelmine unravelled in the last years of Eberhard Ludwig's reign as a crisis over the succession approached. His only son was mortally ill and the next heir was his cousin, Karl Alexander of Württemberg-Winnental. The problem was that Württemberg was Protestant (Lutheran) but Karl Alexander had converted to Catholicism. Nervous courtiers schemed to replace Wilhelmine with a younger mistress who would be more easily controlled⁸. In 1731 Eberhard Ludwig repudiated Wilhelmine, banished her from court, and officially reconciled with his wife after more than twenty years of separation. It was too late for an heir as Johanna Elisabeth was now over fifty. She did claim a pregnancy and preparations were made. But it came to nothing⁹.*

*Eberhard Ludwig's last years were unhappy. He thrashed out at Wilhelmine, accusing her of witchcraft. The charges didn't stick. Eberhard Ludwig died at Ludwigsburg in 1733 after fifty-six years on the throne. Karl Alexander was the next duke of Württemberg and reigned for less than four. He moved the capital from Ludwigsburg back to Stuttgart.*

The guided tour at Ludwigsburg is so long it is spilt into two. You can take the King Friedrich tour, which starts in the king's rooms in the New Corps de Logis and goes clockwise around the courtyard; or take the Queen Mathilde tour which starts in the queen's rooms (adjacent to his) and goes the other way (anti-clockwise). We did both tours back-to-back and it was arduous! There is much else to see at Ludwigsburg including a fashion museum, the sparkling rococo rooms of Duke Karl Eugen, and the

28. Favorite was built by Duke Eberhard Ludwig in the gardens of Ludwigsburg.

*Blooming Baroque* and *Fairy-tale Garden* displays. If you choose to take only one tour, go for Queen Mathilde because this includes the not-to-be-missed Ancestral Gallery of portraits. The English handout has a helpful floorplan but, with seventy to cover, the description of each room is limited to a sentence. We were lucky to be with German friends who translated the guide's commentary (thank you Gert and Uli!).

I was initially somewhat confused about the identity of Queen Mathilde. I knew King Friedrich of Württemberg (1754-1816) was married to Princess Charlotte of Great Britain (1766-1828) – so who was the person called Queen Mathilde? It turned out they are the same; in England Charlotte was known as 'Royal' (from her title as princess royal) but in Württemberg one of her second names was used (Mathilde). To avoid further confusion, I will call her Charlotte Mathilde. Friedrich and Charlotte Mathilde were the first king and queen of Württemberg and the rooms at Ludwigsburg are shown as they left them. One of the first things to notice is that all of the chairs are oversized. Friedrich was a mountain of a man with an enormous belly. The guide gave his personal statistics as six feet eleven inches tall (over two metres) and thirty stones (two hundred kilos). There is a story that at their first meeting, Napoleon said (something like) he had never realised that human skin could stretch so far without bursting! Friedrich retorted that he never knew that anything so small as Napoleon's brain could cause so much trouble! Charlotte Mathilde was also hefty – her statistics were given as six feet one inch (over one point eight metres) and twenty-three and a half stones (one hundred and fifty kilos). The queen fell and broke her hip in middle age and afterwards used a wheelchair[10]. There is one standing in her rooms at Ludwigsburg by the door to her private garden.

Charlotte Mathilde was the eldest of the six daughters of King George III and Queen Charlotte of Great Britain. She was married to Friedrich at the Chapel Royal in St James's Palace, London, in May 1797 when she was thirty years old. Friedrich was forty-two, heir to the duchy of Württemberg, and a widower. When Friedrich first applied to George III with a proposal of marriage for the king's eldest daughter, he was peremptorily refused. His first marriage, to a niece of George III, had ended in scandal leaving Friedrich with a reputation as an abusive husband. King George's response was that ...

> Knowing the brutal and other unpleasant qualities of this prince, I could not give an encouragement to this proposal. ... and if he will not take a gentle hint, I have no objection to adding that after the very unhappy life my niece led with him, I cannot as a father bequeath any daughter of mine to him.[11]

Even today the circumstances of the end of Friedrich's first marriage are shocking. In 1780 he had married fifteen-year-old Princess Auguste of Brunswick-Wolfenbüttel (whose mother was George III's sister). Friedrich was an officer in the Prussian army and third in line for the Württemberg throne. Later he was appointed a regional governor in Finland by Empress Catherine the Great of Russia. His sister was married to Catherine's heir, later Tsar Paul. During a visit to St

Petersburg in 1786, Auguste fled to Catherine seeking protection and claiming that her husband beat her. Whatever she said, the empress believed it. Catherine told Friedrich to leave Russia and he took their three children back to Württemberg, effectively abandoning his wife. What happened next is even murkier. Sometime later Auguste disappeared from the Russian court and her whereabouts were unknown. Eventually it was announced that she had died at the remote castle of Lohde in Estonia. Rumour abounded about this hushed-up death. Only later did the full story emerge and much of this was not known at the time Friedrich proposed for his second wife. Auguste had fallen out of favour with Catherine who sent her to live on a faraway royal estate in the custody of a court official. Auguste died giving birth to his stillborn baby after he refused to call medical attention for fear of their intimate relationship being discovered.

Despite the initial rejection by George III, Friedrich persisted in his proposal. He strenuously denied he was a wife beater and engaged an English barrister to put his side of the case[12]. All he had tried to

29. A card commemorating the centenary of
the kingdom of Württemberg lists its five queens –
Mathilde, Katharina, Pauline, Olga, and Charlotte.

do, he claimed, was to control his first wife's flirtatious and totally inappropriate behaviour. He was helped in his suit by Charlotte Mathilde's unhappiness at home and desperate desire to be married and have her own establishment. Friedrich was a man with a bad temper that he found difficult to control. He was hated by his only son, Friedrich Wilhelm (Auguste's child), who was on the receiving end as a child[13]. When he came to the throne he deliberately did not take his father's name and reigned as King Wilhelm I. Charlotte Mathilde's mother (Queen Charlotte) said she disliked Friedrich because of his temper, and it was suspected that Friedrich didn't always treat his second wife well[14]. But Charlotte Mathilde stoutly defended her husband. She was much happier in her new life in Württemberg, where she could shine as first lady, than she had been back in Britain as an unmarried girl under her parents' close supervision. George III wanted to protect his daughters and keep them unmarried; only two more of the six would escape through marriage and the next not until nearly twenty years later. Charlotte Mathilde became pregnant soon after her marriage, but this ended in the birth of a stillborn baby girl and there were no more pregnancies. The two sets of baby clothes brought from England with her trousseau (one each for a boy and a girl) were never used. She kept them until her death, when they were sold[15]. But she got on well with her stepchildren, particularly Friedrich's only daughter, Katharina. Queen Mathilde was mature, intelligent, and did not expect too much from her marriage[16].

There are many 'star' rooms to see at Ludwigsburg. I remember the cool and elegant Marble Hall redecorated in classical style by King Friedrich. Wild birds on the ceiling hold up the crystal chandeliers; clap your hands in the centre of the room to hear them flutter away. Also, the court theatre of Duke Karl Eugen, where blue satin shoes stood on the stage. Karl Eugen was a womaniser and had so many liaisons that the women were required to wear blue shoes so he could remember those he had slept with[17]. His marriage to Elisabeth Friederike of Brandenburg-Bayreuth did not last and after a few years she left him.

## The Württemberg succession – the duchy

From the eighteenth century, the Württemberg succession very often did not follow a straight line from father to son. After Eberhard Ludwig died in 1733, the next duke was his first cousin (their fathers were brothers – see chart 9). Karl Alexander (1684-1737) had joined the imperial army at the age of twelve and was considered the right-hand-man of Prince Eugen of Savoy[18]. He gave all his sons the name of Eugen (as a second name) in tribute to his patron. At the time of his accession, Karl Alexander was forty-nine years old, an imperial field marshal, and governor of Serbia on behalf of the emperor. Württemberg was a Protestant state, but Karl Alexander had converted to Catholicism in 1712 to further his career in the service of the Hapsburgs. He was required to give guarantees that he would respect and not try to interfere in the religion of his state.

Karl Alexander died unexpectedly on 12 March 1737 in his rooms at Ludwigsburg (included in the Mathilde tour) after only three years as duke. He was a good military commander but not a successful duke and unpopular with his subjects. The cause of death was fluid on the lungs[19] (he had tuberculosis as a child[20]) but the suddenness fostered all sorts of rumours about how he met his end. His Protestant subjects even blamed it on his Catholic religion![21]

Karl Alexander was succeeded by the eldest of his three sons, nine-year-old Karl Eugen (1728-1793). Karl Eugen reigned for fifty-five years and presided over one of the most brilliant courts in Europe, much to the detriment of his small country which had to pay for it. But he failed to produce an heir. So Karl Eugen was succeeded as duke by each of his two brothers in turn. Ludwig Eugen (1731-1795) and Friedrich Eugen (1732-1797) were both elderly and each reigned for two years or less. Ludwig Eugen had only daughters, but Friedrich Eugen produced no less than eight sons, the eldest of whom succeeded him as duke and later became King Friedrich (1754-1816). Although his father was Catholic, Friedrich was brought up as Protestant and the ruler's religion was once more aligned with that of his state.

If you like looking at royal portraits (as I do), don't miss the Ancestral Gallery at Ludwigsburg with portraits of the dukes and duchesses, kings and queens, from Eberhard the Bearded (first duke of Württemberg in 1495). The stand-out portrait for me was Queen Olga (1822-1892), the wife of King Karl (1823-1891), painted by Franz Xaver Winterhalter in 1852. Olga was a grand duchess of Russia (the daughter of Tsar Nikolai I) and immensely rich. In the portrait her dress is littered with pearls! There are strings of pearls hanging from the shoulders, loops and swirls of pearls all over the bodice and skirt, and an edging of pearls around the long train. Queen Olga's marriage was not a happy one and her face looks lugubrious, but this portrait is all about the dress!

## Monrepos

Sometimes the nicest things happen quite by accident. The hotel in Ludwigsburg where we had hoped to stay was full and the receptionist suggested we try instead the hotel at Domäne Monrepos. This is the private estate of the duke of Württemberg some three miles (five kilometres) out of Ludwigsburg centred on Schloss Monrepos. The Domäne is a tremendous amenity for local people. As well as the duke's winery and the offices of the family trust (the Hofkammer des Hauses Württemberg) there is a restaurant, boating lake, fishing, wonderful walks, an equestrian centre, golf course, and of course the Schlosshotel Monrepos. We liked this so much that we stayed there for a week. At the weekend the vast car park for the Domäne was full but in the week we had the place almost to ourselves. The serene and sylvan Domäne is a magical place and has an enthralling history as the party venue of King Friedrich of Württemberg. Monrepos is my favourite schloss in this book.

Monrepos was built in two phases and is a blend of architectural styles. The exterior was built by Duke Karl Eugen of Württemberg (1728-1793) in baroque style in the early seventeen sixties. He was a restless personality and a compulsive builder. Karl Eugen had the

30. Schloss Monrepos was built by Duke Karl Eugen
in baroque style in the early 1760s.

whole area surrounding Ludwigsburg criss-crossed with a pattern of
straight, connecting, avenues. One of these led directly from Schloss
Ludwigsburg out to a pond at Eglosheim where previous dukes had
hunted duck. Karl Eugen reshaped the pond into a rectangular basin
large enough to take gondolas (he had travelled to Venice) and built
an exquisite small schloss on a terrace out into this lake. His court
architect was French (Philippe de la Guêpière) and when Empress
Josephine visited the schloss decades later, she said it reminded her
of the Petit Trianon at Versailles. Called the Seehaus (Lake House),
the schloss was intended to be Karl Eugen's private get-away from the
etiquette and formality of the court.

The exterior was completed in 1762 but then Karl Eugen lost
interest; the interior decoration slowed and ceased altogether in 1765.
His focus had shifted to the next building project – a new summer
residence at Schloss Solitude (see Hohenheim below). The next two
dukes of Württemberg were elderly and each reigned for only a short
time (see chart 9). The Seehaus was left derelict until it was revived
by Duke Friedrich II (1754-1816) starting in 1801. Friedrich was not a
builder like his uncle, Karl Eugen, but did update his palaces in the
latest style. He completed the interior of the Seehaus in classical

empire style and surrounded it with an English landscape park. When it was finished he renamed it Monrepos (the French for My Rest) after his estate when governor of Finland[22]. This small schloss by the lake would be the setting for magnificent court entertainments in summer as Duke Friedrich rose in rank, first to elector and then to king.

31. King Friedrich and Queen Charlotte Mathilde of Württemberg.

Friedrich succeeded his father as duke of Württemberg in December 1797. The issue of the day was revolutionary France and Friedrich will have hoped that his recent marriage to the princess royal of Great Britain (in May 1797) would bring him a powerful ally. As a member of the Holy Roman Empire, Friedrich initially followed the traditional alliance with Austria but this had disastrous consequences when French troops invaded Württemberg. In May 1800 Friedrich, his wife Duchess Charlotte Mathilde, and the entire court were forced to flee the country from their summer residence at Ludwigsburg[23]. Friedrich was a realist and reached an accommodation whereby he relinquished any claim to the county of Montbéliard on the left of the river Rhine (held by the house of Württemberg for centuries but recently annexed by France). In return, under a Holy Roman Empire statute of 1803 compensating its princes for losses of territory ceded to France, Württemberg was increased in size and Friedrich elevated to the rank of elector.

Work on the reconstruction of Monrepos began after the court returned to Ludwigsburg from exile in May 1801. There were a number of problems to overcome – the schloss was damp from the lake, the baroque style of the gardens completely out of date, and more entertaining space was needed. Friedrich's court architect (Nikolaus Thouret) solved them in style. He reduced the water level, to enable the building to dry out, by draining the lake and hollowing out a new, much smaller, basin in the bottom. The schloss foundations so exposed were concealed by a new arcade of arches (see illustration 32). With equal innovation, Thouret remodelled the gardens in the newly fashionable English landscape style by using the digging spoil to build islands in the lake and create a softer, more natural looking shoreline. We walked all the way round the lake on our first day at Monrepos and did not guess it was man-made. From the shore a church steeple on one of the islands is just visible above the trees. The church was transported here by Thouret from another schloss, ready-made[24]. It was damaged by a

32. In the first years of the nineteenth century the lake and grounds were remodelled to an English landscape park.

stray bomb during World War II and only the steeple remains today. Monrepos itself (as well as Schloss Ludwigsburg) was untouched. Ludwigsburg was a military town and the allies wanted to be able to take over the facilities intact.

The court journals for Württemberg record that the renovated Monrepos was first used for entertaining on 2 May 1802 when an afternoon party called a 'gouter' was held[25]. Here is a description (translated from the journals) of the birthday celebrations at Monrepos later that year for Friedrich's heir, Prince Friedrich Wilhelm (later King Wilhelm I).

> At 4:00 pm His Serene Highness was pleased to proceed to the Lakeside Palace and at 6:30 pm he was followed to that very place by His Highness the Prince, heir to the throne, Princess Catarine [Friedrich's daughter], Princess Albertine [Friedrich's sister-in-law] and the court. The arrival there of these persons of highest rank was announced by the thunder of the cannon that had been placed on the island in the lake. The shores of the lake and also the boats [sloops] situated on it were illuminated most tastefully and Turkish music was played by the Grenadier and Seckendorff battalions alternately.[26]

In May 1803 there was a banquet at Monrepos to celebrate Friedrich's new title of prince-elector[27]. The new elector used his new schloss more and more as a showcase for official receptions and court entertainments in a spectacular and unusual setting[28]. The architect solved the problem of a lack of entertaining space by dismantling another schloss and re-erecting this on the shore side of Monrepos as a vast party hall[29]. When the thirty-eighth birthday of Electress Charlotte Mathilde (September 1804) was celebrated with a banquet and court ball at Monrepos, she was ceremonially received at the door of this hall by the elector and his full court to the sound of drums and trumpets[30]. How happy she must have been to be playing the leading role to which she was born after years of frustrated spinsterhood[31]. Later, Thouret added a re-erected theatre which led out of the party hall[32]. The back wall of this theatre could be taken down so that the landscape behind the stage became part of the scenery. During the state visit of Tsar Alexander I of Russia and Emperor Franz II of Austria to Monrepos in 1814, several hundred Württemberg soldiers took part in the battle scenes of an opera called 'The Conquest of Mexico' by Gaspare Spontini[33]. Wow!

33. An old postcard shows the island and the church transported there ready-made to enhance the view.

In October 1805, Napoleon made a surprise visit to Ludwigsburg to negotiate an alliance between France and Württemberg. Friedrich resisted but was forced to give way as Napoleon laid it on the line – be my ally or take the consequences! The rewards were considerable. Württemberg was given even more territory, as Napoleon consolidated the patchwork of small territories in south Germany to create bigger satellite states, and Friedrich received the title of king. On 1 January 1806 all the church bells in Stuttgart rang as he was proclaimed the first king of Württemberg. But the price was very high. Friedrich was forced to provide soldiers for Napoleon's army and more than fifteen thousand Württembergers lost their lives in the Russian campaign of 1812[34].

*One hundred years of royal marriages that linked Württemberg and Russia*

On 26 September 1776, Sophie Dorothee of Württemberg married Grand Duke Paul of Russia in St Petersburg. It was a great match for the niece of the duke of a small German state[35]. The wedding was only five months after the agonising death in childbirth of Paul's first wife but he was the sole heir and his mother, Empress Catherine the Great, could not afford to hang around. Sophie Dorothee was required to give up her fiancé[36], change her religion, and take a new name. As Maria Feodorovna she was the mother of ten children and became empress on Catherine's death in 1796. Four more marriages between the descendants of Sophie Dorothee and the house of Württemberg (see chart 11) would link this German state with one of Europe's great powers and bring wealth in the form of Russian dowries.

In 1816 Maria Feodorovna's fourth daughter, Ekaterina (Katharina), married her cousin Wilhelm (King Friedrich's elder son) and they became king and queen of Württemberg later that year. Katharina was queen for less than three years before her death in 1819 aged thirty. Nonetheless she achieved almost legendary status for her charitable work. A few years later, in 1824, Maria Feodorovna's youngest son, Mikhail, married Friedrich's granddaughter Charlotte (daughter of his younger son, Paul). As Elena Pavlovna she became a respected intellectual in Russia who encouraged Tsar Alexander II in his reforms; but her marriage was not happy.

In 1846, Maria Feodorovna's granddaughter Olga (daughter of Tsar Nikolai I) married Friedrich's grandson Karl (son of King Wilhelm I). Olga was a successful queen but her private life with Karl, who was homosexual, was unhappy and they had no children. The final wedding in one hundred years of marriages to link Württemberg and Russia was when Grand Duchess Vera (daughter of Tsar Nikolai's younger son Konstantin) married Wilhelm Eugen (great-grandson of King Friedrich's younger brother, Eugen) in 1874. As a child Vera was extremely difficult to manage and had been given away by her parents and adopted by her aunt and uncle, Queen Olga and King Karl. Vera's husband died in 1877, but she lived on in Württemberg as an eccentric but rich widow until her own death thirty-five years later.

The newly elevated king became the enemy of his brother-in-law (the prince-regent, later George IV) and Charlotte Mathilde's British family refused to recognise her as a queen. The Württemberg royal family were also required to cement the French alliance through the marriage in 1807 of King Friedrich's only daughter, Katharina, to Napoleon's youngest brother Jérôme, then king of Napoleon's puppet state of Westphalia. In fact Jérôme was already married to an American called Elizabeth Patterson but Napoleon did not approve and had simply ordered his brother to desert her.

Monrepos is privately owned by the house of Württemberg and used for events. We were privileged to be offered a private tour of the interior with the custodian (castellan) who has maintained and restored the schloss for more than twenty-five years. His knowledge and passion were truly impressive and an unforgettable tour is one reason why this is a favourite schloss. Monrepos is quite small – just eleven rooms on the main floor with kitchens underneath and servants' rooms upstairs. The main rooms on the enfilade face south-west and have wonderful views of the lake. They were decorated for King Friedrich on a Greek theme. In the centre is the oval-shaped dining room (called the Kuppelsaal or Cupola Hall), painted in cool colours of ivory and pale lemon. Pairs of pilasters line the walls and garlands of plasterwork fruit loop around the frieze. With even more light from windows in the domed ceiling, there was a feeling of calm elegance in this room.

Next door is the Spiegelsaal (Hall of Mirrors) where the light bounces back and forth off the crystal chandelier and tall mirrors on both sides of the room. In one corner, on top of the stove, is a life-sized statue of the famous female poet from ancient Greece called Sappho. She too is cool and elegant with flowing draperies, a lute in one hand, and a laurel wreath in her hair. Both these rooms are used for events and sadly there has sometimes been damage. The frames of the mirrors are decorated with gilded fretwork on top of dark blue glass. The custodian showed us where he has been forced to cover these with perspex panels as event guests break off pieces of the fretwork as souvenirs! One room

34. The Hall of Mirrors with a view into the Cupola Hall.

which is too precious to use for events is the library with walls panelled in mahogany inset with relief sculptures of Carrara marble showing scenes from Greek mythology. This is a smaller room for the king's private use and the original mahogany fitted furniture, made for him, is still in place. I liked the mahogany curved marquetry doors which, after two hundred years, still seem to fit their frames perfectly.

Underneath the main rooms (at the level of the foundations exposed by Nikolaus Thouret) was quite a surprise – the bones of a huge kitchen, untouched since King Friedrich's time, with different areas for roasting, baking, patisserie and so on. Monrepos was too far for the party food to be brought from Ludwigsburg and had to have its own fully functioning kitchens. Another surprise was the lavatories. When it was built Monrepos was fitted out with eighteenth-century toilets flushed with rain water from the roof to channel the effluent away from the schloss. At some point these became blocked and were only rediscovered when Monrepos was wired for electricity. Rest assured that, should you be lucky enough to attend an event here, there are also modern toilets!

King Friedrich was savvy enough to jump ship before Napoleon's defeat. He managed to keep his crown and Württemberg was one of only five kingdoms in the new German Confederation (the others were Bavaria, Hannover, Prussia, and Saxony). Friedrich died in October 1816 aged sixty-one. Charlotte Mathilde used Monrepos as a widow's residence but had the party hall and theatre demolished in 1818. All that is left of these today is a grassy mound where I watched horses and riders warm up before entering the ring during an event at the equestrian centre. Perhaps Charlotte Mathilde felt these party rooms were obsolete or she just wanted to keep her memories of the great days of entertaining here when she had played a leading role. She had a happy widowhood[37] and died at Ludwigsburg in October 1828, aged sixty-two.

## Hohenheim

Schloss Hohenheim, south of Stuttgart, was built by Duke Karl Eugen of Württemberg (1728-1793) and his second wife, Franziska (1748-1811). Karl Eugen bought the estate in 1769 and presented it to his then mistress, Franziska von Leutrum, three years later. Hohenheim is a university but it is possible to pre-book a guided tour of the historic rooms and there is also a self-guided historical walk around the grounds. In the last part of his life Karl Eugen liked to spend time at Hohenheim with Franziska, living as a country squire and his lady. This was quite a sea-change from his previous relentless pursuit of pleasure and excessive court display.

35. Hohenheim was built by Duke Karl Eugen and his second wife Franziska.

Karl Eugen came to the throne when he was nine years old, spent his formative years at the court of Frederick the Great of Prussia, and grew up in the firm belief that he derived his right to rule from God alone. He was married for the first time in 1748 to Princess Elisabeth Friederike of Brandenburg-Bayreuth (1732-1780). The bride was a niece of Frederick

36. Portrait of Karl Eugen on horseback with
Schloss Solitude in the distance.

the Great (her mother was Frederick's favourite sister, Wilhelmine) and Frederick arranged the marriage to keep Württemberg within the Prussian orbit. The couple initially took to each other and shared a love of music and theatre. There were performances at the court in Stuttgart in which they both played leading roles[38]. But Elisabeth Friederike did not adapt well to her new environment and also failed to produce an heir. Their only child, a daughter, was born in 1750 and died a year later. Karl Eugen was a womaniser from youth but perhaps this would not have mattered if he had supported his wife's position as first lady of the court. Royal wives were expected to understand the difference between dynastic duty and sexual pleasure. But Karl Eugen insulted his wife, and courtiers followed his lead[39]. When she saw the opportunity in 1756, Elisabeth Friederike decamped back to her home court in Bayreuth. Despite the angry protests of her husband, pressure from her parents and Frederick the Great, and even entreaties from the Württemberg Estates (the parliament), who wanted an heir, she refused to return.

The duke who believed in his divine right to rule, was shown to be unable to govern his wife! If Elisabeth Friederike refused to live with him he could not have an heir. Karl Eugen was a Catholic so divorce was not an option; he could not get the marriage annulled on grounds of non-consummation since his wife had borne a child. Perhaps in defiant retaliation to a situation he did not control, Karl Eugen embarked on an ultra-extravagant lifestyle and an endless string of sexual conquests. Looking back later, the duke himself said he was on a *Lebensgaloppade* (a galloping dance of life)[40]. A writer commented that 'The beast had been aroused in him. And unfortunate Württemberg was in future to be ruled by an unleashed tiger.'[41] The duke and his government were on a collision course.

In 1764 the Württemberg Estates took Karl Eugen to the highest court of the Holy Roman Empire (the Reichshofkammer in Vienna) complaining of his despotic rule and illegal imposition of taxes to fund his extravagant lifestyle. Karl Eugen was incensed at their insolence and lèse-majesté. The trouble was that the absolute style of government to which Karl Eugen aspired (epitomised by King Louis XIV) did not work in Württemberg where the Estates had longstanding constitutional rights granted by a previous duke in 1514. The court found for the Estates but Karl Eugen ignored this setback and carried on regardless. He moved his capital from Stuttgart to Ludwigsburg out of pique, thus deliberately depriving Stuttgart of the trade associated with his court.

## Schloss Solitude

Duke Karl Eugen came to build 'Solitude' through disappointment. The Seven Years' War (1756-1763) did not bring him the hoped-for glory; the Württemberg government were challenging his right to rule; he had no son and heir. The duke turned his back on Stuttgart and moved his court to Ludwigsburg. From 1763 to 1769 he built Solitude as his new summer palace and a refuge from his troubles.

The schloss conceived as a private retreat soon also turned into a venue for conspicuous consumption and lavish entertaining. There were parties at Solitude nearly every evening in the summer. The schloss was connected to Ludwigsburg by an eight miles long avenue (thirteen kilometres) and as the duke arrived at Solitude he was greeted with the roar of canon and a ceremonial reception in the Weisser Saal (White Hall)[42]. The reception rooms were in the schloss itself while two long curving (and far less attractive) buildings behind housed the royal and court apartments and offices. An elaborate baroque garden was created; there was a theatre, banqueting hall, Chinese kiosk, pavilions, indoor riding arena, and huge stables for hundreds of horses. In the grounds Karl Eugen set up a High School (the Hohe Karlsschule) for secondary education. This is where the budding young writer Friedrich Schiller was so unhappy. He rebelled against the duke, ran away, and ended up in Weimar (see 'Schloss II').

The interior of Solitude is gorgeous in sparkling late rococo style. Everything is original and our guide described it as a trip back to the eighteenth-century. The entire schloss was covered by camouflage nets during World War II and survived intact. But I did not enjoy the guided tour as much as I expected. There were so many people that we could not all fit together into some rooms. The guide spoke perfect English and gave her own pen picture of Karl Eugen, saying he ate sparsely, never drank wine, and slept only four hours a night. 'He was big in small things and small in big things.' Almost as soon as it was finished, Karl Eugen lost interest in Solitude. He was starting to make changes in his life and his attention drifted away to Hohenheim.

He embarked on more expensive building projects – a new summer residence at Solitude, a massive opera house in the gardens at Ludwigsburg. By dint of his lavish spending the Württemberg opera and ballet became among the very best in Europe. There was a string of illegitimate children with dancers in the 1760s – Rosette Dugazon and Luisa Toscani each bore him two sons, Anna Maria Salamon a daughter, Katharina Kurz a son, Regina Monti a son, Anna Eleonora Franchi a son and a daughter. His last but one mistress, the Italian singer Caterina Bonafini, gave birth to the duke's son in 1768 and a daughter in 1771[43]. We know about these children because the duke acknowledged them.

37. Karl Eugen was an obsessive builder – Solitude was his creation.

The tussle with the Württemberg Estates could not go on indefinitely and eventually the emperor intervened. The political climate was changing rapidly (the French Revolution was only years away) and on New Year's Day 1770, Karl Eugen signed a settlement agreement with the Estates renouncing absolute rule[44]. His frenetic lifestyle was also slowing up; in 1772 Baroness Franziska von Leutrum, the wife of an official at the Württemberg court, divorced her husband and became Karl Eugen's last mistress. She was created Gräfin (countess) of Hohenheim. After the death of his wife (Elisabeth Friederike) in

1780, considerable difficulties from the Catholic church (Franziska was a divorced Protestant), and the protests of his family (Franziska was not of equal birth), Karl Eugen married his 'Franzele'[45] on 11 January 1785. The cornerstone for their new schloss at Hohenheim was laid on 24 June the same year and can still be seen on display in the foyer.

Franziska von Hohenheim did not attract the opprobrium usual for a royal mistress. Quite the contrary, she was welcomed by his subjects and credited with the duke's reform and greater focus on the welfare of his people. Only the royal family were against her, no doubt concerned she might produce a late heir and displace the succession. She was not recognised as duchess of Wurttemberg until 1791[46]. While Hohenheim was under construction, Karl Eugen and Franziska lived in a modest building on the site called the Spiesemeisterei (now a fine-dining restaurant). This is where Karl Eugen died in October 1793, before his last schloss was completed. The widowed Franziska left Hohenheim and settled in Schloss Kirchheim a few miles away. This is now a college but also has a museum. Despite being shown as open on their website, this turned out to be closed the day we went. Note to schlösser – please keep your websites up to date!

Hohenheim remained an unfinished construction site for twenty-five years until it was put to good use by King Wilhelm I. When he acceded in 1816, freak weather conditions and lack of sun, caused by a volcanic eruption in Indonesia, brought widespread crop failure and famine to Württemberg. 1816 was known as the 'year without a summer'. The new Queen Katharina initiated important welfare projects for which she is still remembered. An exhibition in the foyer at Hohenheim tells her story and she is commemorated by an obelisk in the grounds. The king recognised that agricultural reforms were needed to secure the food supply and in 1818 he founded an agricultural institute in Hohenheim. Starting in 1967, some rooms designed by Karl Eugen and Franziska were restored to grandeur and are used for university events. The delicate plasterwork decoration has a rural theme reflecting Karl Eugen's late-in-life preference for a country lifestyle with Franziska.

*The Sepulchral Chapel on the Württemberg Hill – 'Never-ending Love'*

The sepulchral chapel (mausoleum) on the top of Württemberg hill near Stuttgart was built by King Wilhelm I for his wife, Queen Katharina. He chose the location because it was one of Katharina's favourite spots. The Württemberg hill was the site of his ancestral family schloss and Wilhelm had the ruins cleared away to build a Russian orthodox chapel. Katharina was born a Russian grand duchess (the daughter of Tsar Paul) and had to be buried in the Orthodox faith. Over the door is the inscription 'Die Liebe höret nimmer auf' or 'Never-ending love'.

Their marriage was second time around for both Wilhelm and Katharina. When Napoleon indicated that he was interested in Katharina as his second wife, the Russian royal family were horrified and she was quickly married to her cousin, Duke Georg of Oldenburg in 1809. It was a successful marriage and the couple had two sons. When Georg died of typhoid in 1812 Katharina was devastated and had a breakdown. Wilhelm's first marriage to Charlotte of Bavaria in 1808 was a cynical arrangement and never consummated.

Wilhelm and Katharina were first cousins – her mother, Empress Maria Feodorovna was the sister of his father, King Friedrich. Wilhelm's first marriage was annulled and he married Katharina in January 1816. Their two daughters were born in 1816 and 1818. Katharina caught a cold on a day out in early 1819, developed pneumonia, and died at thirty. There is a story that she surprised her husband with a mistress and this hastened her end.

Wilhelm married a third time, to his cousin Pauline (the daughter of his father's younger brother Ludwig), who resembled Katharina[47]. He had affairs and the couple became estranged. They did have two daughters and an only son who became King Karl.

## Schloss and Kloster Bebenhausen

By Saturday 9 November 1918, the news had filtered through to Stuttgart that the king of Bavaria had been overthrown by a Bolshevik revolution and forced to flee from Munich (see *Schloss in Bavaria*). There was also widespread unrest in the Württemberg capital and demonstrators forced their way into the palace demanding that the Royal Standard be taken down and the Red Flag flown in its place. King Wilhelm II realised that his support had evaporated and left the palace quietly that evening with Queen Charlotte. They went to Schloss Bebenhausen near the town of Tübingen. From here the king abdicated on 30 November and in a last letter to his people wrote '... I myself shall never be a hindrance to the free development and conditions of the country and its well-being. Guided by this thought I will lay down the crown today.'[48] The ex-king and queen were allowed the right to live in Bebenhausen for life. Wilhelm died here in 1921 and Charlotte in 1946.

38. The ex-king and queen of Württemberg were granted the right to live in Schloss Bebenhausen for life.

Bebenhausen is a converted Cistercian monastery founded around 1180. After Duke Ulrich (1487-1550) introduced the Reformation to

Württemberg, the monastery was closed in 1535 and the buildings became a Protestant boarding school. The area around Bebenhausen was excellent for hunting and when King Friedrich (1754-1816) acquired the property in 1807 (following the secularisation of church lands) he turned the old monastery into a royal hunting lodge. From 1868 his grandson, King Karl (1823-1891), converted the former monastery guesthouse into a schloss, with reception rooms on the ground floor and the royal apartments upstairs. The last changes to the schloss were made by King Wilhelm II (1848-1921) who modernised the accommodation during World War I.

Bebenhausen is a walled compound of different buildings, rather like a picturesque small village in the countryside where every building is historically important. Please make sure to allow plenty of time to wander around. Visitors have the option of two guided tours – one of Schloss Bebenhausen showing the royal rooms created by Karl and Wilhelm II; the other of Kloster (monastery) Bebenhausen which visits the cloisters, refectory, and monks' accommodation. I had hoped to see the schloss kitchen installed by Wilhelm II in 1915 and still intact, but this is only included on certain tours at weekends. We were the only visitors on the guided tour of the schloss which turned out to be tremendous fun. The guide was Italian with only a smattering of English but with my husband's schoolboy German, a bit of French thrown in, and goodwill on all sides, we managed! We were having such a good time that the tour overran considerably and the guide's colleague was sent to interrupt us.

The tour begins in the Grüner Saal (Green Hall), designed during World War I as part of the modernisation by Wilhelm II. The décor is very striking with colourful wall paintings illustrating the history of the house of Württemberg. A long, painted, vine curls around one wall carrying the family tree – from the founder of the house, Konrad I, to the last king, Wilhelm II. Other walls have landscapes of schlösser and towns in Württemberg. On display is a bronze statuette illustrating a much-loved fable about of the first duke of Württemberg, Eberhard the Bearded (1445-1496). In this fable the rulers of the small German states are bragging to each other about their riches. One boasts of his valuable silver mines; another of rich agricultural lands and vineyards. But Eberhard claims the greatest treasure of all in the love of his people. The statuette shows Eberhard asleep with his head on the knee of a young shepherd who is watching over him.

> ... in the forests, though so vast
> I can boldly rest my head
> In the lap of every subject.[49]

From the Green Hall the tour goes through two more reception rooms (the Blue Hall and Red Hall) and then up a spiral staircase into the Hirschgang (Stag Corridor) with the private rooms of King Wilhelm II and Queen Charlotte. When he was born, Wilhelm was only fourth in the line of succession to the Württemberg throne; after his cousin, Crown Prince Karl, and Wilhelm's own grandfather and father (see chart 10). But it must have become increasingly clear that Karl (who was homosexual) was unlikely to father children from his marriage to Queen Olga and that Wilhelm would succeed. Wilhelm was educated for the role but was a reluctant heir – reluctant to follow the usual military career for princes and reluctant to be apprenticed to the business of government[50]. He was also reluctant to make the usual dynastic marriage and some historians have suggested that his real inclinations lay with members of his own sex[51].

In 1877 Wilhelm married Princess Marie of Waldeck-Pyrmont (1857-1882). We saw her portrait in the King's Bedroom on the Stag Corridor. Marie was one of six sisters who are famous for their marriages; her younger sisters married King Willem III of the Netherlands and Queen Victoria's son, the duke of Albany (see Pyrmont in *Schloss III*). The marriage of Wilhelm and Marie was dynastically arranged but turned out to be a success. There was huge rejoicing in the country when their son, Ulrich, was born in 1880. As a Protestant heir to the Württemberg throne the baby was welcomed in the country (the next branch in line to inherit after Wilhelm was Catholic). Both parents were devastated when the little boy died at a few months old and more tragedy followed when Marie died in childbirth with a stillborn daughter in 1882.

Wilhelm resigned his command in the army and tried to retreat into private life with his and Marie's only surviving child – a daughter Pauline born in 1877. He wrote to a friend

> My whole life is broken, shattered. If I were allowed to do so, I would like to throw it away. I have to continue with this tortured existence, though, for my poor, motherless child, this sacred legacy, the only thing that I have left.[52]

We saw a photograph of Pauline, dated 1898, next to that of her mother in the King's Bedroom. This was the year Pauline married Prince Wilhelm of Wied. To my surprise, she looked quite pretty – all photos of her in later life show her as relentlessly fat and ugly[53]. Our tour guide at Ludwigsburg described Pauline as 'masculine' and 'strange'. As a child the guide wanted to be a princess until her mother showed a photo of Princess Pauline. Not at all a little girl's idea of what a princess ought to look like! Wilhelm had no interest in marrying again and robustly declared he was against dynastic marriage. 'I do not wish to give my country the example of a cold loveless marriage!'[54] But he did precisely that. Under pressure from all sides as the heir, Wilhelm married Charlotte of Schaumburg-Lippe in 1886.

39. Bebenhausen is like a picturesque small village.

*The Württemberg succession – the kingdom.*

*Duke Friedrich II (1754-1816) was proclaimed king of Württemberg on 1 January 1806. There were three further kings of Württemberg, all descended from King Friedrich. But quite extraordinarily, by the time the monarchy came to an end, the next heir to the throne was a descendant of his sixth younger brother. All intervening living males were debarred by virtue of morganatic marriage.*

*King Friedrich was succeeded by his elder son, Wilhelm I (1781-1864), and then by Wilhelm's only son, Karl (1823-1891). Karl had no children and was succeeded by his cousin, Wilhelm II (1848-1921), the grandson of King Friedrich's younger son, Paul. Wilhelm II's only son died as an infant and to find the next heir to the throne, the succession had to go back three generations to the younger brothers of King Friedrich.*

*King Friedrich was the eldest of no less than eight sons of Duke Karl Alexander (1684-1737). You might have thought that with so many there would be a multitude of heirs but this was not the case (see chart 12). The descendants of the second son (Ludwig) were not in line for the Württemberg throne because of a morganatic (unequal) marriage. They became dukes of Teck and married into the British royal family. The third son (Eugen) had several eligible male descendants but the last of these died childless in 1892. The fourth son (Wilhelm) also made a morganatic marriage – so his descendants, the dukes of Urach, were not in line to succeed (see Lichtenstein). The fifth son (Ferdinand) had no children and the sixth (Karl Friedrich Heinrich) never married. So the heir to Württemberg in 1918 was Duke Albrecht (1865-1939), the great-grandson of the seventh son (Alexander). Albrecht, from a Catholic branch, became head of house Württemberg on the death of ex-king Wilhelm II in 1921. The current head of house is his grandson Karl, duke of Württemberg, born in 1936.*

Wilhelm and Charlotte kept up appearances but there were no children; Pauline was King Wilhelm II's only child. Queen Charlotte's rooms at Bebenhausen were my favourite part of this schloss and say something about her life. The drawing room has a wall painting of Schloss Nachod in Bohemia where she grew up. Charlotte was a keen hunter and the antechamber is full of hunting trophies and animals she shot. A portrait in her bedroom shows her at fifty; she did not like this picture at all and would have liked to destroy it[55]. The wheelchair beside her bed is a reminder she suffered a stroke and was paralysed towards the end of her life. Charlotte's dressing room and bathroom, modernised in 1915-1916, still look up-to-date and must have been state-of-the-art

40. King Wilhelm II and Queen Charlotte reached their silver wedding in 1911.

a hundred years ago. The dressing room has fully fitted wardrobes and chests of drawers, built-in jewellery safe, and hinged mirrors; the ensuite bathroom has a flush toilet, bidet, and a walk-in shower. I would be happy to have these rooms in my house today!

## Lichtenstein

Lichtenstein is a fairy-tale schloss in the Swabian mountains in central Baden-Württemberg and not to be confused with the country of Liechtenstein (slightly different spelling) further south, sandwiched between Austria and Switzerland. When I first saw Lichtenstein I could hardly believe it was real. Perched on a sheer-sided lump of rock high above the countryside and embellished with tower, turrets, and stepped gables, it looked amazing and the epitome of a medieval knight's castle. In fact Lichtenstein is mock-medieval and was built in the nineteenth century by Count Wilhelm of Württemberg (1810-1869), a cousin of the Württemberg king. It was always inconvenient to live in – the count's mother-in-law complained that there was not enough room for the children and the castle had no water supply[56].

41. Lichtenstein is a fairy-tale schloss in the Swabian Mountains built by Count Wilhelm of Württemberg, later first duke of Urach.

Count Wilhelm was inspired to build Lichtenstein by the popular romantic novel of the same name by the Swabian author Wilhelm Hauff, published in 1826. It must be the only schloss to have its beginnings in a work of literature. The novel tells the story of how, when he was a fugitive in 1519, Duke Ulrich of Württemberg (1487-1550) hid in the old fourteenth-century schloss at Lichtenstein at night and found shelter in nearby caves during the daytime. By the turn of the twentieth century this old schloss was in very bad condition and King Friedrich knocked down the remains and built a half-timbered lodge on the same site using the original foundations. Count Wilhelm bought the lodge and estate from King Friedrich's successor (King Wilhelm I) in 1837. He was interested in German history and the preservation of his country's monuments[57]. In one portrait at Lichtenstein, Wilhelm is depicted wearing medieval armour. On display in the Armoury is the suit of armour made for him in 1846 to wear at a tournament in Stuttgart. The dents in the breastplate show this was actually used for jousting and not just fancy-dress[58].

Wilhelm demolished the lodge and, starting in 1839, built a new schloss, again on the old foundations. It rises directly out of the rock and is reached by a high narrow bridge over the deep moat (see illustration 41). It was one of several schlösser built around that time in an imagined and romanticised vision of the past. Others include Stolzenfels (see *Schloss III*) and Burg Hohenzollern (which we visit in chapter five).

The building and fitting out took only three years and the new Lichtenstein was inaugurated in a ceremony on 27 May 1842. Lichtenstein means light or bright stone and takes its name from the outcrop of white Jurassic limestone on which it stands. The very tip of this rock has been left exposed inside the schloss. Due to the limitations of the site, the interior of the keep is small with just three rooms on the ground level and four at first floor level. The offices and family accommodation were in supplementary buildings in the outer castle courtyard on the landside of the bridge.

Count Wilhelm was the son of Duke Wilhelm of Württemberg (1761-1830), who was a younger brother of King Friedrich. Duke Wilhelm fell in love with a lady-in-waiting at the Württemberg court called Wilhelmine von Tunderfeld-Rhodis and they were married in 1800. As a fourth son (see chart 12), Duke Wilhelm may have thought it unlikely he would be in the line of succession so it was not important for him to make a dynastic marriage. He was not to know that, had it not been for his wife's unequal status, their grandson (Count Wilhelm's son Wilhelm) would have become heir to the Württemberg throne. (It is confusing that all of Count Wilhelm, his father, and his son, have the same first name but I will try to make it clear which is which.)

### Burg Teck

*Of all the schlösser we visited for this book, the one my husband remembers best is Burg Teck. One reason for this was the long walk uphill to get there. The schloss was destroyed in 1525 during the Peasants' War and the ruins are now part of a nature reserve and can only be reached on foot. The footpath zig-zagged up through the trees and each time we turned a corner it was to find yet another steep incline ahead! When we did eventually emerge among the ruins at the top, we found a hiker's cafe and a welcome cup of coffee. And what really made this schloss so memorable was that in the cafe was displayed a family tree showing how Queen Elizabeth II is descended from a morganatic branch of the Württemberg royal family. Her great-grandfather (father of Queen Mary) was Duke Franz of Teck (1837-1900).*

*Franz was the only son of Duke Alexander of Württemberg and his wife, the beautiful Countess Claudine von Rhédey from Transylvania. Their marriage was classified as morganatic (or unequal) and Franz was born with the lessor title of count Hohenstein (rather than prince of Württemberg). Countess Claudine died young, after a few years of marriage, but will always have a place in royal history because of the manner of her tragic end. Claudine's horse bolted during a military review in 1841 and threw her; she was trampled to death by the passing cavalry.*

*It was a great source of discontent to her son that he was debarred from royal privileges because of his mother's lack of royal birth. Franz was eventually created prince of Teck (in 1863) and then duke of Teck (in 1871). Teck was a defunct dukedom and carried no land or revenues. Chart 13 shows how close Franz would have been to the Württemberg throne. King Wilhelm II, who succeeded in 1891, was the last in the male line of King Friedrich's branch of the family. Except for his morganatic status, Franz would then have become the heir.*

*In 1866, Prince Franz married Princess Mary Adelaide of Cambridge, a granddaughter of King George III and first cousin of Queen Victoria. Their eldest child was Queen Mary – the wife of King George V and grandmother of Queen Elizabeth II.*

Wilhelmine von Tunderfeld-Rhodis was of noble birth but she was not a royal, so her marriage to Duke Wilhelm was deemed morganatic or unequal. Duke Wilhelm had to renounce any right to the succession for himself and his descendants; in return his brother, King Friedrich, granted Wilhelmine the title of princess but her children that of only counts and countesses. There were three surviving children – two sons (Count Wilhelm was the younger) and a daughter. Perhaps Count Wilhelm felt his lack of royal status; one suggestion is that building Lichtenstein was part of his case to get a dukedom. He did get a dukedom towards the end of his life and was created first duke of Urach by his cousin, King Karl, in 1867. This was a subsidiary title of the kings of Württemberg and did not carry any lands or ruling rights.

Count Wilhelm married twice, and both his wives have interesting family backgrounds. In 1841, he married Princess Theodolinde of Leuchtenberg (1814-1857). It has been said he needed her dowry to finish building Lichtenstein[59]. Theodolinde (Linda in the family) was the fourth daughter of a marriage forced by Napoleon – that of Josephine's son (and Napoleon's adopted son), Eugene de Beauharnais,

42. The colourful chapel at Lichtenstein is dedicated to St Theodolinde.

to Princess Auguste Amalie of Bavaria, the daughter of King Maximilian I. It was the widowed Auguste Amalie who complained, on a visit to Lichtenstein in 1846, about the inconvenience (and the cost) of this schloss built by her son-in-law. Count Wilhelm, from only a morganatic side-line, was not in the same league compared to the spouses of her other children. The sons of Eugene and Auguste Amalie married the queen of Portugal and the eldest daughter of Tsar Nicholai I of Russia; two daughters were wives of the king of Sweden and emperor of Brazil. Theodolinde was a Catholic and the colourful St Theodolinde Catholic chapel is a highlight of the guided tour. It holds one treasure of the schloss - a painting of Mary with the apostles from 1440 by an artist called the Master of Schloss Lichtenstein. Wilhelm and Theodolinde had four daughters and the corner towers in the outer castle courtyard are named after these – Auguste, Marie, Mathilde and Eugenie. Count Wilhelm was an artillery expert and the Auguste tower houses a display of canon. The finest of the spectacular views to enjoy at Lichtenstein are from outside this tower. Theodolinde died of tuberculosis in 1857.

Count Wilhelm's second wife was Princess Florestine of Monaco (1833-1897). The house rules of the Grimaldi family did not exclude females from the succession and Florestine was next in line to Monaco after her brother, the ruling prince Charles III, and his descendants. Wilhelm and Florestine married in 1863 and had two sons. When Wilhelm (now a duke) died at Lichtenstein in 1869, his eldest son Wilhelm (1864-1928) succeeded him as second duke of Urach. Wilhelm II is remembered for getting close to but never reaching four thrones. He was debarred from the Württemberg succession by virtue of his grandfather's morganatic marriage to Wilhelmine von Tunderfeld-Rhodis. He had a good claim in Monaco until the French government made it clear that they would not tolerate a German duke as ruler of this neighbouring principality. So, instead, the Grimaldi legitimised the illegitimate daughter of Charles III's only grandson and put her in the line of succession. She was the mother of Prince Rainier (Grace Kelly's husband). In 1913, Wilhelm of Urach applied for the throne of a newly independent Albania but was turned down in favour of another German prince (Wilhelm of Wied who in the event only reigned for a few months). His last try was initially successful when in 1918 Wilhelm was elected as King Mindaugas II of Lithuania, which had also just gained independence. But he never got a chance to visit his new country and the invitation to become king was withdrawn after a few months. The current owner of Lichtenstein is his grandson, Wilhelm Duke of Urach, born in 1957.

43. The Knights' Hall with a portrait of Count Wilhelm, aged twenty-five, in the uniform of an artillery officer.

The guided tour of Lichtenstein felt like an adventure. The schloss is off the beaten track so it was a surprise to find that of the total of six visitors assembled for the tour, five of us were from the United Kingdom! The helpful guide suggested she could improvise an English tour by reading from an English script and the sole German visitor (who spoke English) offered to translate further information and questions. The group bonded and it was a real team effort. Lichtenstein was always intended as a showpiece and the rooms are theatrical and distinctive. Most memorable was the glowing Knights' Hall in gothic-style with a portrait of a young Count Wilhelm in uniform as an artillery officer (see illustration 43). I also loved the rustic Drinking Parlour (tavern) where the men retired for drinking bouts after a day's hunting. The walls are painted with drinking scenes and in one of these pictures two men in medieval costume lean upon a barrel quaffing wine. On the barrel is written a drinking toast which says

> Better to drown in beer and wine
> Than in the Danube or the Rhine[60]

I thoroughly recommend a visit to this schloss!

### Hohenstaufen and Kloster Lorch

During the middle-ages, the Hohenstaufen family was the most important dynasty in Europe. For more than a century (between 1138 and 1254) they held the titles of Holy Roman emperor or German king. (German king was the title of the elected Holy Roman emperor before his coronation as emperor by the Pope.) The Hohenstaufen homeland was the duchy of Swabia which encompassed much of present-day Baden-Württemberg and also stretched south into part of Switzerland and east across the Rhine into France. When I saw the sign for Stauferland on the road near Göppingen (east of Stuttgart), I was instantly attracted because Staufer is the alternative family name. We followed the sign and it took us to the ruins of Schloss Hohenstaufen and the family burial place at Kloster (monastery) Lorch.

In 1079, Friedrich I of Hohenstaufen (1047/8-1105) married the daughter of the Holy Roman Emperor Henry IV and was made duke of Swabia in reward for his loyalty. It was his marriage to Agnes of Waiblingen that brought the emperor's crown into the Hohenstaufen family. Agnes's brother Heinrich V was the last Holy Roman emperor from the Salian line. When he died without a direct heir in 1125, Friedrich I and Agnes' sons, Friedrich II and Konrad III, became candidates for the role. There was a rival candidate however and it was not until 1138 (after the interim reign of Lothar of Supplingburg) that the younger son became German king. Konrad III died in 1152, while he was getting ready to travel to Rome for his coronation by the Pope. For four more generations the title of Holy Roman emperor or German king would stay within the Hohenstaufen dynasty (see chart 14).

44. Duke Friedrich I of Swabia built his castle
on the top of Hohenstaufen mountain.

Friedrich I of Hohenstaufen took his name from the schloss he built around 1070 in a commanding position on top of the Hohenstaufen mountain in Swabia. 'Hohen' means high and 'stauf' bell or goblet shaped. The cone-shaped mountain is nearly seven-hundred metres high and a very distinctive landmark in the countryside. Hohenstaufen was destroyed and left in ruins by rebellious farmers in the Peasants' War of 1525. This was an agrarian uprising in south-west Germany by peasants seeking freedom from oppression. It was savagely repressed by the nobility with the slaughter of an estimated one hundred thousand peasants. Hohenstaufen was never rebuilt and the stones were removed piece by piece for use as building material in nearby Göppingen. Excavations on the site between 1935 and 1938 revealed the base of some walls and these are visible today. The mountain is criss-crossed by hiking trails and we walked up to see the ruins, admire the sweeping views, and find the stele (a hexagonal memorial stone) erected in 2002 to mark the seven hundred and fifty year anniversary of the birth of Konradin (1252-1268), the last Hohenstaufen duke of Swabia. This stele is one of a network across Europe marking important Hohenstaufen sites. And not to be missed at the foot of the mountain is the riveting exhibition in the Documentation Centre for Staufen History. This provides a fascinating guide to the history of the dynasty in visual, imaginative, and colourful form; all translated into English!

The exhibition is suited to all ages and levels of interest. I much enjoyed watching a filmed demonstration (with English sub-titles) showing how a medieval knight would have donned all his fighting gear including chainmail armour and underclothing. Another film tells the story of the Hohenstaufen wives. One of the star exhibits on display is a replica of the famous Barbarossa bust – a sculpture bust of the Hohenstaufen emperor, Friedrich I known as Barbarossa or red beard (1122/24-1190). He succeeded his uncle, Konrad III, and was crowned as emperor in 1155. The original gilded bronze sculpture bust was made around 1160 and given by Friedrich Barbarossa to his godfather[61]. It is believed to be a portrait of the famous Holy Roman emperor from life (albeit idealised) and so may give us an idea of what he looked like.

I liked the focus given in the exhibition to the Hohenstaufen wives. These high-born women played an important role in the success of the dynasty by bringing new territories and titles into the family and by giving birth to sons (see chart 14 for a family tree). When Friedrich I of Hohenstaufen married Agnes of Waiblingen in 1079 she brought the duchy of Swabia as her dowry. Her grandson, Emperor Friedrich Barbarossa, became the ruler of Burgundy when he married the sovereign countess, Beatrix of Burgundy, as his second wife in 1156. Their son, Emperor Heinrich VI (1165-1197), was king of Sicily from 1194 following his marriage to Konstanze of Sicily in 1186. Konstanze had remained unmarried until she was past thirty and was forty years old when she gave birth to her son, the future Emperor Friedrich II

(1194-1250). At that time it would have been considered a very late age to have a baby. There is a story that, to prove the child was truly hers and not a substitute, Konstanze gave birth publicly in a tent in a town market place[62]! The baby grew up to marry four times – his second marriage in 1225 to Yolande of Brienne brought Friedrich II the kingdom of Jerusalem.

Another interesting Hohenstaufen wife was Irene Angelos of Byzantium, daughter of the Byzantine emperor Isaac II Angelos. Her contemporary, the poet and singer Walther von der Vogelweide, called Irene 'a rose without a thorn'[63]. (This is the original of the famous saying.) Irene married Philipp of Swabia (1176/7-1208), the brother of Emperor Heinrich VI, in 1195. His own son was only a toddler when Heinrich VI died in 1197 and his brother Philipp became German king.

45. Kloster Lorch is the Hohenstaufen family burial place.

But his election was contested and a period of strife followed. When Philipp was murdered in 1208, a pregnant Irene fled to Hohenstaufen for safety. There she gave birth to a baby girl called Beatrix Posthuma but both mother and baby died shortly thereafter. They were buried in the family burial place of Kloster (monastery) Lorch.

In 1102, Friedrich I of Hohenstaufen founded a Benedictine monastery at Lorch, just a few kilometres from the schloss he built on Hohenstaufen mountain. The monastery church became the Hohenstaufen burial place and Friedrich I and his wife Agnes of Waiblingen are buried here. A family tree at the rear of the knave shows other family members thought also to be interred at Lorch. Like Hohenstaufen, Kloster Lorch was destroyed in the Peasants' War of 1525 but, unlike Hohenstaufen, it was rebuilt and continued to operate until the Reformation. Today the old monastery buildings house a nursing home but the grounds and romanesque church are open to the public.

A brief English handout with a map of the grounds is available from the shop. We were the only visitors to the church and inside was very quiet and serene. There is a memorial to Irene Angelos and large portraits of the Hohenstaufen emperors and kings on the columns of the arches down each side of the nave. In the centre stands the carved stone sarcophagus of the Hohenstaufen from 1475.

46. The Hohenstaufen sarcophagus at Lorch dates from 1475.

The colourful story of the Hohenstaufen is told at Kloster Lorch in an enormous and vibrant modern painting by local artist Hans Kloss. This huge panorama (thirty metres long and over four metres tall) was completed for the nine-hundred-year anniversary of Kloster Lorch in 2002. In a series of episodes the painting depicts the rise and fall of the dynasty; beginning with the foundation of Kloster Lorch in 1102 and ending with the execution in Naples marketplace of sixteen-year-old Konradin in 1268. We looked at Agnes of Waiblingen riding up the hill to Hohenstaufen; the death of her grandson, Friedrich I Barbarossa, by drowning in a Turkish river during the third crusade; the arrival at Lake Constance of Barbarossa's grandson, Friedrich II, after his election as German king, with camels, elephants and other exotic animals in his train (he came from the middle east); and finally the beheading of Friedrich II's grandson Konradin, the last Hohenstaufen duke of Swabia. I bought lots of postcards and have looked at these many times since.

# 5

# HOHENZOLLERN

As kings of Prussia and German emperors, the Hohenzollern dynasty is most associated with north-east Germany and their great capital of Berlin. But the family's early beginnings were in Swabia in south-west Germany at the eleventh-century ancestral schloss in Baden-Württemberg from which they take their name. In the early thirteenth century the house of Hohenzollern divided into two with one line remaining in Swabia and the other moving north and east to Brandenburg and Prussia. The Prussian Hohenzollerns would have the greater destiny and eventually become pre-eminent as kaisers (emperors) of a united Germany. But the Swabian line also held sovereign territories in south-west Germany until the middle of the nineteenth century.

This chapter visits the flagship schloss of the house of Hohenzollern, remodelled by a Prussian king to symbolise his glorious family history. It also discovers the surprising history of the Catholic south-German Hohenzollerns who intermarried with Napoleon's family and became kings of Romania.

### Burg Hohenzollern

Burg Hohenzollern dates from the mid-nineteenth century when King Friedrich Wilhelm IV of Prussia (1795-1861) rebuilt it as a monument to the history of his mighty house. It is the third schloss on the same site on the crest of Zoller Hill, south of Stuttgart. The king is said to have fallen on his knees in tears when he first visited in 1819 and saw the ruins of the previous schloss[1]. The fabulous hill-top castle he commissioned is a visual feast and a real delight to visit.

47. Burg Hohenzollern dominates the landscape
and is visible from miles away.

Burg Hohenzollern dominates the landscape and is visible from miles away. It really does look like the picture in illustration 47. We must have stopped the car ten times on the way there for photos. We took the shuttle bus from the ticket office to the Eagle Gateway, named after the carved-stone Prussian eagle on the battlements above it. From here there is a further height difference of over eighty feet (twenty-five metres) to the schloss courtyard above and the problem faced by the architect was how to get horses and carriages up with only a limited space available. The solution was an innovative and impressive feat of engineering called the Ramp. I have not seen anything like this in another schloss. Three overlapping, elliptical loops make up a gently sloping carriage drive and an easy ascent. We walked up what seemed like a never-ending spiral to emerge from a tunnel at the end into a theatrical-looking courtyard. In the centre were what looked like giant Easter eggs – huge egg-shaped plant containers covered with colourful pansy flowers.

The guided tour begins in the Ancestral Hall where the walls are painted with the thousand-year genealogy of the house of Hohenzollern (see illustration 48). This has to be the most amazing family tree I have ever seen. With the aid of a light pointer our knowledgeable and enthusiastic guide gave an overview of Hohenzollern dynastic history talking in a mixture of German and English. Here is my attempt at a very short summary, using only three sentences! The first documented record of the house of Hohenzollern is in a medieval chronicle of 1061 which mentions the death in battle of Burchard and Wezil of Zollern. In 1188, the family took a step up when Count (Graf) Friedrich III of

48. The Ancestral Hall is painted with
an amazing Hohenzollern family tree.

Zollern married the daughter of the burgrave of Nuremberg in Franconia (now in Bavaria), and later succeeded to his father-in-law's title and possessions. Friedrich III's sons divided the inheritance into two lines – the senior (Swabian) line, which kept Burg Hohenzollern and stayed

in Swabia; and the junior (Franconian) line, which had lands in Franconia but also later became electors of Brandenburg in 1415, and rose to be Prussian kings in 1701 and German emperors in 1871. (Whew!) Members of the Franconian line (the Prussian royal house) are circled in blue on the family tree in the Ancestral

49. Burg Hohenzollern was rebuilt by King Friedrich Wilhelm IV of Prussia.

Hall; members of the Swabian line (the princes of Hohenzollern) are circled in red. For more about the history of the Swabian line, please see Schloss Sigmaringen below.

The Blue Parlour at Hohenzollern is hung with family portraits from the Prussian royal house, including King Friedrich Wilhelm IV and his wife Princess Elisabeth of Bavaria. This gorgeous room is named after the colour of the upholstery and has golden wallpaper and a golden coffered ceiling. Friedrich Wilhelm was the twenty-three-year-old crown prince of Prussia when he first visited Burg Hohenzollern and saw the dilapidated ruins on a beautiful summer's evening in July 1819. He later wrote that his memories of this visit '... are exceedingly dear to me and like a pleasant dream, especially the sunset we watched from the bastions ...'[2]. The young prince had a strong sense of his family history and was inspired by the nineteenth-century Romantic Movement in architecture, art, and literature. He determined to rebuild the Hohenzollern ancestral schloss in the spirit of the medieval to glorify his dynasty. He called this decision '... a dream of my youth'[3] and it would not be realised for more than thirty years. Friedrich Wilhelm ascended the Prussian throne in 1840 and the foundation stone for the new Burg Hohenzollern was eventually laid on 23 September 1850.

Some of the difficulties were over ownership and funding. There were two surviving independent Hohenzollern principalities in Swabia at that time (Hohenzollern-Hechingen and Hohenzollern-Sigmaringen) and it was not until these relinquished sovereignty to Prussia in 1850 (see Sigmaringen) that Burg Hohenzollern stood on Prussian soil. The financial issues were overcome by a family contract of 1846 whereby the king agreed to fund two thirds of the building costs and the Swabian branches took one third[4]. This deal still holds today – Burg Hohenzollern is privately owned by the house of Hohenzollern, two thirds by the Prussian royal line and one third by the Swabian line. Friedrich Wilhelm's last years were overshadowed by mental and physical disability following a major stroke. In 1858 he was deemed unfit to rule and his next younger brother, Wilhelm, appointed as regent. The king and his wife were childless and Wilhelm was the heir to the Prussian throne. Friedrich Wilhelm did not live to see Burg Hohenzollern completed and died in 1861.

Another portrait in the Blue Parlour to attract my attention was that of Queen Victoria's eldest daughter, also called Victoria or Vicky in the family (1840-1901), who married into the Prussian royal house and became Empress Friedrich III of Germany. She was a talented artist and near to her own portrait is one she painted of her son Waldemar (1868-1879)[5]. Vicky regarded Waldemar as the most promising of her three sons and never fully got over his death from diphtheria at eleven-years-old. On 8th October 1862 Crown Princess Victoria of Prussia (as Vicky then was) visited Burg Hohenzollern with her husband. The schloss was in the later stages of construction and would be officially completed with an inauguration ceremony on 3 October 1867. Vicky wrote about the visit in a letter to her mother and her enthusiastic description does justice to the magic of this hill-top schloss.

Our expedition to Hohenzollern was most successful: anything so grand, so imposing or beautiful I never saw, as the Burg Hohenzollern! Fancy in the midst of the hills called the Rauhe Alp, a pointed hill rising straight up 3000 feet (as high as the Brocken), with the beautiful castle on the top. The day was very fine but at first the clouds quite covered the Hohenzollern and by degrees they cleared away from the top but remained round the summit leaving only the building free; it had a magic effect, looking like a burg built on the clouds! The mist all dispersed by the middle of the day and we had a glorious view from the top.[6]

The great reception room of Burg Hohenzollern is the dazzling Grafensaal or Count's Hall with golden vaulted ceiling, slender marble pillars, and mosaic patterned stone floor in the Hohenzollern heraldic colours of black and white. The candles in the chandeliers are still lit for special occasions and how everything must then glitter! Hohenzollern is close to an earthquake fault-line and a major quake in September 1978 caused millions of pounds of damage and distorted the chimneys, so there is no heating. The Count's Hall is the venue for annual summer charity concerts in aid of the Princess Kira of Prussia Foundation, established in 1952 to bring disadvantaged children from around the world for a holiday at Burg Hohenzollern. Princess Kira (1909-1967) was the wife of Prince Louis Ferdinand of Prussia (1907-1994), son of the last crown prince of Germany and head of the Prussian royal house after his father's death in 1951.

Burg Hohenzollern was always intended as a museum rather than a royal family residence but Friedrich Wilhelm IV wanted a suite of rooms for his own use and these are shown on the guided tour. The only time these rooms have ever been used was for a few months in 1945 when Crown Prince Wilhelm (1882-1951) was interned here under house arrest at the end of World War II[7]. In the autumn, the prince moved into a house in the nearby town of Hechingen and died there on 20 July 1951. He and his wife Cecilie (1886-1954) are buried in the small cemetery at Burg Hohenzollern. The head of the Prussian royal house today is Georg Friedrich Prince of Prussia, born in 1976, who is the grandson of Louis Ferdinand and Kira. The prince lives with his wife and family near Berlin but has an apartment in the schloss for his visits to Burg Hohenzollern.

50. The dazzling Grafensaal or Count's Hall.

There is a legend in the house of Hohenzollern about a ghost called *The White Lady* who appears to family members as a harbinger of death. One possible source of this story is the siege and destruction in 1423 of the original eleventh-century Hohenzollern schloss on Zoller Hill, during a family inheritance feud. An historical painting in the Library depicts an ethereal lady dressed in white walking unharmed through the lines to bring food to the starving garrison[8]. Starting in 1454 a bigger and better schloss was built, but over the centuries this fell into decline as fashions changed and the family moved their residence to the town palace in Hechingen. It was the pitiful state of this fifteenth-century schloss that so upset Friedrich Wilhelm IV. This second schloss was the model for the nineteenth-century reconstruction, but only St Michael's Chapel (Catholic) could be preserved as the oldest part today.

There is so much to see at the fascinating third schloss on the Zoller Hill, built to realise his dream by King Friedrich Wilhelm IV of Prussia. I could have written about the fortified Bastions with breath-taking views; or the Royal Treasury, with stunning court dress of the famous Queen Luise of Prussia; the Prussian king's crown; and other treasures allocated to the house of Hohenzollern in the financial settlement after the monarchy fell. On display here is the uniform worn by King Frederick the Great of Prussia at the 1759 battle of Kunersdorf, together with the snuff box he carried in his breast pocket. Frederick was hit but escaped major injury when the bullet ricocheted off the snuff box. You can see the bullet hole in his jacket. Frederick the Great's coffin rested for forty years in Christ's Chapel (Protestant) at Hohenzollern until it could be taken to Potsdam after German reunification. You must go to Burg Hohenzollern yourself.

## Sigmaringen

Sigmaringen was the residence of the sovereign princes of Hohenzollern-Sigmaringen. Although less well-known than their distant relatives in Prussia, this branch of the house of Hohenzollern also has an illustrious history and was closely linked to several European thrones including Napoleonic France and Romania. Sigmaringen has a dramatic setting on a rocky cliff above the river Danube (see illustration 51) and some truly impressive interiors.

The princes of Hohenzollern-Sigmaringen were a branch of the Swabian line of the house of Hohenzollern. The Swabian line was founded when, after the death of Friedrich III of Zollern in 1201, his two sons split the family inheritance and the elder son, Friedrich IV (1188-1255), retained the ancestral lands in Swabia[9]. Sigmaringen came into the possession of the Swabian line in 1535 and the first count to live here was Karl I (1516-1576). His portrait hangs in the Roter Salon (Red Salon) near that of his wife, Anna of Baden-Durlach, who bore him fifteen children. This salon is part of the suite of state rooms themed by colour (green, blue, black, and red) and where the guests gathered before a grand dinner. On the death of Karl I the Swabian line divided into branches for three of his sons and the middle one, Karl II (1547-1606), became count of Hohenzollern-Sigmaringen. The other two branches were Hohenzollern-Haigerloch (which became extinct in the

51. Sigmaringen on the Danube river was the residence of the sovereign princes of Hohenzollern-Sigmaringen.

male line and was absorbed into Hohenzollern-Sigmaringen in 1634) and Hohenzollern-Hechingen (see below). Karl II's son Johann (1578-1638) was raised to the rank of prince by the Holy Roman emperor in 1623 as a reward for staunch Catholicism.

I liked the way in which the English handout for the guided tour at Sigmaringen used portraits to help tell their fascinating family story. In the Blauer Salon (Blue Salon) I found a portrait of Princess Amalie Zephyrine of Hohenzollern-Sigmaringen. I was looking out for her at the suggestion of the curator at another schloss. Her behaviour as a wife and mother was unconventional and scandalous but she was the saviour of her husband's state and one of the most interesting figures in the history of house Hohenzollern!

Amalie Zephyrine (1760-1841) was the wife of Prince Anton Aloys of Hohenzollern-Sigmaringen (1762-1831). Anton Aloys was preparing for a career in the church but his seven older brothers died and he found himself the heir[10]. His elder sister married Friedrich III of Salm-Kyrburg in 1781 and the following year (1782) Anton Aloys married Friedrich III's sister, Amalie Zephyrine. It was not a success. Amalie Zephyrine had grown up in cosmopolitan Paris and hated her new life in gloomy, old-fashioned, and provincial Sigmaringen. She was strictly supervised by her father-in-law who controlled her whereabouts and spied upon her letters[11]. Just weeks after the birth of their only child in 1785 Amalie Zephyrine left her husband and baby son and went back to live with her brother in Paris. She would not see her son Karl again until he was sixteen[12].

Paris during the French revolution was not a very safe place for an aristocrat. Amalie Zephyrine became a close friend of Josephine de Beauharnais, the future wife of Napoleon. The two ladies lived through the *Reign of Terror* in 1793-1794 when Amalie Zephyrine's brother (Friedrich III of Salm-Kyrburg) and Josephine's first husband (Alexandre de Beauharnais) were both guillotined. Josephine herself was imprisoned and expected to be executed. The friends supported each other and used their wits and connections to survive. Josephine entrusted her children (Hortense and Eugen) to her friend when she thought their lives were at risk and Amalie Zephyrine offered to try to escape with them to England[13]. Josephine did not forget this kindness and, when in a position to, she repaid the favour.

So when Napoleon cut a swathe through the small south German states, the principalities of Hohenzollern-Sigmaringen and Hohenzollern-Hechingen survived. Anton Aloys kept his country and indeed increased his territory owing to his estranged wife's relationship with the French imperial family. The alliance with France was cemented by marriage when in 1808 Amalie Zephyrine and Anton Aloys' son Karl (1785-1853) married Antoinette Murat (1793-1847). She was the niece of Joachim Murat, Napoleon's marshal and brother-in-law (he was married to Napoleon's sister Caroline). Anton Aloys was not happy with a daughter-in-law from such a humble background (her father was an innkeeper) but was in no position to object. Napoleon sent her to Madam Campans's finishing school in Paris[14] and made her a princess just before the wedding[15].

Hohenzollern-Sigmaringen was forced to provide soldiers for Napoleon and Karl fought with the French armies in the Napoleonic Wars. He was on the opposite side to his distant relatives in Prussia. What had begun as a division of the house of Hohenzollern in the thirteenth century based on geography, extended to a religious divide in the sixteenth when Brandenburg became Protestant during the Reformation and the Swabian line remained Catholic. Now the split also became a bitter political divide which would not be mended until Anton Aloys' grandson, Karl Anton, relinquished sovereignty to Prussia[16].

52. Prince Karl married Antoinette Murat, the niece of Joachim Murat, Napoleon's marshal.

One of the most impressive rooms at Sigmaringen is the Ahnensaal (Hall of Ancestors) with twenty-six full-length portraits of the counts and princes of Hohenzollern-Sigmaringen. These include Prince Karl Anton (1811-1885) who refurbished this room in 1877. Karl Anton took over the throne on the abdication of his father in the revolutionary year of 1848 (see chart 15 for a family tree). Karl Anton recognised that his small country could not survive in the long term and was influenced by the liberal dream of a united Germany. He was helped in his decision to sign over sovereignty to Prussia by a close personal relationship with Prince Wilhelm of Prussia, later king of

Prussia and the first German emperor. In his speech at the formal handover on 8 April 1850, Karl Anton said 'no sacrifice is too great' to achieve German unification and ' I lay on the altar of the fatherland the greatest gift I can bring.'[17] Persuaded by Karl Anton, the prince of Hohenzollern-Hechingen followed his lead.

53. Prince Karl Anton decided to relinquish sovereignty of his small country to Prussia (statue outside the schloss).

In return for abdication, Karl Anton was guaranteed personal ownership of his estates and property and granted a handsome annuity. He left Sigmaringen to follow a glittering career, serving as minister president (prime minister) of Prussia and as governor of the Prussian Westphalian and Rhine provinces. He returned to Sigmaringen only in 1871, after Germany had been united. In 1869 the last prince of Hohenzollern-Hechingen died and this principality was absorbed back into Hohenzollern-Sigmaringen. From now on the title became simply prince of Hohenzollern. The last prince of Hohenzollern-Hechingen was Konstantin whose wife was Princess Eugenie of Leuchtenberg (the daughter of Eugene de Beauharnais and Prince Auguste Amalie of Bavaria). They were childless.

In 1834 Karl Anton had also married into Napoleon's family. His wife was Princess Josephine of Baden (1813-1900), the middle daughter of Grand Duke Karl of Baden and Stephanie de Beauharnais (see Barockschloss Mannheim in chapter 2). Their first meeting was at Schloss Arenenberg in Switzerland, on the shore of Lake Constance, the home of Hortense de Beauharnais[18]. The story of Karl Anton and Josephine's children (see chart 15) could fill an entire book on its own. Their portraits are in the Grüner Salon (Green Salon). During the timespan of just twelve years this generation acquired two thrones and came within touching distance of two more. In 1858 the eldest daughter, Stephanie (1837-1859), became Queen of Portugal when she married King Pedro V. Sadly Queen Stephanie died of diphtheria only a year later. In 1866 her brother, Karl (1839-1914), was elected as the ruling prince of Romania. He became King Carol I in 1881 after the country achieved full independence. The younger daughter, Marie (1845-1912) married Count Philippe of Flanders, the younger brother of King Leopold II of Belgium. In 1869 Philippe became heir to the Belgian throne on the death of his brother's only son. Philippe died before Leopold II but he and Marie were the parents of King Albert I. In 1870 a fourth throne came within the family grasp when the eldest son, Leopold (1835-1905) was offered the throne of Spain. His candidacy, first put forward and later withdrawn, was the trigger for the Franco-Prussian War which led to the unification of Germany in 1871 (see Bathhouse Palace Bad Ems in *Schloss III*).

Over the centuries the greatest enemy of schlösser has been fire. In 1893 the east wing of Sigmaringen was badly damaged when a smouldering fire caused by an electrical fault went undetected for three days. When discovered it proved difficult to extinguish as the firefighters' hoses did not fit the schloss hydrants and water had to be brought up from the Danube in a chain of buckets[19]! Prince Leopold of Hohenzollern (the eldest son of Karl Anton and Josephine) undertook the reconstruction. He also built the Portuguese Gallery on the south side of the courtyard, completed in 1906 and named in honour of his wife, Princess Antonia of Portugal (1845-1913). Leopold had married the sister of his own sister Stephanie's widower, King Pedro V, in 1861. The forty-metre long Portuguese Gallery was used for grand entertaining and has three striking mosaic and shell fountains – Neptune at one end and two mermaids at the other. This was the room at Sigmaringen I liked the best. The steps to enter are deliberately shallow so that royalty could appear to glide elegantly in. I could imagine the fountains tinkling and the orchestra playing.

We were unlucky at Sigmaringen to experience a lack-lustre guided tour. There were many positives about it – a small number of people, a guide who spoke English, and a longer and more informative English handout than normal. But we rattled along from room to room so fast I hardly had time to read the handout and the guide was not keen to engage in 'off-script' questions or discussion. I formed the impression that the aim was to get us through to the last room on the tour as quickly as possible. This is the Armoury where visitors are left to explore in their own time and the guide can leave.

# 6

# THE SMALL COURTS OF LAKE CONSTANCE

Lake Constance, called the Bodensee in German, is one of Europe's largest lakes. It forms a triangle between three countries with Germany on the north shore, Switzerland on the south, and Austria at the eastern end. The Lake Constance region of Baden-Württemberg is famous for market gardens, orchards, and vineyards. With its picturesque scenery, mild climate, and many cultural and sporting activities, this is one of Germany's most popular tourist destinations.

As part of the Holy Roman Empire, the Lake Constance region was home to several sovereign territories. The size of these courts was small in comparison to the European superpowers but their rulers had the same aspirations to grandeur and a magnificent lifestyle. During the eighteenth-century they competed to show off their wealth and power through the building of new schlösser in the baroque-style. This chapter visits (among others) a schloss that bankrupted the counts who built it; another that was never completed through lack of funds; and a jewel of the renaissance that miraculously escaped this craze for the baroque.

## Wurzach

Schloss Wurzach in the town of Bad Wurzach near Lake Constance was built between 1723 and 1728 by Count (Graf) Ernst Jakob Truchsess of Waldburg-Zeil-Wurzach (1673-1734). Like so many eighteenth-century rulers of the small German courts, Ernst Jakob was infected by a building dream. He tore down the old castle and built a three-winged baroque palace in its place. This was to be the first part of his grand plan to transform the entire town of Wurzach into a palace complex in imitation of King Louis XIV's Versailles. For want of money, the rest was never realised. In the twentieth century Schloss Wurzach fell on hard times but still boasts a magnificent formal baroque staircase, considered one of the finest in Germany.

54. Schloss Wurzach was the centre of the independent state of Waldburg-Zeil-Wurzach.

I first heard of Wurzach long before I came here, from an elderly neighbour in my village in Cornwall in the United Kingdom. We were chatting at a local event when I happened to mention I was writing a book about German schlösser. To my astonishment, she repleid that as a child she spent part of World War II interned in a schloss in Baden-Württemberg. I knew from my research that some schlösser had been used as prisoner-of-war camps (the most famous example being Colditz), but I was unaware they had also housed British civilian detainees. Gloria was one of hundreds of Jersey civilians (men, women and children) who were deported on the orders of Hitler and interned in Schloss Wurzach. She remembers the staircase, darkened in the wartime blackout, as the trysting place of the young people in the internment camp. They called it Marble Arch.

Waldburg-Zeil-Wurzach was part of the Swabian noble house of Waldburg. This house had its beginnings in the thirteenth century as stewards to the Hohenstaufen dukes of Swabia and Holy Roman emperors[1]. The Waldburg had the title of truchsess (hereditary

55. Tombstone memorial of Georg I Truchsess of Waldburg in the chapel at Wurzach.

steward of the Holy Roman Empire) and truchsess became part of the family name. In 1429 there was a major division when three brothers split the Waldburg family inheritance into three lines and Georg I Truchsess of Waldburg founded the Georgian line. Georg I died in 1467 and his tombstone survives in the chapel in the east wing of Schloss Wurzach. Because of his hairstyle (see illustration 55), he is affectionately known here as *Jörg im hübschen Haar* – George with the pretty hair![2]

### Gloria's Story

In the early hours of Wednesday 16 September 1942, there was a knock on the door of ten-year-old Gloria Webber's home in Jersey. The caller was a local official and he had come to deliver bad news. Her entire family, parents and five young children, were on a list of Jersey residents to be deported by the German occupying forces. The order came directly from Hitler, as a reprisal for the internment by Britain of German nationals in Persia (now Iran). It was effective immediately and the islanders on the list were given only hours to close up their homes and organise their affairs. Gloria and her family had to be at St Helier harbour, ready to embark for France, that same afternoon and were allowed to take only what they could carry.

After a gruelling three-day rail journey across France and Luxemburg to the far reaches of south Germany, and a temporary stay in an old barracks, nearly six hundred Channel Islanders (one hundred and eighty-six men and four hundred and eleven women and children) arrived at their internment camp. Schloss Wurzach was once grand but by World War II it had fallen on hard times and was used as a prison camp. The schloss was cold, damp, in poor condition, and very dirty. No arrangements had been made to accommodate women and children and sanitation was inadequate. Mothers with several children were allocated a room and this is where Gloria lived with her mother and siblings for two and a half years. Another child was born in Wurzach; one of five babies born to the internees. A huge burden fell on Gloria's mother, who had the herculean task of keeping six young children fed, clothed, clean, healthy and happily occupied, when everything was scarce and with absolutely no modern conveniences.

Wurzach civilian internment camp was liberated by Free French troops on 28 April 1945. When the first tank arrived and broke through the barbed wire, the crew were amazed to find themselves surrounded by hundreds of British civilians. They had no idea these would be there and told the internees that their instructions had been to destroy the schloss first should they encounter any resistance in the town. For more about Gloria's story please see my book 'Schloss Wurzach: A Jersey Child Interned by Hitler'.

Waldburg-Zeil-Wurzach was created in 1675 on a sub-division of the Georgian line. Count Ernst Jakob (the builder of Wurzach) was the second of its rulers. In 1803 Count Eberhard I (1730-1807) was elevated to the rank of prince. His eldest son Leopold (1769-1800) died in the courtyard of the schloss when, in the confusion of the war with France, troops of the Holy Roman Empire mistook him for a French officer[3]. When the Empire was disbanded in 1806, Waldburg-Zeil-Wurzach was mediatised and the ruling rights absorbed into the kingdom of Württemberg. The ex-ruling family continued to own the schloss until this sub-branch of the house of Waldburg became extinct in the male line with the death of Eberhard II (1828-1902), the great-grandson of Eberhard I. The schloss buildings were sold off and parts used as a peat works and a brewery. They were neglected and fell into disrepair; by the 1920s ivy and other vegetation was growing up through the roof.

In 1922, Wurzach was purchased by the Catholic Order of Salvatorians. They renovated the buildings as a catholic seminary or boarding school to educate boys in preparation for the priesthood. The Waldburg-Zeil-Wurzach coat of arms on the grand pediment of the front elevation was replaced by a round mosaic with the figure of Christ. The Salvator College opened in 1924 and over the next few years it flourished and expanded. But, as a religious school, its days were numbered when the Nazis came to power in 1933 and took control of the education system. Subject to increasingly restrictive regulation, the school had to close in 1939. The schloss was then commandeered for use as part of the National Socialist camp system and housed French prisoners-of-war before Gloria's group arrived in October 1942.

In Wurzach I was so delighted to meet the local author of an excellent book about the history of Schloss Wurzach and its use in World War II[4]. Gisela very kindly shared her knowledge and showed us the schloss, explaining how everything would have looked in Gloria's time. The schloss is the prominent landmark of Bad Wurzach[5] and fronts directly onto a shopping street. Take a few steps off the pavement and you are in the schloss courtyard. This small space was where the internees exercised, shut off from the life of the town by barbed wire fences. During their confinement Gloria's father painted a record of camp life using paints from Red Cross parcels. One of his paintings

shows a view of Wurzach from the schloss. It looks so normal, with a bank, a hairdresser and a bakery, and it is just yards away; but it was the other side of the barbed wire and so in a different world to the internees. In another picture (see illustration 56) we see his family's room in the west wing with bare boards, single

56. Thomas Webber's painting of the room occupied by his wife and six children.

cupboard, and washing hanging from a string on the wall. Men and women had separate accommodation but he was allowed to spend time with his wife and six children.

Today the schloss is owned by a foundation in which several organisations have a share. These include the Salvatorian Order, a social care trust (who have an old people's home in the grounds) and the town of Bad Wurzach, who use the magnificent staircase as their registry office. The Salvator College in Schloss Wurzach was one of the first schools in south Germany to reopen its doors after World War II. Now a secondary school, it is still based at the schloss with the upper school in the west wing and younger pupils in new buildings in the old schloss park. In the east wing is the chapel with the tombstone of 'George with the pretty hair'. When Count Ernst Jakob built the schloss he preserved the original chapel from the older castle, but this was torn down by the Salvatorians in 1955 when they needed a larger church. Theirs lasted for only forty years and was replaced in 1995 with a modern chapel but following the original size and shape.

### Schloss Zeil

The ancient house of Waldburg survives today in two branches of the Georgian line, called Waldburg-Zeil and Waldburg-Wolfegg. Both Schloss Wolfegg and Schloss Zeil are close to Bad Wurzach and we spent the rest of the day exploring these. There is not much to see at Wolfegg (unless you like automobile museums) but Zeil (although hard to find) is worth a visit.

Schloss Zeil is still owned by the Waldburg-Zeil family and the interior is not open to the public. The garden and grounds are open however and we were able to wander freely. The few places where visitors are not welcome were indicated by a discrete rope chain and polite notice. The Waldburg-Zeil family are wealthy and everything about Schloss Zeil is well-maintained and reeks of quality. The schloss is in renaissance style and the exterior is painted with elaborate architectural motifs around the doors and windows. It all looked as if it had been painted only last week! We were greeted at the main entrance by a gentleman who made me smile – a sentry in period costume leaning nonchalantly on his rifle and smoking a pipe (see illustration). He is a work of art painted on the wall and accurate to the detail, including the shadow thrown by his sentry box. Other impressive works of art here include the stunning metal doors in the internal courtyard and the Marienbrunnen fountain with a fascinating sculpture centrepiece.

There is a lovely garden to explore at Schloss Zeil with viewing terrace and picturesque views. We went into the schloss church, decorated for a wedding, and watched the wedding guests arrive. And when you are ready for a break, there is an atmospheric country inn with waitresses in traditional costume.

57. The magnificent baroque staircase at Wurzach
is considered one of the finest in Germany.

The staircase at Wurzach is open to the public and a very good reason in itself to visit the schloss. In a baroque palace the staircase was designed to impress and much more than just a way of getting upstairs. The staircase was the setting for court ceremonial and one of the grandest and most lavishly decorated rooms. At Wurzach, twin sets of stairs rise in a spiral, one to either side of the room, connecting to curving galleries on each floor. The floorplan is quite compact (that only adds to the impact of the design) and the galleries seem to flow in waves across the space. Everything is light in colour and illuminated by windows on each level. The decoration rises to a crescendo in the vivid ceiling painting where the Greek mythical hero Hercules rides his chariot to the heavens to be received on Mount Olympus by the gods. They are surrounded by a painted balustrade with the flowers and fruits of all the seasons. The names of the artists responsible for all this beauty are no longer known, but they created one of the most beautiful baroque staircases in Germany.

An intriguing thing about Wurzach is what might have been. Between 1784 and 1796 the schloss was home to the Truchsessen Gallery and the fabulous art collection of Count Josef Franz Anton Truchsess of Waldburg-Zeil-Wurzach (1748-1813). Count Josef (a younger son) was a passionate art lover and amassed a famous collection of almost fourteen hundred paintings including Tintoretto, Dürer and other masters. The gallery was housed on the second floor of the schloss and Count Josef redesigned the top of the staircase as the entrance (the windows he installed are still there). But war with revolutionary France disrupted his plans and as French troops advanced Count Josef fled with the collection to safety, taking his paintings to Vienna in 1796. When funds ran short, he was forced to auction much of the collection and his paintings are now dispersed in museums all over the world[6]. But just think – if things had been different, we would all now be flocking to Wurzach as one of the great art galleries of Europe! Instead only a list of his paintings exists today in the archives of nearby Schloss Zeil.

### Tettnang Neues Schloss

Tettnang Neues (new) Schloss was not the easiest place to visit for a non-German speaker. There was no information in English, the portraits were not labelled, and the tour guide spoke so quickly that my husband (who speaks a smattering of German) was defeated. I might have missed the story of what happened here altogether had it not been for an enthusiastic attendant in the ticket office. After the tour was over she took me back to the wonderful ballroom (called the Bacchus Room) to explain the Montfort family portraits. Here were Count Franz Xaver (1722-1780), who went bankrupt and lost his country when the Austrian Hapsburgs called in the mortgage on this schloss; the young wife (his third) who left him because of their reduced circumstances; and his only child (a girl) who died unmarried in a religious house. This visit turned out to be a voyage of discovery about a country and a family I had never heard of before.

58. Tettnang Neues Schloss with the unusual slim towers
set diagonally on each corner.

The new schloss at Tettnang was built between 1712 and 1728 by
Count Anton III of Montfort (1670-1733), the grandfather of Franz
Xaver (see chart 16). He did not have the money to pay for it and you
might argue that he did not even need a new schloss, as his father
(Count Johann X) had built the Altes (old) Schloss (just across the
road) only fifty years before (in 1667)[7]. But Count Anton was the
scion of an ancient noble house. The Montfort were once the most
important ruling family in the region of Lake Constance and in the
fourteenth century their territories stretched from Tettnang north to
Tübingen and south to the San Bernardine Pass in Switzerland[8]. By the
eighteenth century Montfort had shrunk to just a small area around
Tettnang and their financial resources had dwindled accordingly. But
the counts retained their rank and illustrious history. Count Anton's
honour required that he keep up appearances and compete with the
other German courts in his style of living. So, a lavish court and a grand
new baroque palace it had to be!

Count Anton chose the court architect of the prince-bishop of
Konstanz who had already built the first baroque schloss in the Lake

Constance region at Meersburg (see below)[9]. His new schloss at Tettnang is a striking building with strong decorative features. The layout did not follow the prevailing fashion in the baroque, for three wings in horse-shoe shape, but instead harked back to the renaissance style with four symmetrical wings around an internal courtyard. On the outside of this square are four most unusual slim towers set diagonally on each corner (see illustration 58). The small rooms these contain (called cabinets) are exquisitely embellished and a highlight of the tour. All the facades at Tettnang are decorated with heavy ornamental pilasters between each row of windows. You can tell that money was an issue because on the less important sides of the building these pilasters are simply painted on and not the real thing.

Count Anton employed the best artists and craftsmen, many of whom had previously worked on the magnificent new schloss at Pommersfelden in Franconia built by Archbishop-elector of Mainz Lothar Franz von Schönborn (see Weissenstein in *Schloss in Bavaria*). Count Anton visited Pommersfelden after his daughter married the prince-bishop's nephew in 1717[10]. The noble Schönborn family were keen builders and Lothar Franz once said he was infected by the 'devilish building worm'[11]. Another

59. The Altes Schloss is within a stone's throw of the Neues Schloss at Tettnang.

of his nephews built two of the schlösser included in this book (see Schloss Bruchsal in chapter 7 and Neues Schloss Meersburg below). Count Anton spent out vast sums on his magnificant new schloss at Tettnang and by the time work stopped, his debt stood at a dizzying four hundred and fifty thousand guilders[12]. It was a burden that would ruin his successors.

Further disaster struck his son, Count Ernst (1700-1758), in the early hours of 11 November 1753 when a catastrophic fire broke out under the roof and Tettnang Neues Schloss burnt down to a ground-floor shell. For hours Count Ernst stayed put, hoping the flames would be extinguished, but when the fire reached their apartments on the first floor he was forced to leave and take his wife to safety in the Altes Schloss[13]. All the beautiful interiors and most of the contents were lost; Count Ernst faced the daunting prospect of raising yet more money to start all over again. He canvassed the courts of Europe and in 1755 Empress Maria Theresa of Austria came to his financial aid with a loan of half a million guilders. It was an impossibly high figure that the count could never hope to service from his income. The Hapsburgs were always interested in acquiring more territory in south Germany as a counterbalance to Prussia and this huge mortgage put the Montfort in their thrall. But Tettnang Neues Schloss could be rebuilt.

Count Ernst retired in 1755 and was succeeded by his son Franz Xaver – the last ruling count of Montfort. Like his grandfather, Franz Xaver commissioned leading artists of the day who created some of the most important rococo interiors in the Lake Constance region. The painter Johann Joseph Kaufmann and his famous daughter Angelika Kaufmann worked in Tettnang between 1758 and 1761. The exquisite Grünes Kabinett (Green Cabinet) in the east corner tower is panelled in green glass painted with flowers and covered with a diamond-shaped lattice of delicate plasterwork by the famous stuccoist Josef Anton Feuchtmayer (stucco is decorative plasterwork). This intimate space is flooded with light from windows on three sides and sparkles from tiny mirrors in the latticework. Over the door is an extraordinary plasterwork relief showing Zeus (in the form of an eagle) grappling with Ganymede and Hebe (in the form of cupids). The eagle nibbles the tummy of Ganymede with his beak and grabs the backside of Hebe with a claw[14]. Even more extraordinary is the Vaganten-Kabinett (Vagabonds Cabinet) in the south corner tower with green and blue spotted walls and paintings of itinerant pedlars and showmen by the

60. Franz Xaver was the last ruling count of Montfort;
he lost his state when the mortgage on the Neues Schloss fell in.

artist Andreas Brugger. His subjects include a tinker, lemon-seller, girl with a barrel organ, and a 'peepman' with a magic lantern surrounded by a curious crowd. This gallery of subjects from the lowest stratum of society is thought to be unique in a schloss![15]

Last to be furbished (in 1769) was a new ballroom on the first floor called the Bacchussaal or Bacchus Room. It takes its name from a large black stucco statue of the fat drunken god of wine (Bacchus) who sits astride a stove in the shape of a wine barrel at one end of the room. This gorgeous room glows in blush pink and grey with marble and stucco work by Johann Caspar Gigi. The ceiling fresco and six full-length Montfort family portraits are also by Andreas Brugger who was born locally (in Langenargen – see page 133) and picked out as a child and sent to study in Vienna. The portraits include Count Ernst and his wife Antonia, their son Franz Xaver and his third wife Elisabeth, and his younger brother, Anton IV. Franz Xaver married three times but failed to get an heir. (For his wives and children see chart 16). The sixth portrait is thought to be of Franz Xaver's only surviving child – a daughter from his first marriage called Maria-Josepha (1753-1773). She entered a religious abbey as a secular pupil or canoness and died young.

61. The Bacchus Room takes its name from the god of wine
who sits astride a stove in the shape of a wine barrel.

In 1776, it all came to an end when Count Franz Xaver went bankrupt with a staggering debt of over one million one hundred thousand guilders. He was forced to leave Tettnang Neues Schloss and abdicate his state. By a contract dated 13 August 1779 Austria took over the government of Montfort having agreed to make a settlement with the other creditors and grant Franz Xaver a pension[16]. Countess Elisabeth refused to acquiesce in their reduced lifestyle. She was thirty years younger than her husband and this was not what she expected from her marriage. After their separation Franz Xaver lost heart and said he was ready for god to call him from this world[17]. Count Franz Xaver of Montfort died on 24 March 1780.

### Schloss Montfort at Langenargen

*Schloss Montfort is a fantasy castle built by King Wilhelm I of Württemberg on the shoreline of Lake Constance at Langenargen (six miles or ten kilometres from Tettnang). There was a Montfort castle here from around 1300 and Langenargen remained part of their state until the end. After the take-over of Montfort by Austria the schloss became derelict and local people filched the stones for building. Wilhelm I had the ruins cleared away and from 1861 built a small schloss on the site in Moorish style and called it Villa Argena. It is an unusual-looking building with fine brickwork in horizontal stripes of red and yellow and decorative terracotta tiles. Wilhelm I died before the new villa was finished and his son, King Karl, renamed it Schloss Montfort.*

*This schloss has such a romantic location with the waters of Lake Constance lapping its terraces on three sides. Although the style is alien to south-west Germany, the little schloss seems quite in keeping with its setting. In 1873 Schloss Montfort was sold to Princess Luise of Prussia who spent her summers here for the next thirty years. Luise was a cousin of Queen Olga of Württemberg, the wife of King Karl[18]. The schloss is now owned by the town of Langenargen*

*and used as an event venue and café. The link with the old counts of Montfort is remembered by their coat of arms on the wrought-iron gates. We were permitted to peep into the event rooms by a charming gentleman on the information desk. Afterwards we whiled away the time, sitting on the café terrace and looking at the lake. Lake Constance is popular with tourists and Langenargen is a peaceful spot on a lake shore that can often seem choked with visitors. Schloss Montfort is a place for dreaming.*

After Franz Xaver's death, his younger brother, Anton IV (1723-1787), was allowed to return to Tettnang where he lived in a large house in some comfort on an Austrian pension until his own death seven years later. Anton IV never married and was the last in a six-hundred-year line of counts of Montfort. The family disappeared from history but left a legacy of fine buildings in the region and their coat of arms that we saw everywhere (it looks like three rings sitting on top of a portcullis). Montfort was under Austrian rule until 1806 when as part of the break-up of the Holy Roman Empire it became part of Bavaria and later, from 1810, of Württemberg. After the Napoleonic Wars the name of Montfort was revived by King Friedrich of Württemberg for his daughter Katharina and her husband Jérôme Napoleon (the French emperor's youngest brother – see Monrepos in chapter 4). Loyal Katharina adamantly refused to divorce Jérôme so, to get rid of the tainted name of Napoleon, her father made them duke and duchess of Montfort. They did not live at Tettnang and, after Franz Xaver left, the Neues Schloss was never used again as a royal residence.

For two hundred years Tettnang Neues Schloss contained only government offices until in the 1970s the historic first floor apartments were opened as a museum and gradually restored. The latest addition is a lively information room complete with up-to-date technology. As I looked at the gallery of (reproduction) family portraits, the figures begin to talk and move in their frames – just like the portraits in Harry Potter! Fabulous!

### Neues Schloss Meersburg

At the end of August 1526, the Catholic prince-bishop of Konstanz turned his back on the Protestant city of Konstanz and moved across Lake Constance to the medieval castle at Meersburg on the opposite shore[19]. This old castle (now called the Altes Schloss) had belonged to his predecessors for centuries and used by them as a secondary residence. After this move in 1526 the Altes Schloss Meersburg became their main residence and the capital of their state. The prince-bishops were the spiritual leaders of a religious diocese but also the rulers of a sovereign state in the Holy Roman Empire. They were concerned to have a lifestyle befitting a secular prince in the setting of a magnificent schloss. At the beginning of the eighteenth century the incumbent prince-bishop decided that the Altes Schloss was not grand enough and began work on a new building on the adjoining site.

62. In 1526 the prince-bishop of Konstanz relocated his residence to the Altes (old) Schloss at Meersburg.

Three prince bishops would play a role in creating the Neues Schloss Meersburg – Johann Franz von Stauffenberg, who built the original building; Damian Hugo von Schönborn, who engaged the famous baroque architect Balthasar Neumann to add a ceremonial staircase and the chapel; and Franz Conrad von Rodt, who gave the building a rococo make-over and finally moved in after nearly sixty years of construction in 1762. But the prince-bishops' new grandeur would last for only forty years before their state was secularised and Meersburg became part of the grand duchy of Baden in 1803.

When he became the prince-bishop of Konstanz in 1704, Johann Franz von Stauffenberg (reigned 1704-1740) decided that the Altes Schloss was too cramped and instructed master builder Christoph Gessinger to put up a new building on the terrace to the east. Gessinger was a lay monk from the Benedictine monastery at Isny in Baden-Württemberg. He worked at Meersburg and later at Tettnang (see above) until his disgrace and flight to Switzerland in 1730 following accusations of financial irregularity[20]. At Meersburg Gessinger constructed a single wing building in baroque style with a garden parterre and double garden staircase leading down to the Altes Schloss. He gave us the garden façade and the terrace of the Neues Schloss with terrific panoramic views across Lake Constance to the Swiss Alps in the distance. But his new building housed only offices and supplementary accommodation. Gessinger laid it out with room for state apartments but these were not yet designed. So the prince-bishop remained stuck living in the Altes Schloss[21].

The next prince-bishop was Cardinal Damian Hugo von Schönborn (reigned 1740-1743). As prince-bishop of Speyer, Schönborn had built the superb schloss at Bruchsal (see chapter 7) and wanted an equivalent royal residence at Meersburg. He reigned at Konstanz for only three years but pressed on with the conversion of Gessinger's new building, working with the favourite architect of the Schönborn family, Balthasar Neumann. The architect never in fact visited Meersburg and his involvement was only possible because of a detailed plan and inventory drawn up on site in 1740 by master builder Francesco Pozzi and called the Pozzi Plan[22]. Neumann sketched his designs on the Pozzi Plan and these were implemented locally. The architect reoriented the building away from the lake to face the town and created a new entrance with elaborate baroque ceremonial staircase leading to the intended prince-bishop's apartments on the second floor. Neumann also designed a new schloss chapel where the stables had been in Gessinger's building.

The prince-bishop who finally completed the building of Neues Schloss Meersburg and moved out of the Altes Schloss in 1762 was

63. In 1762, the prince-bishop moved to the grander setting
of the Neues (new) Schloss Meersburg.

Prince-bishop Cardinal Franz Conrad von Rodt (reigned 1750-1775).
Working with master builder Franz Anton Bagnato, he remodelled
the elevation facing the town in the frothier style of late baroque and
demolished three town houses to create a small schloss platz in front
of it[23]. We emerged from a maze of small streets in the old town of
Upper Meersburg suddenly to find ourselves standing at the entrance
to the Neues Schloss. It is a most attractive building, painted in pink
and white, with curly gables, delicate decorative over-windows, and
pretty wrought-iron balcony. Bagnato furbished the state apartments
on the second floor and finished the grand staircase begun many years
before under Prince-bishop von Schönborn. The statues of lions on the
staircase are taken from the coat of arms of Prince-bishop von Rodt.
Many of the same artists and craftsmen worked at Meersburg as at
Tettnang; Andreas Brugger painted frescos in the state apartments and
Josef Anton Feuchtmayer sculpted plasterwork in the chapel.

The state apartments on the second floor are now home to a museum
about the history of the Neues Schloss and the eighteenth-century
court of the prince-bishops. This museum proved very accessible to a

foreign visitor with translated storyboards and an English audio-guide. Little painted seagulls, representing those on the lake, point visitors to each listening station on the audio-guide. The rooms on the east side of the second floor are well preserved and still feature the original plasterwork installed under Prince-bishop von Rodt. These were the prince-bishop's apartments containing his private suite and the official reception rooms. Stucco and gilded putti (cupids) romp everywhere and they are usually allegories. The four in the Festsaal (Banqueting Hall) represent architecture (holding a plumb line and draughtsman's angle), music (with lute and flute), painting (brush and palette), and sculpture (hammer and chisel). The rooms on the west side (once guest apartments) are laid out as modern exhibition space with each room themed to an important aspect of the prince-bishop's court – hunting, music, wine... My attention was taken by a large table-top model of Lake Constance and by maps showing the political development and reduction of small states in the region during the Napoleonic Wars.

After the prince-bishop's state was dissolved on the secularisation of church states in the Holy Roman Empire, the Neues Schloss and its contents passed to the grand duke of Baden. It was suggested as a new home for ex-King Gustav IV of Sweden following his abdication in 1809; Gustav was married to a princess of Baden[24] (see chart 19). When this plan fell through, some contents were removed or auctioned off and the remainder cleared to Schloss Karlsruhe (see chapter 7) in 1865. The schloss endured a century of use as an institution before being acquired by the state of Baden-Württemberg in 1955.

Meersburg is a picturesque spot and the two schlösser, (the Altes Schloss and the Neues Schloss) share a magical location on the shore of Lake Constance. The two schlösser are close together – descend the steps (built by Christoph Gessinger) from the terrace behind the new castle and you are at the entrance to the old (see illustration 62). The Altes Schloss is also open to the public as a museum. It was sold off soon after coming into the ownership of Baden and remains privately owned today.

### Heiligenberg

When the guided tour entered the chapel at Schloss Heiligenberg I was astounded. It is no exaggeration to use this word. This chapel is the first room on the tour and has carved wooden figures of the apostles dating from 1596, pictures above the choir stalls painted in 1511 as copies of engravings by Albrecht Dürer, and stained-glass windows which were probably made around 1320. Heiligenberg was remodelled in the second half of the sixteenth century in renaissance style and (somewhat miraculously) escaped reworking in a later architectural mode. It was nearly destroyed on 4 January 1644 when retreating French troops lit the fuse to blow it up during the Thirty Years' War. For some unknown reason the fuse fizzled out before it reached the charge[25]. The last room on the guided tour is the Knights' Hall and this will also make you draw in your breath and gasp. Heiligenberg is rightly described as a renaissance jewel.

64. Renaissance Schloss Heiligenberg with a view to the Swiss Alps.

You need to plan a visit to Heiligenberg in advance. There is no access to the schloss or the grounds except as part of a guided tour and there were only three tours on the day we were there. My usual approach to schloss visiting is to arrive early in the morning and have time to take exterior photographs and be sure of a place on the first tour of the day. But at Heiligenberg we could not work out where the entrance was or find a ticket office. Eventually we discovered a small notice directing us to the Sennhof Am Schloss, a modern building on the other side of the square – and this was closed. The first tour of the day got going at eleven o'clock with four of us and it was a revelation. Before coming here I knew nothing about this beautiful building or the Fürstenberg family who own it. The tour was in German with an English handout and no other information whatsoever about the schloss was available. The German guidebook was out of print and I eventually managed to buy a second-hand copy of the 1981 version on the internet! The first big surprise of the tour (or should I say shock) came when the guide unlocked the door to let us in. It turned out that what we had thought was the schloss was merely an outbuilding and not the schloss at all. We found ourselves in a large forecourt and in front of us, over a bridge across the moat, was the renaissance jewel. The guided tour at Heiligenberg was full of surprises.

The castle on the Heiligenberg or Holy Mountain was built by Count Berthold of Heiligenberg around 1250 and soon after (1277) sold to Count Otto of Werdenberg. The Werdenbergs were a branch of the house of Montfort and the *Lady on the Light* in the reception hall at Heiligenberg holds the Montfort/Werdenberg coat-of-arms (three rings on top of a portcullis – see Tettnang Neues Schloss). The lady is part of a thirteenth-century carved wooden chandelier and her role is to greet guests and ward off misfortune[26]. After the death of the last count of Werdenberg without male offspring in 1534, Heiligenberg passed by inheritance to Count Friedrich of Fürstenberg (1496-1559) who had married the last count's daughter, Anna of Werdenberg, in 1516. The Fürstenberg were an important noble family in south-west Germany. Count Friedrich planned to enhance his new schloss but it was his son Joachim (1538-1598) who transformed the ancient castle at Heiligenberg into a (then) modern renaissance palace. The

65. The shimmering Knights' Hall with intricate
coffered ceiling and tantalising family portraits.

Fürstenbrunnen (Princes' Fountain) in the square outside the schloss
has a statue commemorating him (see illustration 66).

Count Joachim built three new wings around an internal courtyard
– the west wing with the chapel, the south wing where the Knights'
Hall takes up the top two floors, and the east wing with reception hall
(and fascinating kitchen). He integrated parts of the old castle into the
fourth (north) wing of his new schloss. This wing faces the forecourt
and the tour goes along a curved passageway through it to reach the
internal courtyard and entrance to the chapel. The work was largely
completed when Count Joachim died, but by then his son had already
moved to another part of the family estates in Austria where he had
close ties at the imperial court in Vienna[27]. Heiligenberg would be barely
lived in for two centuries. This is what preserved it as a renaissance
building and why it was not rebuilt in baroque style as we have already
seen in this chapter at Wurzach, Tettnang, and Meersburg.

At the end of the eighteenth-century, Princess Elisabeth of
Fürstenberg (born Thurn and Taxis) selected Heiligenberg as her
widow's residence following the death in battle of her husband during
the French Revolutionary Wars. The princess was a fan of the medieval

and repaired and restored the renaissance schloss. Only a suite of rooms in the south wing was redecorated in the prevailing French Empire style as living accommodation. Princess Elisabeth was the mother of Karl Egon II (1796-1854) who succeeded his uncle as head of house in 1804 at the age of seven. His statue also adorns the Fürstenbrunnen. The name of Egon is traditional in the Fürstenberg family and dates back to the eleventh-century founder of the house, Count Egino of Urach in Württemberg[28]. The young boy reigned as prince of Fürstenberg for a short period before the principality was mediatised in 1806. When her son came of age in 1817, Princess Elisabeth retired to Heiligenberg and is buried in the chapel.

66. The Princes' Fountain with statues of Count Joachim
on the left and Prince Karl Egon II on the right.

The tour at Heiligenberg proceeded at an unhurried pace and there was time to look at everything. The guide led us into the sixteenth-century chapel in the west wing of the schloss where we sat in the choir stalls to listen to her talk. The elaborate renaissance decoration of the chapel is almost overwhelming. It is a small room and the pews at the back are a later addition by extending into a living room. High in the ceiling above the altar is an opening for sick people in the room above to hear the service; another in the floor is for the music to go down to the dead in the burial vault below[29]. Also buried here are Prince Maximilian Egon II of Fürstenberg (1863-1941) and his wife Irma. Max Egon became the close friend of Kaiser Wilhelm II of Germany after the disgrace in 1907 of his previous best friend, Prince Philipp von Eulenburg, amid accusations of homosexuality. Wilhelm was one of the hunting party at Max Egon's principal residence of Schloss Donaueschingen (also in Baden-Württemberg) in 1908 when another scandal had to be hushed-up. The close aide and chief of Wilhelm's Military Cabinet, General Count Dietrich von Hülsen-Haeseler, died of a heart-attack while dressed up in drag to dance for and entertain the kaiser and other guests. One version has the general wearing a ballerina's tutu; another, Princess Irma's ballgown and feathered hat[30]!

In the east wing we spent some time in the huge kitchen equipped with all the latest gadgets at the beginning of the twentieth century and still in use today. Our gentle guide demonstrated a hundred-year-old potato peeler, knife sharpener, ice-cream maker, machine for slicing runner beans, and other labour-saving devices. The huge stove is fired by charcoal, but I noticed tucked away to the side were a modern electric oven and microwave. We stopped in the Blue Gallery upstairs for the guide to outline the Fürstenberg family history by reference to a map showing the twenty-three castles they owned in this area in the seventeenth century. It was apparent that there were many branches at different times but none of this history was covered in the English handout for the tour. The guide could sense my frustration; she apologised for not speaking English and I to her in return for not speaking German.

The tour ended in the shimmering and expansive Knights' Hall on the top floor of the south wing. This vast room (thirty-six metres long and eleven metres wide) has huge south facing windows and is swimming with light. Heiligenberg is miles from Lake Constance but we could see right across the lake waters to the Swiss Alps. The

Knights' Hall was completed in time for a family wedding in 1584[31]. The intricate and colourful coffered ceiling is carved with one thousand two hundred fantastical creatures. I saw what looked like mermaids and pagan folk growing out of trees. The inlaid parquet floor was slippery and to my dismay we had to wear the dreaded felt overshoes (a personal bête noir). We shuffled down the long room in a group past a line of tantalising family portraits (not labelled). This visit aroused but did not wholly satisfy my curiosity to find out more about the house of Fürstenberg.

The head of house today is Prince Heinrich, born in 1950, who lives in Schloss Donaueschingen with his wife. Their eldest son lives with his wife and young family at Heiligenberg. On our way out we passed children's toys in the courtyard.

### Kloster and Schloss Salem

In 1802 the old monastery at Salem near Lake Constance was secularised and taken over by the state of Baden. This was part of the break-up of the Holy Roman Empire when the church states were dismantled and their sovereignty given to the large secular states. Margrave Karl Friedrich of Baden (1728-1811) gave Salem to his sons and it became a summer residence for the Baden royal family. Since the fall of the German monarchy in 1918 this has been their main home. Salem is known as Kloster and Schloss Salem because it was originally a monastery (kloster) and later a royal residence (schloss). In 1920 Prince Max of Baden (the last chancellor of the German Empire who announced the abdication of Kaiser Wilhelm II) established a boarding school at the schloss with the progressive educationalist Kurt Hahn. Salem was acquired by the state of Baden-Württemberg in 2009 but the head of house Baden still lives in part of the building.

The Cistercian Abbey at Salem was founded in 1134 and became one of the richest and most important monasteries in Germany. The names of its forty abbots over more than six hundred years are

67. View of Schloss Salem seen across the schloss garden.

engraved on a tablet in the Abbey Minster. The first was Frowin (died 1165), said to have been a companion of Bernard of Clairvaux who formed the Cistercian order as a reform movement of Benedictine monasticism[32]. The abbots of Salem were secular rulers of their lands as well as religious leaders of the monks although, unlike the prince-bishops of neighbouring Konstanz (also secularised to Baden), they never obtained the rank of prince of the Holy Roman Empire. After a devastating fire in 1697 the monastery was rebuilt by Abbot Stephan I (died 1725) in the baroque style. He built two four-winged buildings, called the Prälatur (Prelacy) and Konventbau (Monastery building) which are joined together by a connecting wing. The Monastery building was the monk's accommodation and is now used by the school. The Prelacy housed the abbot's living quarters and state rooms and these are shown on the guided tour.

Salem was the busiest of the schlösser we visited around Lake Constance. From the entrance we could see the Prelacy building, peeping through the trees on the other side of the formal garden (see illustration 67). As a foreign visitor, I found the guided tour a bit of a puzzle. Salem is a complex of different buildings and museums and visitors have a choice of tour depending on what they want to see. We chose the long tour (ninety minutes) because this seemed to include more of the historic rooms. The tour guide spoke very good English but it was a big group and understandably she did not have much time to spend on us. Even with the help of the English handout I struggled to work out where we were on the plan of the buildings or which room we were in. After the others had gone at the end of the tour the guide took pity on me and talked through the plan showing where we had been. Then it all made much more sense!

68. An old picture of the east wing of the Prelacy building
which houses the abbot's rooms, Imperial Hall and
private home of the margrave of Baden.

The guided tour started in the baroque schloss garden where the monks grew vegetables and herbs. It was a hot afternoon and, for her introduction, the guide shepherded us into the shade of a large tree on the lawn outside the Minster. The design and decoration of this thirteenth-century church illustrates the central dichotomy of the monastery – how did the abbots reconcile the humility and austerity of a monastic life with their worldly wealth and hauteur as secular rulers? The answer is that they didn't, at least in the eighteenth century. The gothic exterior of the church is fairly plain but the interior is ostentatiously decorated. Abbot Anselm II (died 1778) embellished it with twenty-seven altars carved from alabaster. Many royal families were forced to use imitation marble on the grounds of cost and alabaster is even more expensive than the real thing! The last monks' chant was heard here on 23 November 1804[33] and the Minster became a Catholic parish church.

The Minster connects to St Bernhard's Cloister in the Monastery building where the monks collected before a religious service. This was the first part of the abbey to be restored after the fire of 1697. The long passageway has a beautiful stucco ceiling and a series of paintings about the life of St Bernhard by Andreas Brugger, whose work we had already seen at Tettnang and Meersburg. Many of the same artists and craftsmen who worked at these palaces also worked at Salem. From the cloister we turned into the connecting wing to see the monks' Summer Refectory or dining room. This is now used as a Protestant church. There are fine views of the margrave of Baden's vineyards from the tall south-facing windows. Local people assured us that the best wines in Germany come from the Lake Constance region. The old cooperage in the former monastery outbuildings (where they made the wine barrels) has a huge wine press dating back to 1706.

In the summer refectory the guide pointed out a table carved with names of pupils of Schule (school) Schloss Salem who were killed or listed as missing in action in World War II. This elite boarding school was started at the schloss in 1920 to educate a post-World War I generation of young Germans to be independent thinking and socially responsible[34]. The headmaster, Kurt Hahn, was an outspoken critic of Adolf Hitler and had to leave Germany to avoid persecution after he was arrested in 1933. He moved to Scotland and founded the Salem school at Gordonstoun. Prince Philip, Duke of Edinburgh, was briefly a pupil at Salem before transferring to Gordonstoun. Philip was the brother-in-law of Margrave Berthold of Baden who became head of the house in 1929 on the death of his father, Prince Max. Berthold married Philip's sister, Princess Theodora of Greece and Denmark. The school was re-established at Salem after World War II and counts several other royals among its alumni including ex-King Constantine of Greece and Prince Ernst August (senior) of Hannover[35].

The guided tour also included the Abbot's rooms on the second floor of the Prelacy building. The study was redecorated in rococo style by Abbot Anselm II. He reigned as abbot for thirty-two years and rose to be imperial privy councillor to Empress Maria Theresa of Austria[36]. A door from the study leads to the abbot's private suite of rooms – a bedroom, sacristy and private chapel. These are more austere in style reflecting his religious role. Also on the this floor is the magnificent state room of the abbey called the Imperial Hall with gorgeous stucco-work decoration by Franz Josef Feuchtmayer. He was the father of Josef Anton Feuchtmayer who worked at Tettnang and Meersburg. Down either side of the long room, on the piers between the windows, are life-sized full-length statues of the Holy Roman emperors. These are the secular rulers from whom the abbots held their territory. Above the windows are bust medallions of the popes, the religious leaders to whom they owed allegiance. Strange-looking wall sconces with a single protruding human arm hold candles to light the room.

The guide emphasised that everything we see is original from the time it was created after the fire of 1697. The reason Salem was not bombed during World War II or plundered by the French occupying forces, she alleged, was that the margrave of Baden was related to the British royal family and the British government directed it not be touched. The guided tour ended in the library, renovated at the end of the eighteenth-century by Abbot Robert (died 1802). Salem Abbey was a centre of learning and there were between forty and sixty thousand books here when it was secularised. They were given to the university at Heidelberg and the only books I saw belonged to the local government who have their cultural office in the Prelacy.

### Prince Max of Baden

On 9 November 1918 Prince Max of Baden (1867-1929), the last chancellor of the German Empire, announced the abdication of Kaiser Wilhelm II. Max made the announcement without the full agreement of the recalcitrant kaiser in a (vain) attempt to preserve the monarchy and to ensure an orderly handover of power. Events were moving fast and hours later the new German republic was proclaimed. Prince Max resigned the same day and the Social Democratic leader, Friedrich Ebert, took over. Max had been chancellor for just one month.

Prince Max (Maximilian) was heir presumptive to the throne of Baden. His cousin, Grand Duke Friedrich II (1857-1928) was married but had no children and Max was the next heir. His father was the younger brother of Grand Duke Friedrich I (Friedrich II's father) – see chart 17. Friedrich I had been married to Wilhelm II's aunt (the sister of his father), so Max and the kaiser were related by marriage. During World War I Max did not have a military or political role but worked for prisoners-of-war as part of the German Red Cross. He was a critic of Germany's war policies and of the Army High Command. He was called in as chancellor only when it became clear that Germany was facing inevitable defeat and a neutral civilian figure was needed to sue for peace so that the High Command would not take the blame for failure. Max was unaware of this when he agreed to take office on 1 October 2018 but nevertheless signed the request for an armistice on 3 October as being in the national interest[37]. In later years a myth would take hold that the High Command could have won the war if it had not been 'stabbed in the back' by the civilian government of Prince Max. This was totally untrue.

On 22 November 1918 Grand Duke Friedrich II of Baden officially abdicated. Prince Max renounced any claim to the succession for himself and his heirs and retired to Schloss Salem. He played no further role in political life and kept a dignified silence to the accusations laid against him by the vindictive ex-kaiser. Before he died Prince Max did publish a full account of his actions during that fateful month as chancellor.

There is much to explore at Salem in addition to the guided tour. Each building has a label (with English translation) explaining its date and use and some aspects of the monastery's history are covered in more detail on storyboards around the site – for example how a faulty stove in a servant's room caused the great fire disaster of March 1697. This fire is the reason why Salem is also now home to a Fire Brigade museum. When the fire broke out the monastery fire precautions were shown to be inadequate. Strong winds quickly spread the fire and the wood panelling, wooden ceilings, and stucco work all added to the flames. The oil paintings had been recently restored and the linseed oil used was highly flammable. The monastery had no water pump and when one did arrive from a nearby town it was too late to save the monastery buildings. The monks only just managed to save their Minster from destruction. When the monastery was rebuilt the latest fire prevention measures were incorporated including fire walls, iron

doors, stone floors and brick ceilings. The monks installed a fire pump in the Prelacy and kept a fire-watch on the staircase.

My favourite part of Salem was (quite surprisingly) the stables, built between 1734 and 1736 by Abbot Konstantin (died 1745) to high standards

69. The baroque stables at Schloss Salem.

of comfort and hygiene. Each of the twenty-eight horses had its own elaborate carved wooden stall and hay manger with a colourful mural on the wall behind featuring a horse. The stables are lofty and airy, face south to keep out the draught, and were connected to running water and to the sewers for waste disposal. The horses were, of course, important working animals and I was pleased to know how well the abbots looked after them.

# 7

# THE GRAND DUCHY
# OF BADEN

The grand duchy of Baden was created out of several territories from the disbanded Holy Roman Empire. It was one of the three large states in south Germany sponsored by Napoleon[1]. As well as the previous (and much smaller) margraviate of Baden, the territory of the grand duchy comprised that of other ex-royal states in this book such as the Palatinate in chapter 2 and the prince-bishopric of Konstanz (Neues Schloss Meersburg) in chapter 6. The new grand duchy now stretched all the way down the Rhine; from Mannheim and Heidelberg in the north, through the Black Forest, to the Swiss border and Lake Constance in the south.

This chapter includes such scions of the royal house of Baden as Ludwig Wilhelm of Baden-Baden, who changed the course of European history and is known as *Turkish Louis* for his victories over the Ottoman Empire (Turks); and Karl Friedrich of Baden-Durlach, who reigned even longer than Queen Elizabeth II of Great Britain (so far). Our tour of fascinating schlösser in Baden-Württemberg ends at the magnificent palace of the prince-bishops of Speyer at Bruchsal.

## Karlsruhe

Legend has it that Schloss Karlsruhe began with a dream. While he was out hunting in the forest one day, Margrave Karl Wilhelm of Baden-Durlach (1679-1738) took a nap under a tree. He dreamt of building a new schloss in the forest with a city radiating out from it in the shape of a fan[2]. The legend might be true, but more likely Karl Wilhelm decided to move his residence to spite the city of Durlach with which he was in dispute and also because he wanted to get away from his wife. The foundation stone for his schloss was laid on 17 June 1715 and Karlsruhe (Karl's Repose) became the new capital of Baden-Durlach in 1719. Margravine Magdalene stayed behind in the old schloss at Durlach (called Karlsburg or Karl's Castle).

70. Karlsruhe was built to a radical design: thirty-two streets flare out in all directions from the central tower, like the rays of the sun.

A large map at the entrance to the schloss illustrates how Karlsruhe was built to a radical design. Karl Wilhelm saw himself as ordained to rule by God and the street plan of his new city is a statement of his absolutist principles. From the schloss, thirty-two streets flare out in all directions like the rays of the sun. The nine streets between its two outstretched wings create the fan shape of Karl Wilhelm's dream. At the centre of the circle is the Lead Tower behind the main wing (see illustration 70). This was named after the lead metal used on its roof. It says something for Karl Wilhelm's self-indulgent lifestyle as an eighteenth-century ruler that the Lead Tower was supposed to be the accommodation for his many mistresses[3]. In 1709 he had entered into a bigamous marriage with Eberhardine Luise von und zu Maddenbach even though his 'official' wife was very much alive. Karl Wilhelm and Eberhardine Luise later 'divorced'[4]. Much of Karlsruhe was built of wood in order to save money. Baden-Durlach had suffered badly at the hands of the French in two wars over a quarter of a century (the War of the Palatinate Succession (1688-1697) and the War of the Spanish Succession (1701-1714)). The skimping on materials meant the new schloss could go up quickly but inevitably it caused problems later. Everything had to be rebuilt in stone during the reign of Karl Wilhelm's grandson and successor, Karl Friedrich.

The new city of Karlsruhe was a landmark in town planning and became an inspiration for the building of the new US capital at Washington DC. When he was US ambassador to France (the later) President Thomas Jefferson visited and took the plans home with him[5]. Karl Wilhelm gave incentives and exemptions to encourage new residents to come to the city and build homes on his street plan and to his set design. The layout of the schloss gardens was a break with the royal norm. In baroque palaces the gardens were usually at the rear for use by only the prince and his entourage. At Karlsruhe the gardens were at the front and open to everyone. The side wings are set at a slant to the main building to symbolise that the schloss is welcoming and has open arms. Between the open wings Karl Wilhelm created a fabulous pleasure garden in the formal French style.

Karl Wilhelm was a keen botanist and plant collector. The botanical gardens he founded at Karlsruhe became famous across Europe. The margrave tasked his court gardener to find seeds and plants from around the world and these still have descendants in the botanic gardens in the schloss grounds. One is the agave which is known as the century-plant because it takes decades to grow and flowers only once. With great timing, it bloomed for the coming of age of the next margrave, Karl Wilhelm's grandson, in 1747[6]. His greatest botanic love was the tulip and the garden at Karlsruhe was planted with nearly five thousand different varieties before he died[7]. Tulip bulbs were very expensive in the eighteenth century and Karl Wilhelm made so many trips to Holland to buy bulbs that he had his own house in Haarlem. Baroque gardens were a form of ostentatious consumption as only the wealthiest could afford to garden for pleasure. The margrave's passion for gardening and for tulips must have eaten up a significant chunk of his country's revenues. Karl Wilhelm died after suffering a stroke in his gardens at Karlsruhe while hoeing his tulip beds[8].

Karlsruhe was badly bombed during World War II and when the schloss was rebuilt in the 1950s only the front was recreated as a facsimile of the original; the interior was fitted out as museum space. Karlsruhe is now home to the vast Badisches Landesmuseum (Baden State Museum) with diverse exhibits ranging over time from antiquity to the twenty-first century. This museum was based on the collections of the grand dukes of Baden and still has content to interest royal history lovers. But my goodness is it hard to find! No-one on the information desk spoke English and there was nothing for sale in English in the shop. The only thing on offer was a half-page floor plan and, as we soon discovered, this was confusing. On my way out I spotted a desk with foreign language audio-guides. How I wished someone had shown me this on the way in! Karlsruhe is a huge building with several staircases and a complicated floor plan. I wanted to see the Turkish Booty Room on the first floor (with loot brought back by Margrave Ludwig Wilhelm of Baden-Baden) but we could not find it. The only way there was up the main stairs to the second floor, along the full length of the wing, and down steep stairs (like a fire-escape) to the first floor. We would never have found it without a chance encounter with a museum attendant.

## The royal house of Baden

The house of Baden can be traced back to Berchtold of Zähringen (died 1078). His grandson Hermann (died 1130) was the first to use the title margrave of Baden. He built the old Hohenbaden castle at Baden-Baden as his residence. Over the following centuries the margraviate of Baden gained new territory but was also divided and reshuffled between branches. Everything was reunited under Christoph I (died 1527) but divided again between his sons. Christoph I built the Neues (new) Schloss at Baden-Baden. His son Bernhard founded the senior line of Baden-Baden with its residence at the Neues Schloss and from 1705 at Rastatt. Another son, Ernst, founded the junior line of Baden-Durlach with the residence first at Pforzheim, then Durlach, and from 1719 at Karlsruhe. Religious differences developed after Baden-Durlach became Protestant and Baden-Baden remained Catholic.

In 1771 the Baden-Baden line died out and was absorbed back into Baden-Durlach. Margrave Karl Friedrich of Baden-Durlach (1728-1811) became ruler of a united Baden with his residence at Karlsruhe. But the new state was still only a small territory comprising a collection of disconnected parcels of land. This changed dramatically during the Napoleonic Wars when Baden benefited from the breakup of the Holy Roman Empire and an alliance with Napoleon's France. Baden emerged from the Congress of Vienna as a four-times-larger grand duchy with joined-up territory[9].

In the early nineteenth century the house faced a dynastic crisis when it became clear that the surviving Baden line was also running out of male heirs. The crisis was resolved by declaring the sons of a morganatic marriage as eligible for the succession. The last grand duke of Baden was Friedrich II (1857-1928). In November 1918, when revolution spread to Baden, he and his family quietly left Karlsruhe by the back door and fled to Zwingenberg (see chapter 2) for safety[10]. Friedrich II and his wife had no children and the next heir was his first cousin, Prince Max (Maximilian) of Baden (1867-1929). When Max succeeded his cousin as head of house in 1928, he reverted to using the ancient title of margrave of Baden. The current head of house is his grandson, Maximilian Margrave of Baden, born in 1933.

Our impromptu guide was a part-time museum attendant and part-time town-planner, and passionate about this aspect of Karlsruhe's history. Under his friendly direction we found our way to the Lead Tower where a film show tells the story of Karl Wilhelm and the founding of the city. Visitors can also ascend the tower to get a bird's eye view of the thirty-two radiating avenues. The Tower Wing has a very interesting exhibition called 'Palace and Court'. This includes mock-ups of some historic rooms with pieces of the original furniture. We saw the study of Grand Duke Friedrich I (1826-1907) and the salon of his wife, Grand Duchess Luise (1838-1923). In 1849 (before they married), Luise's father (Wilhelm, Prince of Prussia, later Kaiser Wilhelm I) invaded Baden with Prussian troops to reinstate Friedrich's father (Grand Duke Leopold I of Baden) on the throne. Leopold had fled Karlsruhe and left the country during the Baden revolution of 1848-1849. Another

71. Grand Duke Karl Friedrich of Baden was on the throne for seventy-three years.

room, in the early nineteenth-century French Empire style, showed portraits of Grand Duke Karl of Baden and his wife Stephanie de Beauharnais, as well as the cradle of their children. Nearby was a portrait labelled as the children of Countess Luise of Hochberg. I asked several attendants who they were, but no one could tell me. What a pity they did not know the riveting royal story of the Baden succession crisis, involving allegations of baby-snatching and nefarious dealings, which brought one of these children to the throne in 1830 as Grand Duke Leopold I (1790-1852).

The story centres on the marriages of Grand Duke Karl Friedrich of Baden (1728-1811). He was one of the longest-reigning monarchs in royal history and presided over an extraordinary upgrading of his country. He succeeded his grandfather (Karl Wilhelm) as margrave of Baden-Durlach at nine years old and died as grand duke of a quadrupled-in-size Baden aged eighty-two. In the last years of his long reign Karl Friedrich was elevated in rank from margrave to prince-elector of the Holy Roman Empire in 1803 and (on its demise) to grand duke in 1806. From his two marriages Karl Friedrich produced five sons who survived childhood so you might have thought the succession would be secure. But it was as not as simple as that. Please see chart 17 for the two families of Karl Friedrich and the succession crisis.

Karl Friedrich's three sons from his first marriage in 1751 to Karoline Luise of Hesse-Darmstadt were all in line for the throne but the last of them would die within twenty years of his father leaving no more male heirs on this side of the family. His second marriage in 1787 (after the death of his first wife) was to the forty-years-younger Luise Karoline Geyer von Geyersberg, later created Countess of Hochberg. This marriage was morganatic because Countess Hochberg was not of equal royal birth and their two sons were not eligible to succeed. The countess has been cast as a villain in royal history with accusations that she schemed to bring her eldest son to the throne, including having a baby heir taken from his cradle and a dying baby substituted instead. This is the basis of the famous royal mystery of Kaspar Hauser who it is claimed was the stolen baby (see Ansbach in *Schloss in Bavaria*). It is intriguing that this claim has never been disproved. DNA tests a few years ago could not rule out the possibility that Kaspar was related to the Baden family.

In 1811 Karl Friedrich died and was followed by his grandson. An annoying trait of Germany's royal families is that they tended to use and reuse only a few names. It is confusing that Karl Friedrich, his son, and his grandson, all have similar names. The son was Karl Ludwig who had predeceased his father in a fatal accident. The grandson was Karl (Ludwig Friedrich) and he succeeded his grandfather as Grand Duke Karl (1786-1818). Karl and his wife Stephanie de Beauharnais

(1789-1860) produced two sons, born in 1812 and 1816, but both died as babies. It was the elder of the two it is alleged was stolen from his cradle. (See chart 18 for the children of Karl and Stephanie.)

As Grand Duke Karl was an only son and had no surviving sons himself, the next in line to inherit Baden were his uncles (his father's two younger full brothers) called Friedrich and Ludwig. Friedrich made a dynastic marriage to Luise of Nassau, but they had no children. Friedrich died before his nephew so it was the younger of the two uncles who became Grand Duke Ludwig I (1763-1830) on Karl's death in 1818. The fifty-four-year-old new grand duke was in a relationship with a teenager called Katharina Werner and married her in 1822[11]. It was a morganatic marriage and their son Ludwig, born in 1820, was not dynastically eligible.

72. Grand Duke Friedrich I and his wife Luise in old age. Luise was the only daughter of Kaiser Wilhelm I.

So, who would next follow Grand Duke Ludwig? King Maximilian I of Bavaria claimed to be the next heir to Baden on the grounds he was married to Grand Duke Karl's eldest sister[12]. It was completely unacceptable for Baden to lose its independence and be absorbed by Bavaria, so in 1817 (before he died) Karl issue a decree declaring his two half-uncles (the sons of countess Hochberg) as dynasts of the house. Countess Hochberg was no longer alive to enjoy the triumph when her elder son became Grand Duke Leopold I of Baden (1790-1852) in 1830. All later grand dukes and heads of house Baden are descended from Leopold I.

*The marriages of the granddaughters of Grand Duke Karl Friedrich*

The eldest son of Karl Friedrich by his first marriage was Count Karl Ludwig of Baden (1755-1801). Karl Ludwig married Amalie of Hesse-Darmstadt and they had seven children who survived infancy – six daughters and one son. Karl Ludwig died before his father and his only son inherited Baden on the death of his grandfather. The daughters made important marriages and three became an empress or queen (see chart 19).

The first to marry was Luise in 1793 to the heir to the Russian throne. He became Tsar Alexander I on the murder of his father (Tsar Paul) in 1801. Luise had converted to Russian Orthodoxy and became Tsarina Elizaveta Alexeievna. The couple had two daughters but neither survived.

In 1797 Karoline became the second wife of Maximilian IV Joseph of Zweibrücken-Birkenfeld. In 1799 he succeeded as elector of both Bavaria and the Palatinate; in 1806 he became king of Bavaria. Maximilian's heir was his son by his first marriage, but his daughters by Karoline made good dynastic marriages. They were queens of Prussia and Saxony and also mothers of Emperor Franz Josef of Austria and of his wife Empress Elisabeth.

Also in 1797, Friederike became queen of Sweden on her marriage to King Gustav IV Adolf. It was on a visit to his daughter in Sweden that Count Karl Ludwig died following a sledging accident in 1801[13]. Gustav IV was forced to abdicate in 1809. His son was also debarred from the throne. Friederike and Gustav came back to Baden but they divorced in 1812.

The two youngest daughters both married German sovereign princes. In 1802 Marie married Friedrich Wilhelm who succeeded as duke of Brunswick on the death of his father from battle wounds in 1806; Friedrich Wilhelm also died fighting Napoleon in 1815 (see Braunschweig in Schloss II). Both Marie's sons became duke, but both died unmarried and the line died out.

The last to marry was Wilhelmine in 1804 to Ludwig of Hesse-Darmstadt. He became Grand Duke Ludwig II in 1830. Wilhelmine's daughter became tsarina of Russia (wife of Alexander II); her grandson became sovereign prince of Bulgaria; and granddaughters were queens of Spain and Sweden. (For more about Wilhelmine's story see Heiligenberg in Schloss III.)

## Rastatt

Schloss Rastatt was built by Margrave Ludwig Wilhelm of Baden-Baden (1655-1707). He was an important figure in the history of Europe and is known as *Türkenlouis* (Turkish Louis) or *Shield of the Empire* because of his victories over the Turks (Ottoman Empire). Ludwig Wilhelm was the first commander to enter Vienna in September 1683 when the siege by Turkish troops was lifted by the imperial armies. In 1689 Emperor Leopold I appointed him supreme commander of the Holy Roman Empire army against the Turks. Without Turkish Louis the history of Europe might have been very different. But while he was busy fighting Turks on the eastern frontier of the empire, the French were devastating his home country in the south-west during the War of the Palatinate Succession (1688-1697). In 1693 the emperor sent Ludwig Wilhelm home to Baden in charge of the empire's western defences against the French. His schloss at Baden-Baden (the Neues Schloss) had been destroyed by the French in 1689. Ludwig Wilhelm decided to build a new residence on a different and less hilly site at Rastatt in the Rhine valley. High on the roof of his magnificent new schloss stands a golden statue of Jupiter (representing the emperor) brandishing his thunderbolts at hostile France across the river.

Ludwig Wilhelm originally intended to build a hunting lodge, but changed his mind in 1700 and commissioned a vast baroque palace complete with satellite new town. Rastatt was one of the earliest German versions of Versailles. Ludwig Wilhelm died in 1707 from the effects of an old war wound and Rastatt was completed by his young widow. It is a very good-looking building in gorgeous colours with terracotta pink stonework, grey-green roofs, and a golden coat of arms on the pediment above the central pavilion. Rastatt was designed to overawe visitors and I did feel awestruck as we walked across the huge cour d'honneur (front courtyard) to reach the entrance.

The guided tour begins in the ceremonial staircase of the central pavilion and includes the state apartments on the first floor. Here,

73. Schloss Rastatt was built by Margrave Ludwig Wilhelm of
Baden-Baden and his wife Sibylla Augusta.

outside the ballroom, stands the original bronze statue of Jupiter,
much bigger than life-size. It was brought inside to protect it from
the weather, with a replica now mounted on the roof. The highlight of
the tour is undoubtedly the ballroom, called the Ahnensaal (Ancestral
Hall) after the portraits of Ludwig Wilhelm's ancestors. These were a
replacement for the gallery of family portraits lost in the destruction
of the Neues Schloss at Baden-Baden. The theme of decoration in
the Ancestral Hall is the glorification of Ludwig Wilhelm's Turkish
victories. The ceiling fresco depicts him as Hercules arriving on Mount
Olympus (home of the gods). On top of the tall pilasters that line the
walls are the figures of naked and contorted Turkish slaves in chains,
forever condemned to struggle in captivity and hold up the ceiling.

Ludwig Wilhelm of Baden-Baden was born in Paris on 8 April 1655
and named in honour of his grandfather Margrave Wilhelm of Baden-
Baden and his godfather (and later bitter enemy), King Louis XIV of
France (Ludwig is the German version of Louis). He was a few years

older than his first cousin, Prince Eugene of Savoy (1683-1736), who would follow him into the imperial army and eventually supersede him in military fame[14]. The marriage of Ludwig Wilhelm's parents

was not a success and he was their only child[15]. His mother refused to leave Paris for what she regarded as a backwater in Germany so his father took the young boy away from her and he was brought up in Baden. His father suffered a fatal hunting accident in 1669 and Ludwig Wilhelm succeeded as margrave of Baden-Baden when his grandfather died in 1677. But by then he was already fighting in the imperial army and gone from Baden. He would always put military service to the Hapsburg emperor above any duty as sovereign of Baden-Baden. Emperor Leopold I rewarded him with promotion, honours, and the spoils of war. The Turkish Booty Room at Karlsruhe is stuffed full of

74. Ludwig Wilhelm was known as *Turkish Louis* for his victories over the Ottoman Empire.

Turkish treasures he brought home, including oriental carpets, exotic weapons, beautiful saddles, and horse armour. The emperor also arranged Ludwig Wilhelm's marriage to a wealthy young heiress; it was her money that paid to build Rastatt. But Baden-Baden was only a small and impoverished principality and Ludwig Wilhelm never achieved the great royal rank he craved – the coveted role of eighth prince-elector (for which there was frenetic lobbying) went in 1692 to

Hannover instead; and Ludwig Wilhelm's attempt to go one better and become a king was thwarted when his applications for the crown of Poland were rejected[16].

In March 1690 Ludwig Wilhelm married Sibylla Augusta of Saxe-Lauenburg (1675-1733). The bride was fifteen years old, the bridegroom thirty-five. Sibylla Augusta and her elder sister were the sole surviving children of Duke Julius of Saxe-Lauenburg. The small duchy of Saxe-Lauenburg in Schleswig-Holstein was forcibly taken over by the house of Hannover when Duke Julius died in 1689 without a male heir. But he was also one of the wealthiest princes in the Empire from vastly rich lands in Bohemia[17]. As heiresses to these lands his daughters were important assets in the royal marriage market and their father left the right to arrange their marriages to Emperor Leopold I. The emperor thought they would make suitable brides for his two successful generals – Ludwig Wilhelm of Baden-Baden and his cousin, Eugene of Savoy. Ludwig Wilhelm was supposed to marry the elder sister and Sibylla Augusta was intended for Prince Eugene. But when they met everything changed and after only four days Ludwig Wilhelm and Sibylla Augusta were engaged[18]. Her sister, Anna Maria Franziska, flatly refused to marry Eugene on the grounds he was not of sufficiently high rank. She married Philipp Wilhelm of Pfalz-Neuburg (brother of the elector of the Palatinate) and (after his death) Gian Gastone, the last Medici grand duke of Tuscany. Prince Eugene never married.

Ludwig Wilhelm and Sibylla Augusta had nine children, born in the thirteen years between 1694 and 1706. Only the youngest was born at Rastatt which was ready for the family's occupation in 1705. In a dreadfully high rate of child mortality, six of the children died in early childhood. Leopold Wilhelm died in 1696; Charlotte in 1700; Luise in 1701; Wilhelmine in 1702; Karl Josef in 1703; and Wilhelm Georg (after his father's death) in 1709. It is hard to imagine the emotional impact of such loss. The three children to reach adulthood were Ludwig Georg (born 1702), Augusta Maria Johanna (1704) and August Georg (1706). See chart 20 for the children of Ludwig Wilhelm and Sibylla Augusta.

## Neues Schloss Baden-Baden

In October 1995 the entire contents of the Neues (new) Schloss at Baden-Baden were sold at auction from a marquee in the grounds. This massive royal house clearance attracted global media attention[19]. Over fifteen days Sotheby's offered six thousand lots containing more than twenty-five thousand objects ranging from valuable sixteenth-century artworks to cheap nineteenth-century bedpans. The Baden family also put the schloss itself on the market. It was eventually sold in October 2003 to the Kuwaiti Al Hassawi Group with the clear expectation it would be renovated to become a luxury hotel. Sixteen years on, nothing has happened and dissatisfaction about the fate of the Neues Schloss has grown.

The Neues Schloss was built on the Florentinerberg (the hill above Baden-Baden) in the late fifteenth century by Margrave Christoph I. This was the main residence of the Baden-Baden line until Margrave Ludwig Wilhelm moved it to Rastatt. In the settlement of assets when the monarchy fell after World War I, the Neues Schloss was awarded as private property to the

Baden family. Grand Duchess Luise (widow of Grand Duke Friedrich I) lived here until her death in 1923. But for decades before the sale of contents in 1995, the schloss was unused and deteriorating.

On my visits to Baden-Baden, I have walked up the steep Florentinerberg to see the decaying schloss. It is a very sad sight. There was hope when scaffolding went up to repair the roof but since this came down in 2016 nothing more is in evidence. Presumably the financial numbers (costs of renovation against returns from leasing to a hotel operator) do not stack up. But something should be done to save this important building. The town of Baden-Baden or state of Baden-Württemberg need to step in.

The guided tour at Rastatt shows the two sets of royal apartments – the margrave's rooms to the north of the Ancestral Hall and the margravine's to the south. Each suite has an enfilade of formal state rooms overlooking the garden (antechamber, audience room, bedroom, and intimate 'cabinet') and three more simple rooms on the courtyard side for the family's private use. The guide spoke excellent English but omitted to mention that she had decided to do the tour in reverse order to that shown on the English handout. I was very confused until I managed to work this out! Overall she was decidedly unhelpful, saying in English (with a smile) that she would be telling many wonderful stories but only in German! Happily another visitor quietly translated for me.

Ludwig Wilhelm's branch of the house of Baden became extinct in 1771 on the death of his younger son and, by family agreement, Baden-Baden was absorbed into Baden-Durlach. The margrave of the newly combined territory already had his own grand residence at Karlsruhe and Rastatt became redundant only seventy years after it was built. It was rarely used and the contents were sold off or dispersed to other Baden schlösser. The royal apartments still have some of the original décor but are largely empty of contents, although the museum is gradually acquiring suitable items. For some reason, perhaps to fill the space, rooms are peopled with cardboard cut-out figures, painted in monochrome black. In the margrave's study these are displayed sitting around a table and signing a document. This is the Treaty of Rastatt which ended the War of the Spanish Succession (1701-1714) and was signed in this room in March 1714. One of the signatories was Prince Eugene of Savoy. The war was started to prevent a French candidate (grandson of Louis XIV) becoming the next king of Spain, but ended with the Treaty of Rastatt endorsing him in the role after the rival Austrian candidate turned out to be even less desirable! Ludwig Wilhelm suffered the wound that eventually killed him in this war at the Battle of Schellenberg Donauwörth in 1704[20]. The Treaty of Rastatt also confirmed Britain's seizure of Gibraltar from Spain during the war.

In the nineteenth century, Rastatt played a role in one more important historical event. In May 1849, Baden soldiers mutinied against their officers in the courtyard of the schloss and fraternised with local insurgents. The Baden revolution of 1848-1849 was part of a Europe-wide struggle for greater democratic freedom; in Baden it was crushed by Prussian troops. Insurgents, including soldiers, were tried by court martial in the Ancestral Hall at Rastatt; some were executed. One wing of the schloss now houses a Museum of Freedom Movements in German History with particular focus on the 1848-1849 Revolution and on the Peaceful Revolution in the German Democratic Republic (East Germany) in 1989-1990.

### Rastatt Favorite

When her husband died prematurely from an old war wound in 1707, Margravine Sibylla Augusta of Baden-Baden was thirty-one-years old. The young widow became regent for her four-year-old son, Ludwig Georg, and ruled on his behalf for twenty years until he reached his twenty-fifth birthday. She took over the government during the War of the Spanish Succession (1701-1714) and only months after her husband's death, Baden-Baden was invaded by the French[21]. Sibylla Augusta proved an energetic and organised regent who helped the country to recover from the ravages of war[22]. She also found her feet as a schloss builder – completing the work her husband had begun at Rastatt (see above), rebuilding her widow's residence at Ettlingen (see page 173) and building a small pleasure palace called Favorite between 1710 and 1720 in her husband's old hunting grounds just an hour's carriage drive from Rastatt.

The dowager margravine was immensely wealthy and spared no expense at Favorite to create some of the most extravagant and extraordinary interiors I have ever seen. She clearly believed that every available inch of space should be lavishly decorated. But Sibylla Augusta was also fanatically religious and the other side of her character is shown by the strange and spartan Hermitage in the schloss grounds where she retreated alone and took her meals in company with wax models of the Holy Family. Rastatt Favorite was little used after Sibylla Augusta died in 1733 and everything is still original to her creation. Her important collection of porcelain (fifteen hundred items), that earned Favorite the title of a *porcelain palace*, has also survived and is on display. Rastatt Favorite has the Wow factor!

75. View of Rastatt Favorite from across the lake
in the English landscape park.

Favorite is set in the middle of a beautiful garden and there are wonderful views of the building from all angles. The garden was remodelled to an English landscape park in the 1780s, but the bones of Sibylla Augusta's formal baroque garden are still discernible. From the car park we approached down a long walk along the line of the former baroque canal, between twin orangeries and an avenue of topiary lime trees. The outside of Favorite is as elaborately decorated as the interior in colours of brown, caramel, and cream with intricate doorways and window surrounds, balustrades, and cupids. The dowager margravine was interested in unusual decorative techniques and the walls are covered with small pebbles and granite chipping in an early form of pebbledash. The story goes that local children collected the pebbles from the nearby river[23].

The internal layout of the new summer palace was designed around a central banqueting hall called the Sala Terrena which stretches the entire height of the building. The ground floor of this lavish space is darkened to provide a cool retreat from the summer heat of the garden. It has the feel of an expensive upmarket grotto with cool blue-and-white tiled walls and trickling fountains. White sandstone statues in the corner niches represent the four seasons – Flora for spring, with an overflowing horn of plenty; Ceres with burgeoning summer ears of wheat; Pomona holding grapes to show autumn's fruitful abundance; and Vesta representing winter, with an owl for darkness and a frozen-looking cherub. But look upwards and the décor of the Sala Terrena lightens, illuminated by windows in the upper storeys and a lantern roof. A gallery connects the state apartments on the first floor – the margravine's to one side of the Sala Terrena and her elder sons on the other. Visitors reached these rooms by a grand, sweeping, exterior double staircase.

What makes Favorite so distinctive is that Sibylla Augusta experimented with all sorts of unusual decorative materials and techniques. The walls of the Floral Room in the margravine's apartment have folded papier-maché woven into patterns and interlaced with floral sprays fashioned out of silk ribbon. The bedroom in her son's suite is hung with beadwork embroidery using gold and silver thread. It is amazing to think that such fragile materials have survived for three hundred years. There are mirror rooms at other schlösser, but at Favorite Sibylla Augusta cut the mirrors to different shapes and sizes and hung them at crazy angles to intensify the reflections. The Mirror Cabinet was also decorated with small paintings on parchment showing Sibylla Augusta and her children wearing different fancy-dress costumes. Their faces and figures are the same in every picture, but the costumes vary, reminding me of dress-up paper dolls. The margravine is shown as shepherdess, peasant, huntress, and in different national dress. There are more than seventy pictures in the series and these are so fragile they are now displayed in climate-controlled glass cases. When the American writer Mark Twain (1835-1910) visited, he did not like Favorite at all saying, 'There was enough crazy and rotten rubbish in the building to make a true brick-a-bracker green with envy.'[24]. But whether or not Sibylla Augusta's style is to your taste, you will never see anything like it in another schloss.

76. At Rastatt Favorite the widowed Margravine Sibylla Augusta of Baden-Baden experimented with unusual decorative techniques.

The Florentine Cabinet dating from the 1720s is hung with seven hundred and fifty-eight super-expensive pietra dura panels from Florence. Pietra dura is the art of making pictures with inlaid semi-precious stones – marble, mother-of-pearl, lapis lazuli, agate, onyx, jasper, and alabaster. Sibylla Augusta discovered the technique when she visited Florence where her sister's husband ruled as grand duke of Tuscany. These pictures cover a whole range of subjects, from landscapes to still-life, and the level of detail and clarity are impressive.

The Florentine Cabinet is also embellished by mirrors overlaid by golden trellis and under-painted with one hundred and fifty miniature portraits of artists and architects. The pattern on the stunning scagliola (imitation marble) floor is scattered with unexpected items which are so realistic that I wanted to stoop to pick up the fallen playing cards and almost jumped at the lizard slithering away.

The attendants at Rastatt Favorite could not have been more charming and helpful. The tour guide faced a challenge in that the tour was in the German language but none of the visitors were German. Half of our small group were English (my husband and I) and the other half Russian. After the tour we got chatting to the custodian and he kindly offered to give us a private view of the Hermitage in the garden. This is a small, plain, building erected by Sibylla Augusta in 1718. She was extremely pious and the Hermitage is where she retreated from time to time to undertake penance[25]. The interior is very strange and such a contrast to the lavishly decorated schloss. But before we went to see it it the custodian gave us an extract to read from Mark Twain's account of his visit.

In the grounds, a few rods from the palace, stands the Margravine's chapel, just as she left it, – a coarse wooden structure, wholly barren of ornament. It is said that the Margravine would give herself up to debauchery and exceedingly fast living for several months at a time, and then retire to this miserable wooden den and spend a few months in repenting and getting ready for another good time. ...

She shut herself up there, without company, and even without a servant, and so abjured and forsook the world. In her little bit of a kitchen she did her own cooking; she wore a hair shirt next to the skin, and castigated herself with whips, – these aids to grace are exhibited there yet. ...

In another small room is an unpainted wooden table, and behind it sit half-life-size waxen figures of the Holy Family, made by the very worst artist that ever lived, perhaps, and clothed in gaudy, flimsy, drapery. The Margravine used to bring her meals to this table and dine with the Holy Family. What an idea that was! What a grisly spectacle it must have been! Those rigid, shock-headed figures, with corpsy complexions and fishy glass eyes, occupying one side of the table in the constrained attitudes and dead fixedness that distinguishes all men that are born of wax, and this wrinkled, smouldering old fire-eater occupying the other side, mumbling her prayers and munching her sausages in the ghostly stillness and shadowy indistinctness of a winter twilight. It makes one feel crawly even to think of it.[26]

The suggestion of Sibylla's debauched lifestyle is almost certainly false, but the rest of Twain's narrative gives a good impression of this weird building. The wax figures of the Holy Family still sit at table in the dining room as Twain described them and on display are a shirt and whip as he mentioned. The octagonal-shaped Hermitage is laid out with a central chapel and a series of small rooms around it with bare wooden walls. All the rooms connect, and all have open hatches with sight-lines into the central chapel. The sun came out while we were in the chapel, bathing the altar in golden light from the yellow Bohemian glass windows in the dome. White light from underneath the altar illuminated a wax model of Jesus in his tomb. In another wax tableaux Mary Magdalene washes the feet of the Jesus. Above the door to the chapel is a painting of Sibylla Augusta's daughter, Augusta Maria Johanna (1704-1726), on her deathbed.

Augusta Maria Johanna (Johanna) died in childbirth in 1726. The king of France had been her father's enemy (see Rastatt) and Johanna vigorously resisted marrying into the French royal family. But the marriage of princesses was a dynastic issue and she had no choice. In 1724 she married Duke Louis of Orleans; the great-nephew of Louis

XIV and grandson of Liselotte of the Palatinate (see Heidelberg). The French made it clear to her mother that if Johanna did not produce healthy sons she would be shunted off to a remote country palace[27]. Johanna fulfilled the expectations and gave birth to a son in 1725 but died the following year producing a daughter. From her son she was the grandmother of Louis Philippe of Orleans (1747-1793), known as Philippe Égalité, who famously voted for the death of his kinsman, Louis XVI, and died himself on the guillotine.

On 7 June 1727 Sibylla Augusta retired from her role as regent and handed over the government of Baden-Baden to her eldest son, Ludwig Georg (1702-1761). It was his twenty-fifth birthday[28], which does seem a late age to reach his majority. Ludwig Georg did not match his father in fame and is known in history as Jägerlouis (Hunting Louis) because of a passion for the expensive pastime of hunting that

77. Sibylla Augusta retired to her widow's residence at Ettlingen.

would plunge his country into debt[29]. As a boy Ludwig Georg had been very slow to talk (he didn't speak until he was eight) and some people thought he might be mentally impaired[30]. His mother made several pilgrimages to pray for a miracle to the Black Madonna statue at Einsiedeln Abbey in Switzerland. In the corner of the dining room of the Hermitage is a copy of this statue.

When it seems her prayers were answered, Sibylla Augusta gave a huge sum of money to the abbey and sponsored the building of a new church. Hers was the biggest donation in their history[31]. Ludwig Georg married twice but left only a daughter when he died in 1761; he was succeeded as margrave by his younger brother August Georg (1706-1771).

## Ettlingen

Schloss Ettlingen was the retirement home of Dowager Margravine Sibylla Augusta. The renaissance schloss had been badly damaged during the War of the Palatinate Succession when French troops set fire to the town on 15 August 1689. When she gave up the regency in 1727, Sibylla Augusta moved into the habitable rooms and remodelled the schloss in baroque style. She built a new east wing and created a courtyard with a grand new entrance crowned by the coats-of-arms of Baden-Baden and Saxe-Lauenburg (Sibylla Augusta was born a princess of Saxe-Lauenburg). The highlight of the renovation was the new chapel of St Nepomuk in the east wing (now called the Assam room) with frescos by Cosmas Damian Assam. The work was finished in 1733; Sibylla Augusta died of cancer in July that same year. She was buried without pomp in the schloss church at Rastatt in a simple wooden coffin. On her tombstone was inscribed the line 'Pray for the great sinner Augusta'[32].

After her death Schloss Ettlingen endured two hundred and fifty years of neglect and deterioration. The first structural damage appeared within forty years during the reign of her younger son, August Georg, who died in 1771. His widow stayed on in Ettlingen but when she died in 1775 the schloss was stripped of contents and only used occasionally as a guest house. Emperor Napoleon of France was a guest in 1805, during the Napoleonic Wars. From 1808 until the end of World War I the schloss was used by the military as barracks, hospital, or training school. It was then bought by the town and for fifty years used as rough and ready temporary housing. 'By the 1960s' said the young attendant in the museum 'this schloss was trashed'. Photographs on display bear out his words showing insanitary toilets, multiple beds crammed into Sibylla Augusta's state bedroom, and rubbish everywhere. Only in the 1970s did restoration begin.

Schloss Ettlingen is now home to local government offices, the registry office, an art gallery and a museum in Sibylla Augusta's baroque rooms on the second floor. We were not able to see either the courtyard or the Assam room during our visit as these were being set up for the summer music festival held here each year. I feel another visit coming on ...

The younger son of Sibylla Augusta had been pushed by his mother into a religious career for which he was unsuited and disinclined. In 1734, after her death, August Georg obtained a dispensation from the pope to return to secular life and get married to try to perpetuate the family line[33]. But his marriage was childless and August Georg was the last of the Catholic line of Baden-Baden. In 1765, recognising the inevitable, he had entered into a family agreement for the house of Baden to be reunited on his death and Baden-Baden was reabsorbed into Protestant Baden-Durlach (see Karlsruhe).

## Bruchsal

At 1.53pm on the afternoon of 1 May 1945, a squadron of American bombers began a daylight bombing raid on Bruchsal. The city was targeted because of its important railway facilities. The raid lasted forty minutes, destroying the centre of the city and killing more than one thousand people. In the firestorm that raged after the bombing, the eighteenth-century schloss was gutted to a roofless shell. Only the facade of the central block (the Corps de Logis) was left standing and in danger of collapse. The remnants of the baroque staircase, for which Bruchsal is famous, were open to the skies and at the mercy of the elements. With the town in ruins, and inhabitants living in temporary shelters amid the rubble, the idea of rebuilding at first seemed impossible. But by the spring of 1946 there was an emergency roof over the stairwell and work on reconstruction began the following year[34]. It was eventually completed with the reopening of the state apartments seventy years later, in 2017. An exhibition at the schloss entitled *Construction, Destruction, Resurrection* charts the remarkable building story of the magnificent palace of the prince-bishops of Speyer at Bruchsal.

The foundation stone for Bruchsal was laid in 1722. The old residence schloss of the prince-bishops at Speyer on the left bank of the Rhine had been destroyed by French troops in 1689 when they rampaged through the Rhineland during the War of the Palatinate Succession (1688-1697). Also destroyed in this campaign were the schlösser of neighbouring Baden-Baden (see Rastatt), Baden-Durlach (see Karlsruhe); and the Palatinate (see Heidelberg in chapter 2.) Thirty years on, the Catholic prince-bishops of Speyer were still in dispute with the Protestant

78. Bruchsal was the residence palace of the prince-bishops of Speyer.

citizens of the Free City of Speyer. So, when Cardinal Damian Hugo von Schönborn (1676-1743) was elected as prince-bishop in 1719 he decided to build on a different site at Bruchsal on the right bank of the river. The new prince-bishop came from the fascinating Schönborn noble family who specialised in being elected as church princes. He was the nephew of Archbishop-elector of Mainz Lothar Franz von Schönborn (see Bamberg in *Schloss in Bavaria*) and his three brothers between them held high church roles at Bamberg, Trier, Worms, and Würzburg. The Schönborn are also famous as schloss builders and patrons of the arts. Damian Hugo could call on this expertise and on a network of artists and craftsmen who had worked for the family before. The architect for Bruchsal was recommended by his uncle, Lothar Franz; but Damian Hugo also dabbled in the design himself – with disastrous results!

While his architect was away from the site, the prince-bishop decided to solve the problem of lack of office space by inserting a mezzanine floor. Unfortunately, this completely messed-up the architect's plan for the grand staircase in the centre of the Corps de Logis. The staircase was part of the ceremonial of an eighteenth-century court and the route to take visitors from the entrance to the state apartments on the belétage (first floor). But with the extra mezzanine between the ground and first floors, the planned staircase would no longer fit the space and could not connect to the belétage. There seemed to be no solution and for several years there was a hole in the middle of the building where the staircase ought to be[35]. Eventually, at the suggestion of Damian Hugo's brother (who was prince-bishop of Würzburg), the greatest architect of the age was called in to address the knotty issue in 1728. Balthasar Neumann was a Schönborn family favourite and already working for Prince-bishop Johann Philipp Franz von Schönborn on his new palace at Würzburg (today a UNESCO World Heritage site). Now he also became the lead architect at Bruchsal. Neumann is world-famous for his wonderful baroque staircases and the solution he came up with at Bruchsal is inventive, imaginative, and unique.

Neumann placed two symmetrical staircases in the middle of the entrance hall. As the staircases rise through the space, they curve and turn around an oval base. It is so unexpected to enter the hall and see a row of three ornamented arches directly in front of you. The arches to left and right frame the staircases and that in the centre leads to the gloomy area between them (effectively the cupboard under the stairs). Here Neumann made a virtue out of a necessity and created an underground grotto painted with seashells, stalagmites, and oozing rock. The decor on the stairs gets brighter and more exuberant step by step, but windows on the inside of the curves still look down into the darkened grotto. At the top, the stairs reach an oval-shaped platform under the domed roof called the Kuppelsaal (Cupola Room). Floodlit by windows all around, it feels like an island floating on the clouds. Neumann solved the problem of how to reach the belétage by joining

79. Entrance to the famous staircase by Balthasar Neumann.

the Cupola Room to the rooms on either side by bridges. It is an amazing experience to climb the stairs, from the earthbound grotto to the heavenly Cupola Room above, and marvel at Neumann's ingenuity.

Damian Hugo's career as a church prince was sponsored by his uncle, Archbishop-elector of Mainz Lothar Franz von Schönborn. Mainz was the pre-eminent church appointment in the Holy Roman Empire and carried the position of imperial chancellor with the right to crown the emperor. Born in 1676, Damian Hugo joined the German Order (Teutonic Knights) in 1699 (see Mergentheim in chapter 3) and held several positions in this Order. In 1713 he became a cardinal of the Catholic church; in 1716 he was appointed number two and nominated successor at Speyer. On the death of his predecessor in 1719, he was elected as price-bishop. He had kept his options open and was only now ordained as a priest[36]. It was not uncommon for church prelates to hold more than one high position simultaneously and in 1740 Damian Hugo was also elected as prince-bishop of Konstanz (see Neues Schloss Meersburg in chapter 6). Damian Hugo was a close friend of and mentor to the widowed Sibylla Augusta of Baden-Baden at neighbouring Rastatt (see earlier in this chapter).

Damian Hugo did not live to see the masterpiece of his new schloss at Bruchsal in its full glory. When he died in 1743, the staircase and Cupola Room were built but the decor was still unfinished[37]. His successor, Prince-bishop Franz Christoph van Hutten, commissioned the fabulous fresco on the vaulted ceiling of the Cupola Room that glorifies the history of the diocese of Speyer. Over a hundred painted figures fill the tumultuous scene, including those of Prince-bishop Franz Christoph sitting on a throne and Prince-bishop Damian Hugo looking at a building plan with his architect Balthasar Neumann. Above them the clouds part to reveal the heavens. The original fresco was lost in the bombing and repainted in the 1960s before the restored Bruchsal reopened to the public in 1975.

80. Supplementary building at Bruchsal,
today the district court.

After the war Bruchsal was rebuilt as a replica of the original, including the distinctive architectural paintwork on the exterior. But the decision was taken early on to reconstruct the interior décor only in a limited number of rooms in the Corps de Logis – Neumann's staircase, the Cupola Room, and the great reception halls on either side of this, called the Fürstensaal (Princes' Hall) and the Marmorsaal (Marble Hall). The state apartments on the belétage were reconfigured and fitted out as modern space for exhibitions. But this decision began to feel less comfortable as most of the original contents of the Corps de Logis had in fact survived. Bruchsal had been bombed before the catastrophic raid in 1945 and, to save them from destruction, the contents had been evacuated in two tranches. The first consignment went to Schloss Langenstein near Lake Constance in 1939 and the second to a disused prison at Bonndorf in the Black Forest in 1944[38].

Starting in 2008 the state apartments on the belétage were reconfigured to their original floorplan and the contents put back in place. The curators had a tremendous resource in hundreds of photographs dating back to 1870. A fascinating feature of the English audio-guide is a screen which shows an old photo of each room to compare with how it looks today. Restoring the décor in full was not feasible as so much had been lost and the ceilings today are much lower than before the bombing. But an impression of these historic rooms has been recreated in simpler form to put the contents into context.

The ceiling painting in the Marmorsaal celebrates the eternal future of the prince-bishops of Speyer. In a (futile) effort to make time stand still, Hercules binds Fortuna (the goddess of fortune or good luck), and putti try to shackle the feet of the figure of Passing Time[39]. But within decades the bishopric would cease to exist. Damian Hugo von Schönborn was the first of only four prince-bishops of Speyer who resided at Bruchsal before the ecclesiastical state was secularised to Baden in 1803. The last, Prince-bishop Philipp Franz Wilderich von Walderdorff (1739-1810), was granted the ongoing right to live at Bruchsal for life. This proved rather awkward when, in 1806, Princess Amalie of Baden (1754-1832) was also given Bruchsal as her widow's residence. Amalie took over what had been the prince-bishop's rooms and redecorated these in fashionable French Empire style (this is how they are shown today). Philipp Franz was forced to move to another suite and cannot have been pleased when Protestant Amalie converted his private Catholic chapel into her dressing room! They mostly avoided each other with Philipp Franz living at Bruchsal in the winter and Amalie in summer[40].

Amalie was the widowed daughter-in-law of Grand Duke Karl Friedrich of Baden and the mother of Grand Duke Karl who would succeed him in 1811. She is often called *the mother-in-law of Europe* because of the important marriages of her daughters (see Karlsruhe and chart 19 for details of these). In April 1806 her son Karl married Stephanie de Beauharnais in a marriage arranged by Napoleon (see Mannheim in chapter 2). Amalie lost her position as first lady at the Baden court and her nose was out of joint. She had strongly opposed the marriage but felt unable to refuse when Napoleon adopted Stephanie and made her a princess of France. The dowager was faced down by Napoleon at a one-to-one meeting at Karlsruhe. They seemed to have impressed one another – Napoleon said Amalie was the only 'man' he had met at the Baden court; Amalie wrote to her sister that Napoleon could persuade any woman to do what he wanted[41]. So, Amalie retreated from court and formed her own circle at Bruchsal. When she died in 1832, the schloss fell into the shade until the beginning of the twentieth century when it became a museum.

The distinctive exterior painting, in the bright Baden colours of red, white and yellow, make Bruchsal a memorable sight. It was a pleasure to wander through the colourful complex and its gardens. There are many supplementary buildings in addition to the main Corps de Logis and one of these houses the schloss café. A nice way to end our tour!

# 8

# THE RICH LEGACY OF GERMAN SCHLÖSSER

The south west is one of the most beautiful parts of Germany and it is a mystery to me why Baden-Württemberg is far less visited by English-speaking tourists than neighbouring Bavaria. I hope this book may contribute in a small way to changing that. Before World War I, when Germany was a monarchy, what is now the federal state of Baden-Württemberg was made up of numerous kingdoms, duchies, principalities and other sovereign territories. Their fascinating royal history is also not well known, and little has been written in English about the royal families of south west Germany. They all aspired to display their rank and power and have left a rich legacy of beautiful castles and palaces.

By visiting schlösser in Baden-Württemberg I discovered the colourful stories of the Hohenzollerns who never moved to Prussia; the 'other' Wittelsbach, who ruled not Bavaria but a Rhineland state called the Palatinate; the counts of Montfort, who were forced to sell their country to Austria for a pension; the Hohenlohe, dukes of Württemberg, margraves of Baden-Baden and Baden-Durlach and others ... Perhaps the glimpses in this book may encourage you to visit Baden-Württemberg and see these places for yourself. But beware! What I call *Schloss Hunting* is an infectious bug and once you get it (as I have) it can be hard to shake off.

From among the twenty-five schlösser in this book, of course I have some personal favourites. They cover a range of ages, architectural styles, families, and size of visitor numbers. What they have in common is that they were great fun to visit. For me these favourite places have that something special that gives them extra 'oomph', such as the unique interior décor of Sibylla Augusta at Rastatt Favorite; the unforgettable gardens at Schwetzingen; or the enthralling story of Monrepos as a party schloss. I stress they are my personal choice and readers may well have their own favourites.

---

*The author's favourite schlösser in this book (in alphabetical order)*

**Burg Hohenzollern** – *fabulous hill-top castle in the Swabian mountains built by King Friedrich Wilhelm IV of Prussia as a monument to the history of his mighty house.*

**Langenburg** – *ancient Hohenlohe castle that has a close connection to the British royal family.*

**Lichtenstein** – *fairy-tale schloss built by the son of a Württemberg duke and inspired by a romantic novel.*

**Monrepos** – *delightful lakeside party schloss of King Friedrich I of Württemberg and his English wife (the eldest daughter of King George III).*

**Rastatt Favorite** – *quirky retreat where the widowed regent of Baden-Baden used her great wealth to experiment with unusual decorative materials and techniques.*

**Schwetzingen** – *glorious summer palace of the Wittelsbach electors of the Palatinate where the story of an unhappy marriage was played out.*

**Tettnang Neues Schloss** – *grand baroque palace near Lake Constance that bankrupted the counts of Montfort and forced them to sell their state to the Austrian Hapsburgs.*

---

In the last years five I have visited more than two hundred German schlösser in the course of researching my books. My husband suggested we take an overseas trip when I retired from my first career and we decided to explore Germany by car. On our first morning we visited the castle in the town of Celle in Lower Saxony and the rest (as they say) is history – five books on the history of German schlösser so far (and three books on Queen Victoria). Over the series of five books, I have written about one hundred and twenty-five schlösser (twenty-five in each book) sharing my experience as a visitor and some of their colourful royal history. A further fifty or so have been covered more briefly, either in the main narrative or in short text boxes. An index of all the schlösser is included as appendix C and is on my website – www.susansymons.com.

The five *Schloss* books include schlösser in thirteen of Germany's sixteen federal states, the exceptions being Bremen and Hamburg (both historically self-governing Free Cities and not royal states) and the Saarland (the smallest state on the border with France). Some states have been more extensively covered than others; forty schlösser from Baden-Württemberg are mentioned in this book and seven from Rhineland-Palatinate in *Schloss* and *Schloss III* together. With the rich legacy of German schlösser, there are many more castles and palaces still to explore. Already in research are my next books – *Schloss in Saxony-Anhalt* and (my favourite part of the country) *Schloss in Thuringia*.

Every one of the schlösser in my books is distinct and fascinating in its own special way. To remember them all and fix each one in my mind, I use a technique explained by a friend who takes part in memory championships. This is to come up with a phrase or short sentence that encapsulates my memory of it. Using the system for schlösser in this book, for example, Mannheim is where Elector Karl Philipp tried to engineer the future through the marriages of his granddaughters (see page 17); Mergentheim where we enjoyed an impromptu second tour with an expert on the Teutonic Order (page 56); and Heiligenberg quite simply a renaissance jewel (page 139).

81. The Upper Castle Greiz (Reuss elder line) will be in *Schloss in Thuringia*.

As the history of Baden-Württemberg demonstrates so well, the monarchy in Germany was made up of multiple royal families each with sovereign rights over their own territory. My books have highlighted historical stories from many of these, ranging in time from the Hohenstaufen family, who dominated the Holy Roman Empire from the mid-twelfth to thirteenth centuries; to the Prussian royal house of Hohenzollern, who from modest beginnings in Swabia were dominant as German emperors before the monarchy fell at the end of World War I. The index in appendix C indicates with which noble family I most associate each schloss. After the Napoleonic Wars, the political map of Germany was redrawn in 1815 at the Congress of Vienna. In place of the defunct Holy Roman Empire and the Napoleon-sponsored Confederation of the Rhine, the Congress created a new grouping called the German Confederation. The forty-one members of this Confederation included thirty-one sovereign states ruled by a German royal family. The other members were four free cities, (Bremen, Frankfurt, Hamburg, and Lübeck), two duchies ruled by the king of Denmark (Holstein and Lauenburg), and four central European states (Austria, Bohemia, Liechtenstein, and Luxembourg). One ambition for my *Schloss* books is to include schlösser connected with all the thirty-one German royal houses. As indicated in the list on the opposite page, with the two books currently in research this will be achieved.

### The German royal houses

Anhalt-Dessau - Schloss III chapter 4.

Anhalt-Bernburg - Schloss III chapter 4.

Anhalt-Köthen - Schloss in Saxony-Anhalt (to come).

Baden - Schloss V chapter 7 (this book).

Bavaria - Schloss IV chapters 5, 6, and 7. Schloss III chapter 1.

Brunswick - Schloss II chapter 7. Schloss III chapter 3.

Hannover - Schloss chapter 2.

Hesse-Darmstadt - Schloss III chapter 6.

Hesse-Homburg - Schloss chapter 6.

Hesse-Kassel - Schloss III chapter 6.

Hohenzollern-Hechingen - Schloss V chapter 5 (this book).

Hohenzollern-Sigmaringen - Schloss V chapter 5 (this book).

Lippe-Detmold - Schloss III chapter 2.

Mecklenburg-Schwerin - Schloss chapter 3.

Mecklenburg-Strelitz - Schloss II chapter 4.

Nassau - Schloss chapter 6.

Oldenburg - Schloss II chapter 2.

Prussia - Schloss chapters 4 and 6. Schloss II chapter 5. Schloss III chapter 7. Schloss V chapter 5 (this book).

Reuss, elder line - Schloss in Thuringia (to come).

Reuss, younger line - Schloss in Thuringia (to come).

Saxe-Coburg-Saalfeld - Schloss II chapter 6. Schloss IV chapter 3.

Saxe-Gotha-Altenburg - Schloss II chapter 6.

Saxe-Hildburghausen - Schloss in Thuringia (to come).

Saxe-Meiningen - Schloss III chapter 5.

Saxe-Weimar-Eisenach - Schloss II chapter 6. Schloss III chapter 5.

Schaumberg-Lippe - Schloss II chapter 2.

Saxony - Schloss chapter 5.

Schwarzburg-Rudolstadt - Schloss II chapter 6.

Schwarzburg-Sondershausen - Schloss in Thuringia (to come).

Waldeck-Pyrmont - Schloss III chapter 3.

Württemberg - Schloss V chapter 4 (this book).

After seeing so many schlösser in a relatively short time, my husband jokes that I should be *The Schloss Inspector* commenting on the museum experience from the point of view of a foreign visitor. I certainly feel I have learned a lot from this perspective and have strong views. For me, what makes for the best visits is a combination of beautiful surroundings, intriguing historical stories, and (above everything else) a friendly and welcoming staff. Some of the visits I have enjoyed the most were at the least-well-known schlösser that rarely see an English-speaking visitor. The attitude and approach of the staff matters so much more than any other factor – whether the schloss is smart or shabby, how the exhibits are laid out, if there is material in English, or whether visitors can take photos. Fortunately, in most cases we have had a warm welcome from knowledgeable and friendly staff who have helped us to enjoy the visit. It is only in a few cases that we have not.

# APPENDICES

# APPENDIX A
## MAP OF BADEN-WÜRTTEMBERG

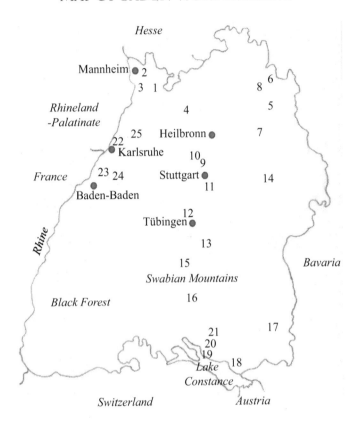

Hand drawn map showing the approximate location of the twenty-five schlösser in this book.

| | | |
|---|---|---|
| 1. Heidelberg | 10. Monrepos | 18. Tettnang |
| 2. Mannheim | 11. Hohenheim | 19. Meersburg |
| 3. Schwetzingen | 12. Bebenhausen | 20. Heiligenberg |
| 4. Neckarbischofsheim | 13. Lichtenstein | 21. Salem |
| 5. Langenburg | 14. Hohenstaufen and Lorch | 22. Karlsruhe |
| 6. Weikersheim | 15. Hohenzollern | 23. Rastatt |
| 7. Neuenstein | 16. Sigmaringen | 24. Rastatt Favorite |
| 8. Mergentheim | 17. Wurzach | 25. Bruchsal |
| 9. Ludwigsburg | | |

# APPENDIX B
## CHARTS AND FAMILY TREES

1. Electors of the Palatinate Part 1 – 1398 to 1685.
2. Electors of the Palatinate Part 2 – 1685 to 1803.
3. The marriages of the granddaughters of Elector Karl Philipp of the Palatinate.
4. Family tree for the von Helmstatt prince-bishops of Speyer.
5. Divisions of the house of Hohenlohe from 1551.
6. The three marriages that connect Schloss Langenburg with Queen Victoria's family.
7. The children of Ernst I and Feodora of Hohenlohe-Langenburg.
8. Family tree for the counts of Hohenlohe-Weikersheim.
9. The dukes of Württemberg from 1628 to 1803.
10. The kings and queens of Württemberg.
11. One hundred years of royal marriages that linked Württemberg and Russia.
12. The Württemberg succession.
13. The relationship between the dukes of Teck and the Württemberg and British royal families.
14. Hohenstaufen family tree.
15. The princes of Hohenzollern-Sigmaringen.
16. The counts of Montfort and the building of Tettnang Neues Schloss.
17. The two families of Grand Duke Karl Friedrich of Baden and the succession crisis.
18. The children of Grand Duchess Stephanie of Baden (born de Beauharnais).
19. The important marriages of the granddaughters of Grand Duke Karl Friedrich of Baden.
20. The children of Margrave Ludwig Wilhelm and Sibylla Augusta of Baden-Baden.

# 1. ELECTORS OF THE PALATINATE Part I – 1398 to 1685

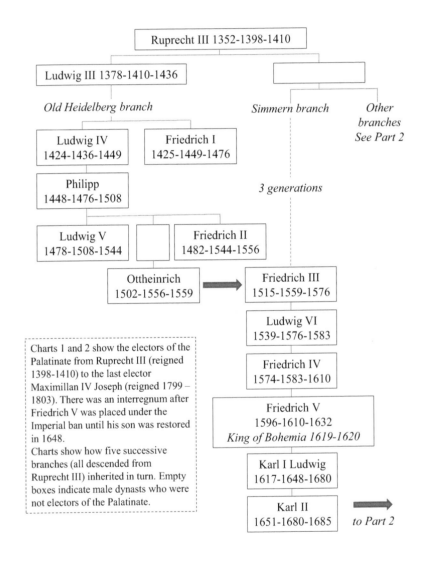

Ruprecht III 1352-1398-1410

Ludwig III 1378-1410-1436

*Old Heidelberg branch*

*Simmern branch*

*Other branches See Part 2*

Ludwig IV
1424-1436-1449

Friedrich I
1425-1449-1476

Philipp
1448-1476-1508

*3 generations*

Ludwig V
1478-1508-1544

Friedrich II
1482-1544-1556

Ottheinrich
1502-1556-1559

Friedrich III
1515-1559-1576

Ludwig VI
1539-1576-1583

Friedrich IV
1574-1583-1610

Friedrich V
1596-1610-1632
*King of Bohemia 1619-1620*

Karl I Ludwig
1617-1648-1680

Karl II
1651-1680-1685

*to Part 2*

Charts 1 and 2 show the electors of the Palatinate from Ruprecht III (reigned 1398-1410) to the last elector Maximillan IV Joseph (reigned 1799 – 1803). There was an interregnum after Friedrich V was placed under the Imperial ban until his son was restored in 1648.

Charts show how five successive branches (all descended from Ruprecht III) inherited in turn. Empty boxes indicate male dynasts who were not electors of the Palatinate.

190

## 2. ELECTORS OF THE PALATINATE Part 2 – 1685 to 1803

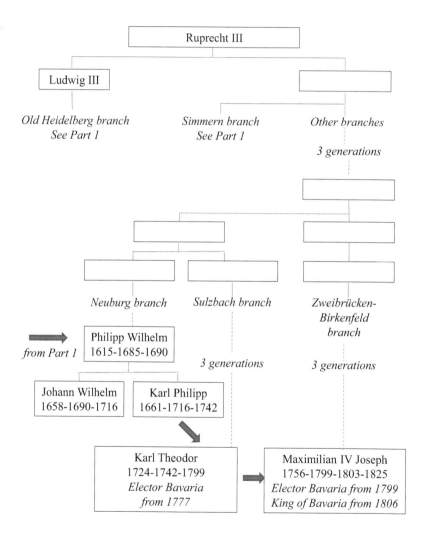

Ruprecht III

Ludwig III

*Old Heidelberg branch*
*See Part 1*

*Simmern branch*
*See Part 1*

*Other branches*

*3 generations*

*Neuburg branch*

*Sulzbach branch*

*Zweibrücken-*
*Birkenfeld*
*branch*

*from Part 1*

Philipp Wilhelm
1615-1685-1690

*3 generations*

*3 generations*

Johann Wilhelm
1658-1690-1716

Karl Philipp
1661-1716-1742

Karl Theodor
1724-1742-1799
*Elector Bavaria*
*from 1777*

Maximilian IV Joseph
1756-1799-1803-1825
*Elector Bavaria from 1799*
*King of Bavaria from 1806*

### 3. THE MARRIAGES OF THE GRANDDAUGHTERS OF ELECTOR KARL PHILIPP OF THE PALATINATE[1]

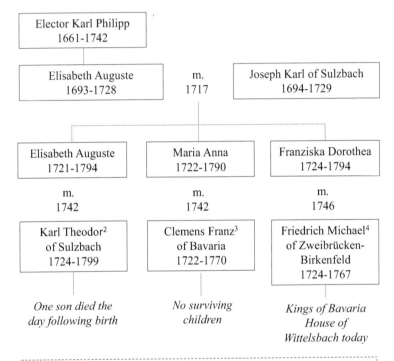

1. All three marriages were within the house of Wittelsbach and were arranged by Karl Philipp.
2. Karl Theodor succeeded Karl Philipp as elector of the Palatinate.
3. Clemens Franz was the grandson of Elector Maximillian II Emanuel of Bavaria. If this couple had produced a surviving son, he would have succeeded as elector of Bavaria.
4. Maximillian IV Joseph, who succeeded Karl Theodor in 1799 and became the first king of Bavaria in 1806, was the younger son of this couple.

## 4. FAMILY TREE FOR THE VON HELMSTATT PRINCE-BISHOPS OF SPEYER

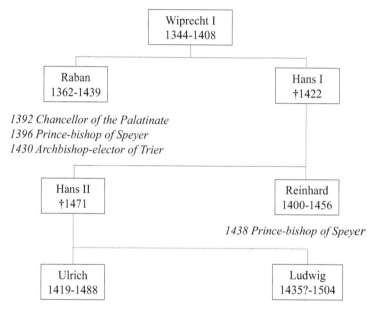

Wiprecht I
1344-1408

Raban
1362-1439

*1392 Chancellor of the Palatinate*
*1396 Prince-bishop of Speyer*
*1430 Archbishop-elector of Trier*

Hans I
†1422

Hans II
†1471

Reinhard
1400-1456

*1438 Prince-bishop of Speyer*

Ulrich
1419-1488

*1456 Elected Prince-bishop of Speyer*
*But did not take up the position*

Ludwig
1435?-1504

*1478 Prince-bishop of Speyer*

Chart shows the elected prince-bishops of Speyer from the family of
ritter von Helmstatt and their descent from Wiprecht I.

## 5. DIVISIONS OF THE HOUSE OF HOHENLOHE FROM 1551

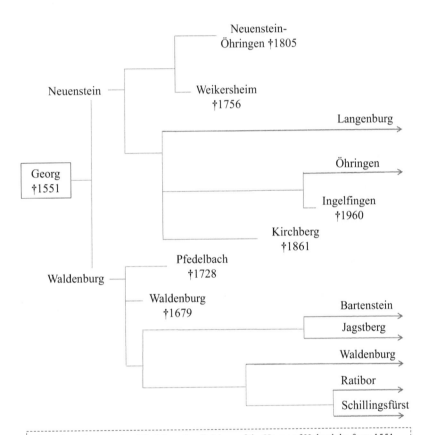

Chart shows in very simplified form the divisions of the House of Hohenlohe from 1551.
Chart shows branches that died out † and the seven branches that survive today –
Langenburg, Öhringen, Bartenstein, Jagstberg, Waldenburg, Ratibor, and Schillingsfürst.
Source: "Hohenlohe" by Friedrich Karl Fürst zu Hohenlohe-Waldenburg (see bibliography)

## 6. THE THREE MARRIAGES THAT CONNECT
## SCHLOSS LANGENBURG WITH QUEEN VICTORIA'S FAMILY

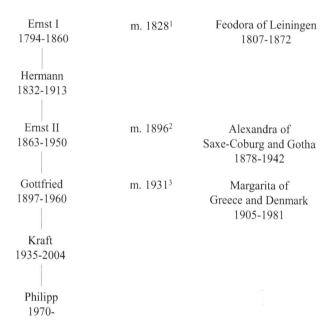

| Ernst I | m. 1828[1] | Feodora of Leiningen |
| 1794-1860 | | 1807-1872 |
| | | |
| Hermann | | |
| 1832-1913 | | |
| | | |
| Ernst II | m. 1896[2] | Alexandra of |
| 1863-1950 | | Saxe-Coburg and Gotha |
| | | 1878-1942 |
| Gottfried | m. 1931[3] | Margarita of |
| 1897-1960 | | Greece and Denmark |
| | | 1905-1981 |
| Kraft | | |
| 1935-2004 | | |
| | | |
| Philipp | | |
| 1970- | | |

Chart shows the princes of Hohenlohe-Langenburg from Ernst I to the present day and the marriages of three of these to members of Queen Victoria's family.
1. Feodora was the half-sister of Queen Victoria; Ernst I was the first cousin of Queen Adelaide of Great Britain.
2. Ernst II was Queen Victoria's great nephew; Alexandra was her granddaughter (the third daughter of Victoria's second son Alfred).
3. Gottfried was Queen Victoria's great-grandson; Margarita was her great-great-granddaughter (one of the four sisters of Prince Philip).

## 7. THE CHILDREN OF ERNST I AND FEODORA
## OF HOHENLOHE-LANGENBURG

Karl
1829-1907

Abdicated his rights immediately following his father's death to make a morganatic marriage to Maria Grathwohl, the daughter of a Weikersheim grocer.

Elise (Eliza)
1830-1851

Died young from tuberculosis. Unmarried.

Hermann
1832-1913

Inherited when his elder brother abdicated. Married Leopoldine of Baden; the present prince of Hohenlohe-Langenburg is their descendant.

Viktor
1833-1891

Joined the Royal Navy as a teenager; when later forced to resign due to ill health, he became a sculptor. Also gave up his rights to make a morganatic marriage to Laura Seymour, the daughter of a British admiral.

Adelheid (Ada)
1835-1900

Married Duke Friedrich VIII of Schleswig-Holstein-Sonderburg-Augustenburg; they were the parents of Auguste Viktoria, the last queen of Prussia and empress of Germany.

Feodora (Feo)
1839-1872

Married Duke Georg II of Saxe-Meiningen as his second wife. Died from scarlet fever.

## 8. FAMILY TREE FOR THE
## COUNTS OF HOHENLOHE-WEIKERSHEIM

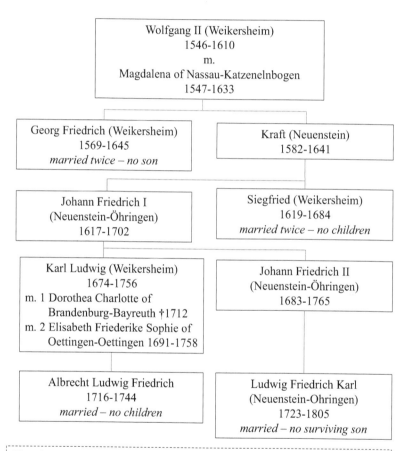

Wolfgang II (Weikersheim)
1546-1610
m.
Magdalena of Nassau-Katzenelnbogen
1547-1633

Georg Friedrich (Weikersheim)
1569-1645
*married twice – no son*

Kraft (Neuenstein)
1582-1641

Johann Friedrich I
(Neuenstein-Öhringen)
1617-1702

Siegfried (Weikersheim)
1619-1684
*married twice – no children*

Karl Ludwig (Weikersheim)
1674-1756
m. 1 Dorothea Charlotte of
Brandenburg-Bayreuth †1712
m. 2 Elisabeth Friederike Sophie of
Oettingen-Oettingen 1691-1758

Johann Friedrich II
(Neuenstein-Öhringen)
1683-1765

Albrecht Ludwig Friedrich
1716-1744
*married – no children*

Ludwig Friedrich Karl
(Neuenstein-Ohringen)
1723-1805
*married – no surviving son*

Chart shows the counts of Hohenlohe-Weikersheim from Wolfgang II (1546-1610) to Karl
Ludwig (1674-1756). When this branch of the house of Hohenlohe died out in 1756
Weikersheim was inherited by the Neuenstein-Öhringen branch. After this died out in turn
in 1805, Weikersheim went to Hohenlohe-Langenburg.

## 9. THE DUKES OF WÜRTTEMBERG FROM 1628 TO 1803

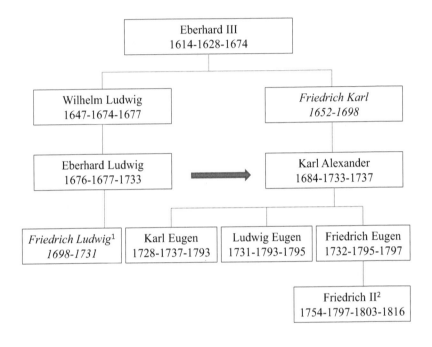

Chart shows the eight dukes of Württemberg from the accession of Eberhard III in 1628 to the change of status to an electorate in 1803. Male dynasts whose names are shown *in italics* did not reign as duke.
1. Friedrich Ludwig died before his father with no surviving son.
2. Duke Friedrich II became Elector Friedrich in 1803 and King Friedrich in 1806.

# 10. THE KINGS AND QUEENS OF WÜRTTEMBERG

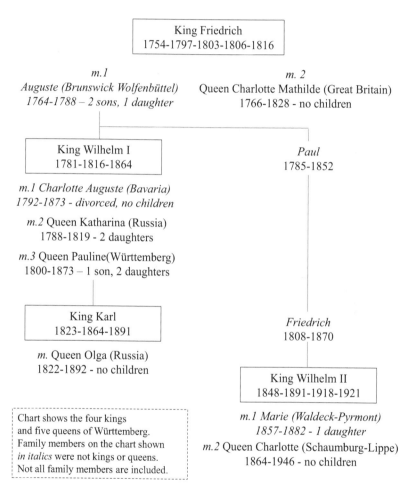

King Friedrich
1754-1797-1803-1806-1816

*m.1*
*Auguste (Brunswick Wolfenbüttel)*
*1764-1788 – 2 sons, 1 daughter*

*m. 2*
Queen Charlotte Mathilde (Great Britain)
1766-1828 - no children

King Wilhelm I
1781-1816-1864

*Paul*
*1785-1852*

*m.1 Charlotte Auguste (Bavaria)*
*1792-1873 - divorced, no children*

*m.2* Queen Katharina (Russia)
1788-1819 - 2 daughters

*m.3* Queen Pauline(Württemberg)
1800-1873 – 1 son, 2 daughters

King Karl
1823-1864-1891

*Friedrich*
*1808-1870*

*m.* Queen Olga (Russia)
1822-1892 - no children

King Wilhelm II
1848-1891-1918-1921

Chart shows the four kings
and five queens of Württemberg.
Family members on the chart shown
*in italics* were not kings or queens.
Not all family members are included.

*m.1 Marie (Waldeck-Pyrmont)*
*1857-1882 - 1 daughter*

*m.2* Queen Charlotte (Schaumburg-Lippe)
1864-1946 - no children

## 11. ONE HUNDRED YEARS OF ROYAL MARRIAGES
## THAT LINKED WÜRTTEMBERG AND RUSSIA

| Württemberg | | Russia |
|---|---|---|
| Sophie Dorothee (Maria Feodorovna) 1759-1828 sister of King Friedrich | m. 1776 | Paul (later Tsar of Russia) 1754-1801 |
| King Wilhelm I 1781-1864 son of King Friedrich | m. 1816 first cousins | Ekaterina (Katharina) 1788-1819 daughter of Tsar Paul and Maria Feodorovna |
| Charlotte (Elena Pavlovna) 1807-1873 daughter of King Friedrich's younger son, Paul | m. 1824 first cousins, once removed | Mikhail 1798-1849 son of Tsar Paul and Maria Feodorovna |
| King Karl 1823-1891 son of Wilhelm I, grandson of King Friedrich | m. 1846 second cousins | Olga 1822-1892 daughter of Tsar Nikolai I, granddaughter of Tsar Paul |
| Wilhelm Eugen 1846-1877 great-grandson of Eugen, King Friedrich's younger brother | m. 1874 distant cousins | Vera 1854-1912 daughter of Konstantin, Tsar Nikolai I's son, great-granddaughter of Tsar Paul |

## 12. THE WÜRTTEMBERG SUCCESSION

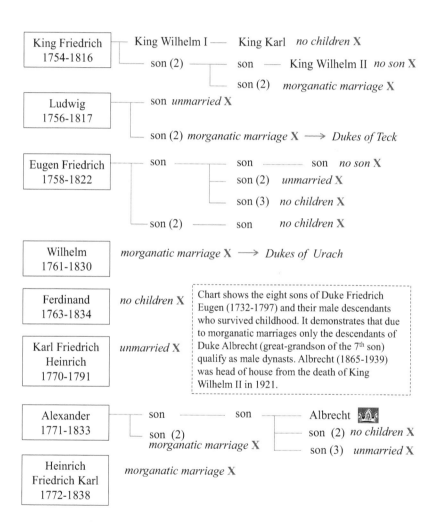

King Friedrich 1754-1816 — King Wilhelm I —— King Karl  *no children* X
— son (2) —— son —— King Wilhelm II  *no son* X
— son (2)  *morganatic marriage* X

Ludwig 1756-1817 — son *unmarried* X
— son (2) *morganatic marriage* X ⟶ *Dukes of Teck*

Eugen Friedrich 1758-1822 — son —— son —— son  *no son* X
— son (2)  *unmarried* X
— son (3)  *no children* X
— son (2) —— son  *no children* X

Wilhelm 1761-1830  *morganatic marriage* X ⟶ *Dukes of Urach*

Ferdinand 1763-1834  *no children* X

Chart shows the eight sons of Duke Friedrich Eugen (1732-1797) and their male descendants who survived childhood. It demonstrates that due to morganatic marriages only the descendants of Duke Albrecht (great-grandson of the 7th son) qualify as male dynasts. Albrecht (1865-1939) was head of house from the death of King Wilhelm II in 1921.

Karl Friedrich Heinrich 1770-1791  *unmarried* X

Alexander 1771-1833 — son —— son —— Albrecht
— son (2) *morganatic marriage* X
— son (2) *no children* X
— son (3) *unmarried* X

Heinrich Friedrich Karl 1772-1838  *morganatic marriage* X

## 13. THE RELATIONSHIP BETWEEN THE DUKES OF TECK AND THE WÜRTTEMBERG AND BRITISH ROYAL FAMILIES

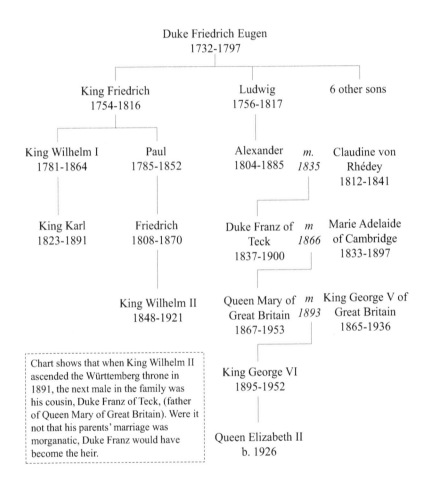

Duke Friedrich Eugen
1732-1797

King Friedrich
1754-1816

Ludwig
1756-1817

6 other sons

King Wilhelm I
1781-1864

Paul
1785-1852

Alexander
1804-1885

*m.*
*1835*

Claudine von
Rhédey
1812-1841

King Karl
1823-1891

Friedrich
1808-1870

Duke Franz of
Teck
1837-1900

*m*
*1866*

Marie Adelaide
of Cambridge
1833-1897

King Wilhelm II
1848-1921

Queen Mary of
Great Britain
1867-1953

*m*
*1893*

King George V of
Great Britain
1865-1936

Chart shows that when King Wilhelm II ascended the Württemberg throne in 1891, the next male in the family was his cousin, Duke Franz of Teck, (father of Queen Mary of Great Britain). Were it not that his parents' marriage was morganatic, Duke Franz would have become the heir.

King George VI
1895-1952

Queen Elizabeth II
b. 1926

## 14. HOHENSTAUFEN FAMILY TREE

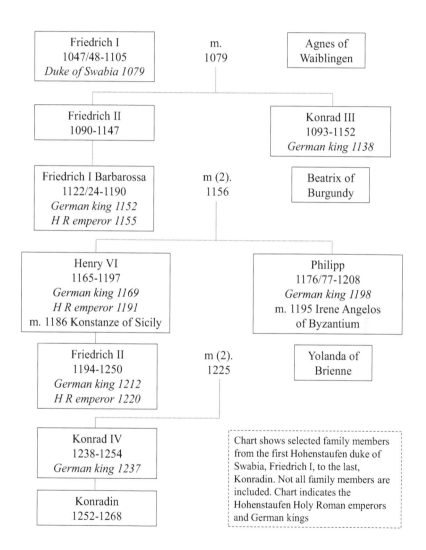

| | | |
|---|---|---|
| Friedrich I<br>1047/48-1105<br>*Duke of Swabia 1079* | m.<br>1079 | Agnes of<br>Waiblingen |

| | |
|---|---|
| Friedrich II<br>1090-1147 | Konrad III<br>1093-1152<br>*German king 1138* |

| | | |
|---|---|---|
| Friedrich I Barbarossa<br>1122/24-1190<br>*German king 1152*<br>*H R emperor 1155* | m (2).<br>1156 | Beatrix of<br>Burgundy |

| | |
|---|---|
| Henry VI<br>1165-1197<br>*German king 1169*<br>*H R emperor 1191*<br>m. 1186 Konstanze of Sicily | Philipp<br>1176/77-1208<br>*German king 1198*<br>m. 1195 Irene Angelos<br>of Byzantium |

| | | |
|---|---|---|
| Friedrich II<br>1194-1250<br>*German king 1212*<br>*H R emperor 1220* | m (2).<br>1225 | Yolanda of<br>Brienne |

Konrad IV
1238-1254
*German king 1237*

Konradin
1252-1268

Chart shows selected family members from the first Hohenstaufen duke of Swabia, Friedrich I, to the last, Konradin. Not all family members are included. Chart indicates the Hohenstaufen Holy Roman emperors and German kings

## 15. THE PRINCES OF HOHENZOLLERN-SIGMARINGEN

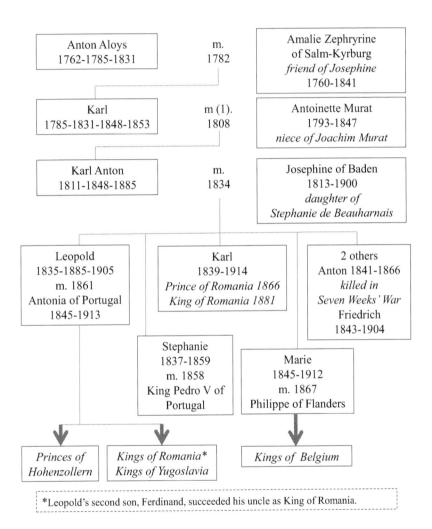

| Anton Aloys 1762-1785-1831 | m. 1782 | Amalie Zephryrine of Salm-Kyrburg *friend of Josephine* 1760-1841 |

| Karl 1785-1831-1848-1853 | m (1). 1808 | Antoinette Murat 1793-1847 *niece of Joachim Murat* |

| Karl Anton 1811-1848-1885 | m. 1834 | Josephine of Baden 1813-1900 *daughter of Stephanie de Beauharnais* |

| Leopold 1835-1885-1905 m. 1861 Antonia of Portugal 1845-1913 | Karl 1839-1914 *Prince of Romania 1866* *King of Romania 1881* | 2 others Anton 1841-1866 *killed in Seven Weeks' War* Friedrich 1843-1904 |

Stephanie 1837-1859 m. 1858 King Pedro V of Portugal

Marie 1845-1912 m. 1867 Philippe of Flanders

*Princes of Hohenzollern*

*Kings of Romania\* Kings of Yugoslavia*

*Kings of Belgium*

\*Leopold's second son, Ferdinand, succeeded his uncle as King of Romania.

## 16. THE COUNTS OF MONTFORT AND THE BUILDING OF TETTNANG NEUES SCHLOSS

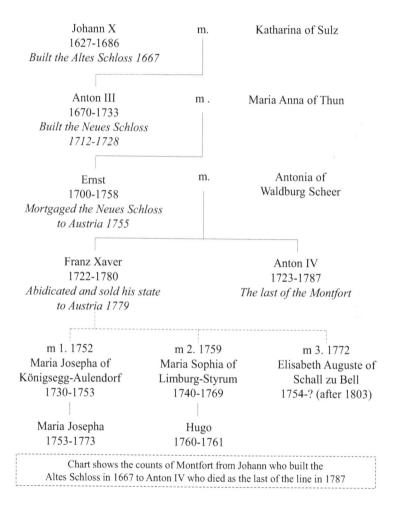

Johann X
1627-1686
*Built the Altes Schloss 1667*

m.

Katharina of Sulz

Anton III
1670-1733
*Built the Neues Schloss
1712-1728*

m .

Maria Anna of Thun

Ernst
1700-1758
*Mortgaged the Neues Schloss
to Austria 1755*

m.

Antonia of
Waldburg Scheer

Franz Xaver
1722-1780
*Abidicated and sold his state
to Austria 1779*

Anton IV
1723-1787
*The last of the Montfort*

m 1. 1752
Maria Josepha of
Königsegg-Aulendorf
1730-1753

m 2. 1759
Maria Sophia of
Limburg-Styrum
1740-1769

m 3. 1772
Elisabeth Auguste of
Schall zu Bell
1754-? (after 1803)

Maria Josepha
1753-1773

Hugo
1760-1761

Chart shows the counts of Montfort from Johann who built the
Altes Schloss in 1667 to Anton IV who died as the last of the line in 1787

## 17. THE TWO FAMILIES OF GRAND DUKE KARL FRIEDRICH OF BADEN AND THE SUCCESSION CRISIS

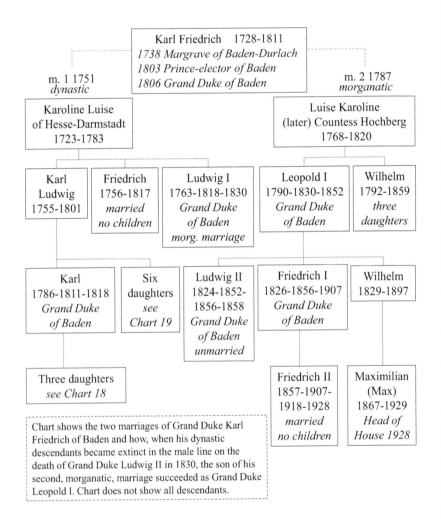

Karl Friedrich   1728-1811
*1738 Margrave of Baden-Durlach*
*1803 Prince-elector of Baden*
*1806 Grand Duke of Baden*

m. 1 1751
*dynastic*

m. 2 1787
*morganatic*

Karoline Luise
of Hesse-Darmstadt
1723-1783

Luise Karoline
(later) Countess Hochberg
1768-1820

| Karl Ludwig 1755-1801 | Friedrich 1756-1817 *married no children* | Ludwig I 1763-1818-1830 *Grand Duke of Baden morg. marriage* | Leopold I 1790-1830-1852 *Grand Duke of Baden* | Wilhelm 1792-1859 *three daughters* |

| Karl 1786-1811-1818 *Grand Duke of Baden* | Six daughters *see Chart 19* | Ludwig II 1824-1852-1856-1858 *Grand Duke of Baden unmarried* | Friedrich I 1826-1856-1907 *Grand Duke of Baden* | Wilhelm 1829-1897 |

Three daughters
*see Chart 18*

Friedrich II
1857-1907-
1918-1928
*married
no children*

Maximilian
(Max)
1867-1929
*Head of
House 1928*

Chart shows the two marriages of Grand Duke Karl Friedrich of Baden and how, when his dynastic descendants became extinct in the male line on the death of Grand Duke Ludwig II in 1830, the son of his second, morganatic, marriage succeeded as Grand Duke Leopold I. Chart does not show all descendants.

## 18. THE CHILDREN OF GRAND DUCHESS STEPHANIE OF BADEN (BORN DE BEAUHARNAIS)

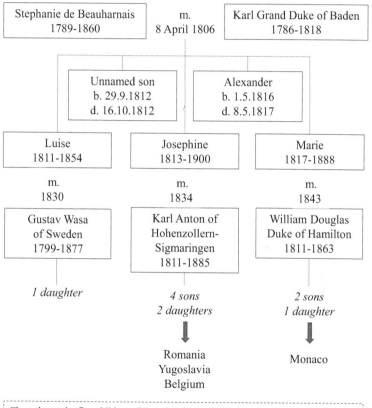

Stephanie de Beauharnais 1789-1860 — m. 8 April 1806 — Karl Grand Duke of Baden 1786-1818

Unnamed son
b. 29.9.1812
d. 16.10.1812

Alexander
b. 1.5.1816
d. 8.5.1817

Luise 1811-1854
Josephine 1813-1900
Marie 1817-1888

m. 1830
m. 1834
m. 1843

Gustav Wasa of Sweden 1799-1877
Karl Anton of Hohenzollern-Sigmaringen 1811-1885
William Douglas Duke of Hamilton 1811-1863

1 daughter
4 sons 2 daughters
2 sons 1 daughter

Romania Yugoslavia Belgium
Monaco

Chart shows the five children of Grand Duke Karl and Grand Duchess Stephanie of Baden (born de Beauharnais).
Chart also shows the marriages of their three daughters and the thrones descended from these.

## 19. THE IMPORTANT MARRIAGES OF THE GRANDDAUGHTERS OF GRAND DUKE KARL FRIEDRICH OF BADEN

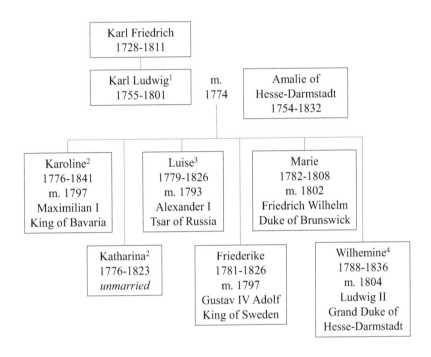

Chart shows the marriages of the granddaughters of Karl Friedrich by his eldest son. Three became queens or empresses.

1. Hereditary Count Karl Ludwig was the heir to Baden-Durlach but died before his father as a result of a sled accident
2. Karoline and Katharina were twins
3. After her marriage, Luise became Tsarina Elizaveta Alexeievna
4. For Wilhelmine's story, see Schloss Heiligenberg in *Schloss III*

Chart does not show all descendants.

## 20. THE CHILDREN OF  LUDWIG WILHELM AND SIBYLLA AUGUSTA OF BADEN-BADEN

| Ludwig Wilhelm 1655-1707 | m. 1690 | Sibylla Augusta 1675-1733 |
|---|---|---|

Leopold Wilhelm — Born 1694; died 1696

Charlotte — Born 1696; died 1700

Karl Josef — Born 1697; died 1703

Wilhelmine — Born 1699; died 1702

Luise — Born 1701; died 1701

Ludwig Georg — Born 1702; died 1761
Margrave 1707; regency of mother to 1727
married twice; one daughter

Wilhelm Georg — Born 1703; died 1709

Augusta Maria Johanna — Born 1704; died 1726
married Duke Louis of Orleans
Grandmother of Philippe Egalité

August Georg — Born 1706; died 1771
Margrave of Baden-Baden 1761
married; no children
The last of the line

# APPENDIX C
## INDEX OF SCHLÖSSER IN THE *SCHLOSS* BOOKS

Listed in alphabetical order by federal state and showing the noble family with which I most associate each.

| Name (location if different) | Family | Book | Page no. |
|---|---|---|---|
| ***Baden-Württemberg*** | | | |
| Baden-Baden Neues Schloss | Baden | *Schloss V* | 164 |
| Bebenhausen (Tübingen) | Württemberg | *Schloss V* | 88 |
| Bruchsal | Prince-bishops Speyer | *Schloss V* | 174 |
| Ettlingen | Baden | *Schloss V* | 173 |
| Heidelberg | Palatinate | *Schloss V* | 10 |
| Heiligenberg | Fürstenberg | *Schloss V* | 139 |
| Hohenbaden (Baden-Baden) | Baden | *Schloss V* | 155 |
| Hohenheim (Stuttgart) | Württemberg | *Schloss V* | 81 |
| Hohenstaufen (Göppingen) | Staufer | *Schloss V* | 100 |
| Hohenzollern | Hohenzollern | *Schloss V* | 106 |
| Karlsruhe | Baden | *Schloss V* | 152 |
| Kirchheim (Kirchheim unter Teck) | Württemberg | *Schloss V* | 86 |
| Langenburg | Hohenlohe | *Schloss V* | 36 |
| Lichtenstein | Württemberg | *Schloss V* | 93 |
| Lorch | Staufer | *Schloss V* | 100 |
| Ludwigsburg | Württemberg | *Schloss V* | 64 |
| Ludwigsburg Favorite | Württemberg | *Schloss V* | 65 |
| Mannheim | Palatinate | *Schloss V* | 17 |
| Meersburg Altes Schloss | Prince-bishops Konstanz | *Schloss V* | 134 |
| Meersburg Neues Schloss | Prince-bishops Konstanz | *Schloss V* | 134 |
| Mergentheim (Bad Mergentheim) | Teutonic Knights | *Schloss V* | 56 |
| Monrepos (Ludwigsburg) | Württemberg | *Schloss V* | 72 |
| Montfort (Langenarden) | Montfort | *Schloss V* | 133 |
| Neckarbischofsheim | von Helmstatt | *Schloss V* | 30 |
| Neuenstein | Hohenlohe | *Schloss V* | 50 |
| Öhringen | Hohenlohe | *Schloss V* | 55 |
| Rastatt | Baden | *Schloss V* | 160 |
| Rastatt Favorite | Baden | *Schloss V* | 166 |
| Salem | Baden | *Schloss V* | 144 |
| Schwetzingen | Palatinate | *Schloss V* | 24 |
| Sigmaringen | Hohenzollern | *Schloss V* | 112 |
| Solitude (Stuttgart) | Württemberg | *Schloss V* | 84 |
| Stetten | Stetten | *Schloss V* | 40 |
| Teck (Owen) | Württemberg | *Schloss V* | 96 |
| Tettnang | Montfort | *Schloss V* | 127 |

| | | | |
|---|---|---|---|
| Villa Hohenlohe (Baden-Baden) | Hohenlohe | *Schloss V* | 43 |
| Weikersheim | Hohenlohe | *Schloss V* | 44 |
| Wurzach (Bad Wurzach) | Waldburg | *Schloss V* | 120 |
| Zeil (Leutkirch im Allgäu) | Waldburg | *Schloss V* | 125 |
| Zwingenberg | Palatinate | *Schloss V* | 29 |

### Bavaria

| | | | |
|---|---|---|---|
| Ansbach | Brandenburg-Ansbach | *Schloss IV* | 37 |
| Bamberg New Residence | Prince-bishops Bamberg | *Schloss IV* | 8 |
| Berchtesgaden | Wittelsbach | *Schloss IV* | 158 |
| Berg | Wittelsbach | *Schloss IV* | 125 |
| Burghausen | Wittelsbach | *Schloss IV* | 89 |
| Burgraves Castle (Nuremberg) | Burgraves Nuremberg | *SchlossIV* | 34 |
| Callenberg (Coburg) | Saxe-Coburg and Gotha | *Schloss IV* | 59 |
| Dachau | Wittelsbach | *Schloss IV* | 112 |
| Donastauf | Thurn und Taxis | *Schloss IV* | 75 |
| Ehrenburg (Coburg) | Saxe-Coburg and Gotha | *Schloss IV* | 46 |
| Forchheim | Prince-bishops Bamberg | *Schloss IV* | 30 |
| Fürstenreid (Munich) | Wittelsbach | *Schloss IV* | 147 |
| Füssen | Prince-bishops Augsburg | *Schloss IV* | 177 |
| Greifenstein (Heiligenstadt) | Stauffenberg | *Schloss IV* | 25 |
| Herrenchiemsee | Wittelsbach | *Schloss IV* | 140 |
| Hohenschwangau | Wittelsbach | *Schloss IV* | 168 |
| Ketschendorf (Coburg) | Saxe-Coburg and Gotha | *Schloss IV* | 65 |
| Landshut Residence | Wittelsbach | *Schloss IV* | 88 |
| Laufen | Prince-bishops Salzburg | *Schloss IV* | 99 |
| Linderhof (Ettal) | Wittelsbach | *Schloss IV* | 132 |
| Neuburg | Wittelsbach | *Schloss IV* | 101 |
| Neuschwanstein (Hohenschwangau) | Wittelsbach | *Schloss IV* | 173 |
| Nuremberg | Holy Roman emperors | *Schloss IV* | 32 |
| Nymphenburg (Munich) | Wittelsbach | *Schloss IV* | 113 |
| Palais Edinburgh (Coburg) | Saxe-Coburg and Gotha | *Schloss IV* | 53 |
| Possenhofen | Wittelsbach | *Schloss IV* | 124 |
| Rosenau (Rödental) | Saxe-Coburg and Gotha | *Schloss IV* | 51 |
| Roseninsel Casino (Lake Starnberg) | Wittelsbach | *Schloss IV* | 124 |
| Royal Villa (Berchtesgaden) | Wittelsbach | *Schloss IV* | 160 |
| Schleissheim (Munich) | Wittelsbach | *Schloss IV* | 106 |
| Seehof (Memmelsdorf) | Prince-bishops Bamberg | *Schloss IV* | 15 |
| Seeon (Seeon-Seebruck) | Leuchtenberg | *Schloss IV* | 152 |
| St Emmeram (Regensburg) | Thurn und Taxis | *Schloss IV* | 68 |
| Tegernsee | Wittelsbach | *Schloss IV* | 138 |
| Tittmoning | Prince-bishops Salzburg | *Schloss IV* | 95 |
| Trausnitz (Landshut) | Wittelsbach | *Schloss IV* | 82 |
| Veste Coburg | Saxe-Coburg and Gotha | *Schloss IV* | 54 |
| Weissenstein (Pommersfelden) | Schönborn | *Schloss IV* | 20 |
| Wildenwart (Frasdorf) | Wittelsbach | *Schloss IV* | 144 |

**Berlin & Brandenburg**

| | | | |
|---|---|---|---|
| Altes Palais (Berlin) | Hohenzollern | *Schloss* | 56 |
| Cecilienhof (Potsdam) | Hohenzollern | *Schloss* | 78 |
| Charlottenburg (Berlin) | Hohenzollern | *Schloss* | 67 |
| Kronprinzenpalais (Berlin) | Hohenzollern | *Schloss* | 59 |
| Neues Palais (Potsdam) | Hohenzollern | *Schloss* | 63 |
| New Pavilion (Berlin) | Hohenzollern | *Schloss* | 75 |
| Paretz (Ketzin) | Hohenzollern | *Schloss* | 76 |
| Rheinsberg | Hohenzollern | *Schloss II* | 96 |
| Sanssouci (Potsdam) | Hohenzollern | *Schloss* | 60 |

*Hesse*

| | | | |
|---|---|---|---|
| Bad Homburg | Hesse-Homburg | *Schloss* | 124 |
| Darmstadt | Hesse-Darmstadt | *Schloss III* | 114 |
| Friedberg | Hesse-Darmstadt | *Schloss III* | 134 |
| Friedrichshof (Kronberg i/Taunus) | Hesse-Kassel | *Schloss* | 112 |
| Heiligenberg (Jugenheim) | Battenberg | *Schloss III* | 126 |
| Burgruine Königstein | Nassau | *Schloss* | 120 |
| Kranichstein (Darmstadt) | Hesse-Darmstadt | *Schloss III* | 121 |
| Kronberg | Lords of Kronberg | *Schloss* | 118 |
| Luxembourg (Königstein i/Taunus) | Nassau | *Schloss* | 122 |
| Rosenhöhe (Darmstadt) | Hesse-Darmstadt | *Schloss III* | 119 |
| Wilhelmshöhe (Kassel) | Hesse-Kassel | *Schloss III* | 138 |
| Wilhelmsthal (Calden) | Hesse-Kassel | *Schloss III* | 144 |
| Wolfsgarten (Langen) | Hesse-Darmstadt | *Schloss III* | 125 |

*Lower Saxony*

| | | | |
|---|---|---|---|
| Ahlden | Hannover | *Schloss* | 13 |
| Bevern | Brunswick-Bevern | *Schloss III* | 56 |
| Braunschweig | Brunswick-Wolfenbüttel | *Schloss II* | 151 |
| Bückeburg | Schaumburg-Lippe | *Schloss II* | 10 |
| Celle | Hannover | *Schloss* | 6 |
| Fallersleben (Wolfsburg) | Brunswick-Lüneburg | *Schloss II* | 178 |
| Herrenhausen (Hannover) | Hannover | *Schloss* | 16 |
| Jever | Anhalt-Zerbst | *Schloss II* | 33 |
| Kaiserpfalz (Goslar) | Holy Roman emperors | *Schloss II* | 169 |
| Marienburg (Pattensen) | Hannover | *Schloss* | 21 |
| Oldenburg | Oldenburg | *Schloss II* | 19 |
| Pyrmont | Waldeck-Pyrmont | *Schloss III* | 48 |
| Rastede Palais | Oldenburg | *Schloss II* | 24 |
| Rastede Schloss | Oldenburg | *Schloss II* | 24 |
| Little Richmond (Braunschweig) | Brunswick-Wolfenbüttel | *Schloss II* | 157 |
| Salzdahlum | Brunswick-Wolfenbüttel | *Schloss II* | 166 |
| Stadthagen | Holstein-Schaumburg | *Schloss II* | 13 |
| Wolfenbüttel | Brunswick-Wolfenbüttel | *Schloss II* | 162 |
| Wolfsburg | Schulenburg-Wolfsburg | *Schloss II* | 174 |

### Mecklenburg-Pomerania

| | | | |
|---|---|---|---|
| Bad Doberan | Mecklenburg-Schwerin | *Schloss* | 30 |
| Blücher (Göhren-Lebbin) | Blücher | *Schloss II* | 94 |
| Gamehl | von Stralendorff | *Schloss* | 52 |
| Gelbensande | Mecklenburg-Schwerin | *Schloss* | 46 |
| Güstrow | Mecklenburg-Güstrow | *Schloss* | 44 |
| Hohenzieritz | Mecklenburg-Strelitz | *Schloss II* | 76 |
| Ludwigslust | Mecklenburg-Schwerin | *Schloss* | 33 |
| Mirow | Mecklenburg-Strelitz | *Schloss II* | 68 |
| Neustrelitz | Mecklenburg-Strelitz | *Schloss II* | 82 |
| Prinzenpalais (Bad Doberan) | Mecklenburg-Schwerin | *Schloss* | 32 |
| Schwerin | Mecklenburg-Schwerin | *Schloss* | 41 |
| Burg Stargard | Mecklenburg-Strelitz | *Schloss II* | 90 |
| Wiligrad (Löbstorf) | Mecklenburg-Schwerin | *Schloss* | 50 |

### North Rhine-Westphalia

| | | | |
|---|---|---|---|
| Altena | von Mark | *Schloss III* | 33 |
| Augustusburg (Brühl) | Wittelsbach | *Schloss III* | 10 |
| Bensberg (Bergisch-Gladbach) | Wittelsbach | *Schloss III* | 24 |
| Detmold | Lippe | *Schloss III* | 38 |
| Falkenlust (Brühl) | Wittelsbach | *Schloss III* | 17 |
| Nordkirchen | von Plettenberg | *Schloss III* | 20 |
| Türnich (Kerpen) | von Hoensbroech | *Schloss III* | 19 |
| Vischering (Lüdinghausen) | zu Vischering | *Schloss III* | 30 |

### Rhineland-Palatinate

| | | | |
|---|---|---|---|
| Bathhouse Palace (Bad Ems) | Nassau-Diez | *Schloss III* | 150 |
| Diez | Nassau-Diez | *Schloss III* | 162 |
| Marksburg (Braubach) | Hesse/Nassau | *Schloss* | 135 |
| Oranienstein (Diez) | Nassau-Diez | *Schloss III* | 157 |
| Phillipsburg (Braubach) | Hesse-Rheinfels | *Schloss* | 136 |
| Stolzenfels (Koblenz) | Hohenzollern | *Schloss III* | 163 |
| Vier Turme (Bad Ems) | von Thüngen | *Schloss III* | 152 |

### Saxony

| | | | |
|---|---|---|---|
| Colditz | Wettin | *Schloss* | 102 |
| Pillnitz (Dresden) | Wettin | *Schloss* | 98 |
| Residenzschloss (Dresden) | Wettin | *Schloss* | 86 |
| Rochlitz | Wettin | *Schloss* | 107 |
| Burg Stolpen | Wettin | *Schloss* | 95 |
| Taschenbergpalais (Dresden) | Wettin | *Schloss* | 88 |

### Saxony Anhalt

| | | | |
|---|---|---|---|
| Bernburg | Anhalt-Bernburg | *Schloss III* | 82 |
| Luisium (Dessau) | Anhalt-Dessau | *Schloss III* | 72 |
| Johannbau (Dessau) | Anhalt-Dessau | *Schloss III* | 62 |

| | | | |
|---|---|---|---|
| Mosigkau | Anhalt-Dessau | *Schloss III* | 67 |
| Oranienbaum | Anhalt-Dessau | *Schloss III* | 72 |
| Quedlinburg | Abbesses of Quedlinburg | *Schloss III* | 77 |
| Wörlitz Country House | Anhalt-Dessau | *Schloss III* | 71 |

### Schleswig-Holstein

| | | | |
|---|---|---|---|
| Blomenburg (Selent) | von Blome | *Schloss II* | 66 |
| Eutin | Holstein-Gottorf | *Schloss II* | 42 |
| Glücksburg | Holstein-Glücksburg | *Schloss II* | 54 |
| Gottorf | Holstein-Gottorf | *Schloss II* | 53 |
| Hemmelmark | Hohenzollern | *Schloss II* | 54 |
| Husum | Holstein-Gottorf | *Schloss II* | 62 |
| Kiel | Hohenzollern | *Schloss II* | 47 |
| Salzau (Fargau-Pratjau) | von Blome | *Schloss II* | 66 |

### Thuringia

| | | | |
|---|---|---|---|
| Altenstein (Bad Liebenstein) | Saxe-Meiningen | *Schloss III* | 100 |
| Belvedere (Weimar) | Saxe-Weimar-Eisenach | *Schloss II* | 133 |
| Elisabethenburg (Meiningen) | Saxe-Meiningen | *Schloss III* | 94 |
| Friedenstein (Gotha) | Saxe-Gotha-Altenburg | *Schloss II* | 113 |
| Heidecksburg (Rudolstadt) | Schwarzburg-Rudolstadt | *Schloss II* | 138 |
| Palais Weimar (Bad Liebenstein) | Saxe-Meiningen | *Schloss III* | 106 |
| Reinhardsbrunn (Friedrichroda) | Saxe-Coburg-Gotha | *Schloss II* | 120 |
| Saalfeld | Saxe-Coburg-Saalfeld | *Schloss II* | 106 |
| Schwarzburg | Schwarzburg-Rudolstadt | *Schloss II* | 145 |
| Wartburg (Eisenach) | Ludovingian | *Schloss III* | 86 |
| Residenzschloss Weimar | Saxe-Weimar-Eisenach | *Schloss II* | 128 |
| Wilhelmsburg (Schmalkalden) | Hesse-Kassel | *Schloss III* | 106 |

# ILLUSTRATIONS

The illustrations listed below, listed by illustration number (or page number), are reproduced by courtesy of the individuals or organisations shown. All other illustrations are from the author's collection.

10. 11. Heimatverein Neckarbischofsheim, photography Bernhard Lorenz.

13. 14. 15. 16. Archiv Schloss Langenburg.

20. 21. 22. Fürst zu Hohenlohe-Oehringen'sche Verwaltung.

23. also page 55. Stadt Oehringen.

24. Deutschordensmuseum, photography Jens Hackmann, kopfeist-arts.de.

25. 26. Deutschordensmuseum, photography Photo Besserer, Lauda-Königshofen.

30. 31. 32. Archiv des Hauses Wuerttemberg Schloss Altshausen, Germany.

41. 42. 43. Schloss Lichtenstein.

45. 46. Kloster Lorch.

47. 48. 49. 50. © Roland Beck/Burg Hohenzollern.

54. 57. Stadtverwaltung Bad Wurzach.

55. Stadt Bad Wurzach.

56. Personal collection of Gloria Bullen.

60. 61. Landesmedienzentrum Baden-Württemberg.

Page 133. JoachimKohlerBremen, Wikipedia.

# NOTES

*Chapter 2*

1. The Palatinate stretched across both banks of the river Rhine and comprised parts of the present-day states of Rhineland-Palatinate and Hesse, as well as Baden-Württemberg.
2. German king was a title given at the time to the elected Holy Roman emperor before he was crowned.
3. Schloss Heidelberg English audio-guide.
4. Ibid.
5. Rosalind K. Marshall, *The Winter Queen: The Life of Elizabeth of Bohemia 1596-1662* (Edinburgh: Scottish National Portrait Gallery, 1998), 36.
6. Ibid, 47.
7. It remains in the Vatican today.
8. Wolfgang Wiese and Karin Stober (edited), *Heidelberg Castle* (Berlin München: Deutscher Kunstverlag GmbH, 2014) 27.
9. Before the Thirty Years' War, the Palatinate consisted of two distinct areas – the Lower Palatinate along the Rhine, and the Upper Palatinate (today part of Bavaria). After Friedrich's defeat the Upper Palatinate plus his role as an elector were given to the Catholic Duke Maximilian of Bavaria. When Karl I Ludwig was restored to his inheritance after the war, he was given back only the Lower Palatinate (the Upper Palatinate remained with Bavaria). An extra elector role was created for Karl I Ludwig but this was less prestigious than that retained by Bavaria.
10. Also called the Nine Years' War or the War of the Augsburg Alliance.
11. Maria Kroll (edited), *Letters from Liselotte: Elisabeth Charlotte, Princess Palatine and Duchess of Orléans, 'Madame' 1652-1722* (London: Victor Gollanz Ltd, 1970), 46. Letter from Versailles to Electress Sophia of Hannover, 3 January 1687.
12. Ibid, 51. Letter from Versailles to Electress Sophia of Hannover, 20 March 1689.
13. Audio-guide at Barockschloss Mannheim. Mannheim is located at the confluence of the rivers Rhine and Neckar.
14. He was the third (and last) elector from the Neuburg branch and followed his father Elector Philipp Wilhelm (1615-1690) and older brother Elector Johann Wilhelm (1658-1716).
15. The War of the Palatinate Succession (1688-1697) after Elector Karl II died – see Heidelberg.
16. Eleonore Kopsch, *Pfälzische Wittelsbacher* (Mannheim, Verlag Wellhofer, 2013, 2015), 110.

17. Ibid 111.
18. Ibid, 115.
19. When the Palatinate was dissolved in 1803 its territory on the right bank of the Rhine became part of Baden.
20. Carola Oman, *Napoleon's Viceroy: Eugène de Beauharnais* (London: Hodder and Stoughton, 1966), 490.
21. Theo Aronson, *The Golden Bees: The Story of the Bonapartes* (Greenwich, Connecticut: 1964), 75.
22. Kathrin Ellwardt, *Das Haus Baden in Vergangenheit und Gegenwart* (Werl: Börde-Verlag, 2015), 33.
23. Guided tour at Schwetzingen.
24. Ibid. George II, born 1683, was brought up in Hannover and only moved to England after his father became George I in 1714.
25. Hartmut Troll and Uta Schmitt, *Schwetzingen Palace Gardens* (Michael Imhof Verlag), 12.
26. Ibid, 72.
27. Ibid, 54.
28. Elisabeth Auguste was born on 17 January 1721 and Karl Theodor on 11 December 1724.
29. Guided tour at Schwetzingen. Elisabeth Auguste's younger sister, Maria Anna, married Clemens Franz of Bavaria in the double wedding of 1742.
30. Peter Fuchs, *Karl Theodor* in Neue Deutsche Biographie 11 (1977), S. 252-258, Online-version.
31. Guided tour at Schwetzingen.
32. Ibid.
33. Ulrich declined the position because he felt himself to be unworthy of the role. A contemporary chronicler, Jakop Wimpheling, praised his goodness, scholarship and charity. Email correspondence with the Heimatverein Neckarbischofsheim.
34. The seven electors were the ecclesiastical archbishop-electors of Cologne, Mainz and Trier and the secular prince-electors of Bohemia, Brandenburg, the Palatinate, and Saxony. Four of the seven were located in an area around the Rhine (Cologne, Mainz, Trier and the Palatinate) making them a particularly powerful block.
35. Guided tour at Altes Schloss Neckarbischofsheim.

## Chapter 3

1. Alexandra was the third daughter of Victoria's second son, Alfred, who became duke of Saxe-Coburg and Gotha in 1893. Alexandra (called Sandra in the family) is rather overshadowed in royal history by her two elder

sisters – Queen Marie of Romania (Missy) and Grand Duchess Victoria Melita of Russia (Ducky).

2. Letter from Princess Feodora of Hohenlohe-Langenburg to her sister Princess Victoria of Kent, Langenburg, 23 March, 1828. Harold A. Albert, *Queen Victoria's Sister: The Life and Letters of Princess Feodora* (London: Robert Hale: 1967), 60.

3. Ibid 63.

4. For a discussion about Feodora's arranged marriage see Cecil Woodham-Smith, *Queen Victoria, Her Life and Times: Volume I, 1819-1861* (London: Hamish Hamilton, 1972), 59-62.

5. Queen Adelaide's mother was a princess of Hohenlohe-Langenburg; she was the sister of Ernst I's father.

6. On his marriage, Viktor renounced his rights and took the title of Count Gleichen (a subsidiary family possession). He was a favourite nephew of Queen Victoria and he and his wife were treated by her as junior members of the British royal family. She later encouraged them to resume the title of prince and princess of Hohenlohe-Langenburg, although this was not recognised in Germany. Viktor and his wife had three children. For their family story see three fascinating articles by Marlene Eilers-Koenig in *Eurohistory: The European Royal History Journal*, August 2012 (Part 1), October 2012 (Part 2), and December 2012 (Part 3).

7. Eliza died single but Feo married Duke Georg II of Saxe-Meiningen in 1858 (see Schloss Elisabethenburg in *Schloss III*).

8. Albert, *Queen Victoria's Sister*, 199.

9. Queen Victoria's journal. RA VIC/MAIN/QVJ(W) Wednesday 29 March 1876 (Princess Beatrice's copies), retrieved 30 December 2018.

10. Queen Victoria's journal. RA VIC/MAIN/QVJ(W) Thursday 30 March 1876 (Princess Beatrice's copies), retrieved 30 December 2018.

11. Albert, *Queen Victoria's Sister*, 240.

12. Klaus Merten, *Weikersheim Castle* (Munich Berlin: Deutscher Kunstverlag), 1996, 2.

13. Udo Speth and Rebecca Simpfendörfer, *Bilder einer Ausstellung: 4000 Jahre Schloss Öhringen, 300 Jahre Hofgarten* (Öhringen: Druckerei Speh Öhringen, 2012),13.

14. Marcus Binney, *Great Houses of Europe: From the Archives of Country Life* (London: Aurum Press, 2003), 70.

15. Georg Friedrich commanded an imperial regiment in the Hungarian campaign of 1595-1560 against the Ottoman Empire. Carla Fandrey, *Schloss Weikersheim* (Berlin München: Deutscher Kunstverlag, 2010), 11.

16. Weikersheim was given to the Deutscher Orden (Teutonic Knights) in 1637 and restored to Hohenlohe in the Treaty of Westphalia of 1648.
17. Fandrey, *Schloss Weikersheim*, 14.
18. Elisabeth Friederike Sophie was Karl Ludwig's second wife. In 1711 he married as his first wife Margravine Dorothea Charlotte of Brandenburg-Bayreuth but she died eight months later. Fandrey, *Schloss Weikersheim*, 17.
19. Prince Constantin of Hohenlohe, *The Hohenlohe Museum at Neuenstein Castle* (München Berlin: Deutscher Kunstverlag, 1992), 4.
20. Ibid 12.
21. Guided tour at Neuenstein.
22. Ibid.
23. William Urban, *The Teutonic Knights: A Military History* (Barnsley: Frontline Books, 2011), 251.
24. Ibid 252.
25. Schloss Marienburg was lost to the Order in 1457 and the residence of the grand master moved to the castle at Königsberg, now Kaliningrad in Russia.
26. William Urban, *Tannenberg and After: Lithuania, Poland, and The Teutonic Order in Search of Immortality* (Chicago: Lithuanian Research and Studies Center, 2003), 433.
27. Deutschordensmuseum in Schloss Mergentheim.
28. Holger Kempkens, 'Clemens August of Bavaria, Master of the House' in *Augustusburg Palace, Brühl* (Berlin and Munich: Deutscher Kunstverlag, 2010), 7-8. Clemens August became prince-bishop of both Paderborn and Münster in 1719, archbishop-elector of Cologne in 1723, prince-bishop of Hildesheim in 1724, and prince-bishop of Osnabrück in 1728.
29. Email correspondence with Deutschordensmuseum in Schloss Mergentheim.
30. Franz Thiele; expert on the history of the German Order and guide to the Deutschordensmuseum at Schloss Mergentheim.

*Chapter 4*
1. Michael Wenger, *Ludwigsburg: The Entire Complex* (Berlin München: Deutscher Kunstverlag, 2004), 4. Hannover became an electorate in 1692.
2. Adrien Fauchier-Magnan, *The Small German Courts in the Eighteenth Century* (London: Methuen & Co, 1958), 129. This is an allusion to the mistress of Louis XIV.
3. Peter H. Wilson, 'Women and Imperial Politics: the Württemberg Consorts 1674-1757.' *Queenship in Europe 1660-1815: The Role of the Consort*. Edited by

Clarissa Campbell Orr (Cambridge: Cambridge University Press, 2004), 229.

4. Called the Grävenitz Palais, this is still there, in Marstallstrasse.

5. www.schloss-ludwigsburg.de

6. Fauchier-Magnan, *The Small German Courts in the Eighteenth Century*, 131.

7. Johanna Elisabeth's father and main champion, the margrave of Baden-Durlach, died in 1709.

8. Wilson, Women and Imperial Politics, 237.

9. Ibid, 239.

10. Guided tour at Ludwigsburg.

11. Janice Hadlow, *The Strangest Family: The Private Lives of George III, Queen Charlotte and The Hanoverians* (London: William Collins, 2014), 464-5.

12. Ibid, 465.

13. Guided tour at Ludwigsburg. As an adult, Wilhelm also resented the treatment of his mother.

14. Hadlow, The Strangest Family, 468-9, 590-1. Flora Fraser, *Princesses: The Six Daughters of George III* (London: John Murray, 2004), 297

15. Lucille Iremonger, *Love and The Princess* (London: Faber and Faber, 1958), 123.

16. Hadlow, *The Strangest Family*, 469.

17. Guided tour at Ludwigsburg. Also Gabriele Katz, *Herzogin von Württemberg: Franziska von Hohenheim* (Stuttgart: Belser, 2010), 47. And Fauchier-Magnan, *The Small German Courts in the Eighteenth Century*, 202.

18. Fauchier-Magnan, *The Small German Courts in the Eighteenth Century*, 152.

19. Paul Friedrich von Stälin, 'Karl Alexander, ruling Duke of Würtemberg'. *Allgemeine Deutsche Biographie*, Historische Kommission bei der Bayerischen Akademie der Wissenschaften, Volume 15 (1882), 366-372, digital full-text edition in Wikisource, retrieved 28 January 2019.

20. Guided tour at Ludwigsburg.

21. Ibid. Karl Alexander introduced the (catholic) festival of carnival and it was claimed that the dust this created had filled his lungs.

22. Richard Schmidt, *Schloss Monrepos Near Ludwigsburg* (Berlin München: Deutscher Kunstverlag, 1964), 10.

23. Dr. Eberhard Fritz, 'Vom 'Seehaus' zu 'Monrepos': Studien zur Funktion des Seeschlosses unter König Friedrich von Württemberg.' *Ludwigsburger Geschichtsblätter.* 49 (1995), 67-92.

24. Schmidt, *Schloss Monrepos*, 10. The neo-gothic church came from Schloss Hohenheim.

25. Fritz, 'Vom 'Seehaus' zu 'Monrepos''. The court journals kept by the major-domo's office have survived for some years of Friedrich's reign and are held

in the archives of the house of Württemberg. A 'gouter' was an afternoon party with a light meal.

26. Ibid. Translated by Graham Billing.

27. Schmidt, *Schloss Monrepos*, 14.

28. Fritz, 'Vom 'Seehaus' zu 'Monrepos'.

29. Wenger, *Ludwigsburg: The Entire Complex*, 59. Schloss Einsedel built by Karl Eugen near Tübingen was torn down and transported to Monrepos as the Festin building.

30. Fritz, 'Vom 'Seehaus' zu 'Monrepos'.

31. See Ludwigsburg. The electress was the eldest daughter of King George III of Great Britain and did not marry until she was thirty.

32. Wenger, *Ludwigsburg: The Entire Complex*, 59. The theatre came from Schloss Grafeneck, also built by Karl Eugen.

33. Schmidt, *Schloss Monrepos*, 14.

34. Hubert Krins, *Kings and Queens of Württemberg* (Lindenberg: Kunstverlag Josef Fink, 2011), 3.

35. Sophie Dorothee was the eldest daughter of Duke Friedrich Eugen who reigned 1795-1797. At the time of her marriage the duke was her uncle Karl Eugen who died in 1793. Another uncle, Ludwig Eugen, reigned 1793-1795 (see chart 9).

36. This was Ludwig of Hesse-Darmstadt who was the brother of Paul's deceased first wife.

37. Fraser, *Princesses*, 298.

38. Fauchier-Magnan, *The Small German Courts in the Eighteenth Century*, 181.

39. Gabriele Katz, *Herzogin von Württemberg: Franziska von Hohenheim* (Stuttgart: Belser, 2010), 43.

40. Ibid, 48.

41. Fauchier-Magnan, *The Small German Courts in the Eighteenth Century*, 184.

42. *Solitude Palace: Short Guide* (Staatliche Schlösser und Gärten, Baden-Württemberg).

43. Katz, *Herzogin von Württemberg: Franziska von Hohenheim*, 46-48.

44. Ibid, 50.

45. Ulrich Fellmeth, *Tour of the Palace: An Insight into Schloss Hohenheim* (Stuttgart: Universität Hohenheim, 2013), 3.

46. Ibid, 3.

47. Krins, *Kings and Queens of Württemberg*, 16.

48. Ibid, 37.

49. The quote is from an 1818 poem about the story by Justinus Kerner. The title of this poem is 'Praising with many a wonderful speech'. Frank Lorenz Müller, *Royal Heirs in Imperial Germany: The Future of Monarchy in*

*Nineteenth-Century Bavaria, Saxony and Württemberg* (London: Palgrave Macmillan, 2017), 124. Also guided tour at Schloss Bebenhusen.

50. Müller, *Royal Heirs in Imperial Germany*, 49, 97.

51. David McIntosh, 'The Fall of Thrones.' *Royalty Digest: A Journal of Record* (November 1998), 147. Hugo Vickers (edited by), *The Quest for Queen Mary: James Pope-Hennessy* (London: Zuleika and Hodder & Stoughton, 2018), 105. From Pope-Hennessy's notes of a conversation with Carol von Radowitz who facilitated his meeting with Princess Pauline of Wied (born Württemberg) on 20 July 1956.

52. Müller, *Royal Heirs in Imperial Germany*, 50.

53. Vickers, *The Quest for Queen Mary*, 106. When he met her in 1956, Pope-Hennessy in his notes described Princess Pauline as '... one of the strangest figures I have ever contemplated. She is enormously fat, with a huge red face like an old baby...'.

54. Müller, *Royal Heirs in Imperial Germany*, 52.

55. Guided tour at Bebenhausen.

56. Katharina Hild and Nikola Hild, *Lichtenstein* (Reutlingen: Oertel und Spörer, 2000), 139.

57. Ibid, 159.

58. Guided tour at Lichtenstein.

59. Hild and Hild, *Lichtenstein*, 136.

60. Ibid, 163.

61. Karl-Heinz Reuss and Anton Hegele, *The Staufen Dynasty: Companion Guide to the Exhibition in the Documentation Centre for Staufen History in Göppingen-Hohenstaufen* (Göppingen: Stadt Göppingen, 2016), 39. His godfather was Graf Otto von Cappenberg and the original bust is in the parish church of Cappenberg Westphalia.

62. Exhibition in the Documentation Centre for Staufen History.

63. Storyboard in the monastery church at Kloster Lorch.

Chapter 5

1. Johann Georg Prinz von Hohenzollern and others, *Hohenzollern, 950 Jahre: One Dynasty – Two Aristocratic Families* (Sigmaringen, Hechingen: Unternehmensgruppe Fürst von Hohenzollern), 5.

2. *Burg Hohenzollern Ancestral Seat of the Prussian Royal House: A Mountain of Surprises*. English Brochure.

3. Ibid.

4. Ulrich Feldhahn, *Burg Hohenzollern: Ancestral Seat of the Prussian Royal House and the Princes of Hohenzollern* (studiodruck Nürtingen-Raidwangen, 2014),10.

5. Guided tour at Burg Hohenzollern.
6. Roger Fulford (edited by), *Dearest Mama: Private Correspondence of Queen Victoria and the Crown Princess of Prussia, 1861-1864* (London: Evans Brothers Ltd, 1981), 109-110. Letter from the crown princess to Queen Victoria dated 10 October 1862.
7. Feldhahn, *Burg Hohenzollern*, 26.
8. Ibid, 24-25.
9. The Swabian line was the senior line of the house of Hohenzollern. The younger son, Conrad, followed his father as burgrave of Nuremberg in Franconia. He founded the junior line that went on to become electors of Brandenburg, kings of Prussia, and emperors of Germany.
10. Hubert Krins, *Das Fürstenhaus Hohenzollern* (Lindenberg: Kunstverlag Josef Fink, 2013), 11.
11. Guided tour at Sigmaringen.
12. Krins, *Das Fürstenhaus Hohenzollern*, 16.
13. Guided tour at Sigmaringen.
14. Madam Campan was a former lady-in-waiting to Queen Marie Antoinette of France. Several of the young ladies in Napoleon's family were sent to her school including his sister Caroline and also Hortense and Stephanie de Beauharnais.
15. Krins, *Das Fürstenhaus Hohenzollern*, 16.
16. Prinz von Hohenzollern and others, *Hohenzollern, 950 Jahre*, 41.
17. Krins, *Das Fürstenhaus Hohenzollern*, 23.
18. Prinz von Hohenzollern and others, *Hohenzollern, 950 Jahre*, 57. Also note that in 1844, Karl Anton's sister Friederike married Joachim Napoleon, Marchese Pepoli (the grandson of Joachim Murat and Caroline Bonaparte).
19. Guided tour at Sigmaringen.

*Chapter 6*

1. www.almanachdegotha.org Mediatised House of Waldburg.
2. Discussions with Gisela Rothenhäusler, Bad Wurzach author and historian.
3. Ibid.
4. Gisela Rothenhäusler, *Reaching across the Barbed Wire: French PoWs, Internees from the Channel Islands and Jewish Prisoners from Bergen-Belsen in Schloss Wurzach, 1940-1945* (Lindenberg: Kunstverlag Josef Fink, Jersey: Channel Islands Publishing), 2012.
5. The prefix Bad was added to the name in 1952 to indicate that the town has medicinal spa facilities. It specialises in hot mud baths to treat joint and bone conditions.
6. Information on the Truchsessen Gallery from discussions with Gisela

Rothenhäusler, Bad Wurzach author and historian, and from Gerda Franziska Kirchner, *Die Truchsessen-Galerie* (Ein Beitrag zur Geschichte des Deutschen Kunstsammelns um 1800: Frankfurt Bern Las Vegas, 1979).

7. The original Montfort castle at Tettnang was destroyed in the Thirty Years War. Count Johann X chose an adjacent site for the Altes Schloss and his son, Anton III, built the Neues Schloss on the old castle site.

8. A series of informative maps in the information room at the Neues Schloss plot the extent of the Montfort territories over time. At their height in the fourteenth century they stretched one hundred and forty kilometres or eighty-five miles north from Tettnang to Tübingen; and two hundred kilometres or one hundred and twenty miles south to the San Bernardine Pass.

9. The architect was Christoph Gessinger c1670-1735.

10. Michael Wenger, Angelika Barth and Karin Stober. *Tettnang Neues Schloss und Stadt* (Berlin München: Deutscher Kunstverlag GmbH, 2004), 9. She married Anselm Franz von Schönborn, 1681-1726.

11. Joachim Zeune, *Castles and Palaces: Germany* (Regensburg: Schmidt Verlag, 2004),100.

12. Wenger, Barth and Stober, *Tettnang Neues Schloss und Stadt*, 11.

13. Konrad Vögele, *Grafen und Gräfinnen von Montfort im 17. und 18. Jahrhundert* (Tettnang: Lorenz Senn Verlag, 2010), 123.

14. Wenger, Barth and Stober, *Tettnang Neues Schloss und Stadt*, 36.

15. Ibid, 41.

16. Vögele. *Grafen und Gräfinnen von Montfort*, 125-126.

17. Ibid, 130.

18. Queen Olga was the daughter of Tsar Nikolai I and Tsarina Alexandra Feodorovna of Russia. Luise's father, Prince Karl of Prussia, was a brother of the tsarina who was born Princess Charlotte of Prussia.

19. This was Prince-bishop Hugo von Hohenlandenberg who reigned at Meersburg from 1526-1529.

20. Christina Huber-Yüzgec, *Neues Schloss Meersburg* (Munich Berlin: Deutscher Kunstverlag, 2012), 11.

21. Ibid, 10.

22. Ibid, 13.

23. Ibid, 61.

24. She was Friederike, the daughter of Hereditary Count Karl Ludwig and the sister of Tsarina Elizaveta Alexeievna of Russia, wife of Alexander I – see chart 19.

25. Graf E. W. zu Lynar, *Schloss Heiligenberg* (München Zürich: Schnell & Steiner, 1981), 10.

26. Guided tour at Heiligenberg.
27. zu Lynar, *Schloss Heiligenberg,* 10.
28. Ibid, 6.
29. Guided tour at Heiligenberg.
30. John C. G. Röhl, *Kaiser Wilhelm II 1859-1941: A Concise Life* (Cambridge: Cambridge University Press, 2014), 114 and note 10 on page 211.
31. zu Lynar, *Schloss Heiligenberg,* 9.
32. Wikipedia, *Salem Abbey,* retrieved 5/3/2019.
33. Guided tour at Salem.
34. *History of Schule Schloss Salem,* www.schule-schloss-salem.de/en
35. Guided tour at Salem.
36. Ibid.
37. Obituary: Prince Max of Baden. Reprinted with permission from *The Times,* November 7, 1929. *Royalty Digest: A Journal of Record.* March 2000, 269.

*Chapter 7*
1. The others were the kingdom of Württemberg (see chapter 4 of this book) and the kingdom of Bavaria (see *Schloss in Bavaria*).
2. Rüdiger Homberg, *Karlsruhe: An Illustrated Travel Guide* (Lübeck: Schoening Verlag), 5.
3. Heinrich Dietrich, *The administration and economy of Baden-Durlach, Charles William in 1709-1738* (Inaugural Dissertation. Heidelberg 1911), 60. From Wikipedia: Charles III William, Margrave of Baden-Durlach.
4. www.almanacdegotha.org Grand Duchy of Baden.
5. Discussion with curator at Schloss Karlsruhe.
6. Homberg, *Karlsruhe,* 11.
7. Anna Pavord, *The Tulip* (London: Bloomsbury, 1999), 80.
8. Wikipedia: Charles III William, Margrave of Baden-Durlach.
9. Casimir Bumiller, Stefan Feucht and Marlene Pelhammer, *Sommerfrische in Salem: Das Hause Baden am Bodensee* (Staatliche Schlösser und Gärten Baden-Württemberg, 2012), 20.
10. John Van Der Kiste, *Daughter of Prussia: Luise, Grand Duchess of Baden and Her Family* (South Brent: A & F Publications, 2017), 88.
11. Bumiller and others, *Sommerfrische in Salem,* 30.
12. Charlotte Zeepvat, 'Baden – A Family Album.' *Royalty Digest Quarterly.* 2 2007, 1.
13. Ibid, 2.
14. Eugen's father, Count Eugen Moritz of Soissons, was the brother of Ludwig Wilhelm's mother.
15. His father was Hereditary Prince Ferdinand Maximilian of Baden-Baden

(1625-1669). His mother was Princess Louise of Savoy-Carignan (1627-1689).

16. Kathrin Ellwardt, *Das Haus Baden in Vergangenheit und Gegenwart* (Werl: Börde-Verlag, 2015), 22.

17. Duke Julius Franz of Saxe-Lauenburg (1641-1689). Anja Stangl, Verena Helfert and Frank Thomas Lang (edited), *Sibylla Augusta; Ein Barockes Schicksal. Die Badische Markgräfin Zwischen Familie, Politik und Kunst 1675-1733* (Stuttgart: Staatsanzeiger, 2008), 5.

18. Ibid, 6.

19. Alan Riding. 'At a Castle in Germany, A King-Size Yard Sale.' *The New York Times*, October 7 1995.

20. Ellwardt, *Das Haus Baden*, 22.

21. Anja Stangl, Verena Helfert and Frank Thomas Lang (edited). *Sibylla Augusta; Ein Barockes Schicksal. Die Badische Markgräfin Zwischen Familie, Politik und Kunst 1675-1733* (Stuttgart: Staatsanzeiger, 2008), 9.

22. Ellwardt, *Das Haus Baden*, 23.

23. Marcus Binney, *Great Houses of Europe: From the Archives of Country Life* (London: Aurum Press, 2003), 65.

24. Mark Twain, *A Tramp Abroad*. First published in 1880, 55.

25. Ellwardt, *Das Haus Baden*, 23.

26. Twain, *A Tramp Abroad*, 55-56.

27. Stangl and others (edited), *Sibylla Augusta*, 13.

28. Ibid, 9.

29. Ibid, 12.

30. Ibid, 12.

31. Discussion with custodian at Rastatt Favorite.

32. Ibid, 9.

33. Stangl and others (edited), *Sibylla Augusta*, 12.

34. Sandra Eberle and Petra Pechaček, *Schloss Bruchsal* (Petersberg: Michael Imhof Verlag, 2017), 35.

35. Sandra Eberle (edited), *Kirchenmacht und Schlösserpracht; Die Fürstbischöfe von Speyer und ihre Bruchsaler Residenz* (Staatliche Schlösser und Gärten Baden-Württemberg, 2010), 19.

36. Ibid, 18.

37. Klaus Merten, *German Castles and Palaces* (London: Thames and Hudson, 1999), 155.

38. Audio-guide at Bruchsal.

39. Ibid.

40. Ibid.

41. Ibid.

# BIBLIOGRAPHY

Albert, Harold A. *Queen Victoria's Sister: The Life and Letters of Princess Feodora.* London: Robert Hale: 1967.

Arnold, Udo. *Deutscher Orden 1180-2000: Ein Führer durch das Deutschordensmuseum in Bad Mergentheim.* Baunach: Spurbuchverlag, 2011.

Aronson, Theo. *The Golden Bees: The Story of the Bonapartes.* Greenwich, Connecticut: New York Graphic Society, 1964.

Binney, Marcus. *Great Houses of Europe: From the Archives of Country Life.* London: Aurum Press, 2003.

Borchardt-Wenzel, Annette. *Die Frauen am Badischen Hof: Gefährtinnen der Grossherzöge zwischen Liebe, Pflicht und Intrigen.* Gernsbach: Casimir Katz Verlag, 2010.

Bumiller, Casimir, Stefan Feucht and Marlene Pelhammer. *Sommerfrische in Salem: Das Hause Baden am Bodensee.* Staatliche Schlösser und Gärten Baden-Württemberg, 2012.

Burmeister, Karl Heinz and others. *Langenargener Geschichte(n): Das Schloss Montfort.* Langenargen: Herausgeber Gemeinde Langenargen, 1993.

Cornelius, Vera and Anja Patricia Helm. *Fascinating Heidelberg: A Journey Through Time.* Heidelberg: abcdruck GmbH, 2013.

Davies, Norman. *Vanished Kingdoms: The History of Half-Forgotten Europe.* London: Allen Lane, 2011.

Eberle, Sandra. *Schloss Rastatt.* Berlin München: Deutscher Kunstverlag, 2010.

Eberle, Sandra and Petra Pechačhek. *Schloss Bruchsal.* Petersberg: Michael Imhof Verlag, 2017.

Eberle, Sandra (edited). *Kirchenmacht und Schlösserpracht; Die Fürstbischöfe von Speyer und ihre Bruchsaler Residenz.* Staatliche Schlösser und Gärten Baden-Württemberg, 2010.

Eilers-Koenig, Marlene. 'The Counts of Gleichen – the Unknown Royal Cousins'. *Eurohistory: The European Royal History Journal.* East Richmond Heights: Kensington House Books, Volumes 15.4, August 2012 (Part 1), 30; 15.5, October 2012 (Part 2), 29; 15.6, December 2012 (Part 3), 10.

Ellwardt, Kathrin. *Das Haus Baden in Vergangenheit und Gegenwart.* Werl: Börde-Verlag, 2015.

Fandrey, Carla. *Schloss Weikersheim.* Berlin München: Deutscher Kunstverlag, 2010.

Fauchier-Magnan, Adrien. *The Small German Courts in the Eighteenth Century.* London: Methuen & Co, 1958.

Feldhahn, Ulrich. *Burg Hohenzollern: Ancestral Seat of the Prussian Royal House and the Princes of Hohenzollern.* studiodruck Nürtingen-Raidwangen, 2014.

Fellmeth, Ulrich. *Tour of the Palace: An Insight into Schloss Hohenheim.* Stuttgart: Universität Hohenheim, 2013. www.uni-hohenheim.de

Fraser, Flora. *Princesses: The Six Daughters of George III.* London: John Murray, 2004.

Fritz, Eberhard. 'Vom 'Seehaus' zu 'Monrepos': Studien zur Funktion des Seeschlosses unter König Friedrich von Württemberg.' *Ludwigsburger Geschichtsblätter.* 49 (1995), 67-92.

Fürst zu Hohenlohe-Waldenburg, Friedrich Karl. *Hohenlohe: Bilder aus der Geschichte von Haus und Land.* Öhringen: Familienverband des Fürstlichen Hauses Hohenlohe, 1983.

Gensichen, Sigrid, Ulrike Grimm, Manuel Bechtold and Sandra Eberle. *Schloss Favorite Rastatt mit Garten und Eremitage.* München, Berlin: Deutscher Kunstverlag, 2007.

Graf zu Lynar, E. W. *Schloss Heiligenberg.* München Zürich: Schnell & Steiner, 1981.

Gräter, Carlheinz. *Hohenlohe.* Tübingen, Silberburg Verlag, 2008.

Hadlow, Janice. *The Strangest Family: The Private Lives of George III, Queen Charlotte and The Hanoverians.* London: William Collins, 2014.

Hanemann, Regina. *Schloss Mergentheim mit dem Deutschordensmuseum.* Berlin München: Deutscher Kunstverlag, 2006.

Hild, Katharina and Nikola Hild. *Lichtenstein.* Reutlingen: Oertel und Spörer, 2000.

Hild, Nikola and Katharina Hild. *Bebenhausen Kloster und Schloss.* Tübingen: Silberburg-Verlag, 2006.

Hild, Nikola and Katharina Hild. *Schloss Sigmaringen: Der Hohenzollernsitz in Donautal und die Residenzstadt.* Tübingen: Silberburg-Verlag, 2008/2015.

Homberg, Rüdiger. *Karlsruhe: An Illustrated Travel Guide.* Lübeck: Schoening Verlag.

Huber-Yüzgec, Christina. *Neues Schloss Meersburg.* Munich Berlin: Deutscher Kunstverlag, 2012.

Iremonger, Lucille. *Love and The Princess.* London: Faber and Faber, 1958.

Kampelmann, Felix. *Das Haus Hohenzollern-Sigmaringen: Über 550 Jahre Gesamtgeschichte mit Stammfolge.* Werl: Börde-Verlag, 2014.

Kampelmann, Felix. *Das Haus Württemberg.* Werl: Börde-Verlag, 2016.

Katz, Gabriele. *Herzogin von Württemberg: Franziska von Hohenheim.* Stuttgart: Belser, 2010.

Knapp, Ulrich. *Salem: Ehemalige Zisterzienserreichsabtei.* Regensburg: Schnell & Steiner, 2007.

Köhler, Mathias, Rainer Y and Carla Fandrey. *Kloser und Schloss Bebenhausen.* Munich Berlin: Deutscher Kunstverlag, 2014.

König, David and Axel Dittrich (edited). *Schloss Langenburg: Erlebnis Hohenlohe.* Langenburg: Schloss Langenburg.

Kopsch, Eleonore. *Pfälzische Wittelsbacher.* Mannheim, Verlag Wellhofer, 2013, 2015.

Krins, Hubert. *Das Fürstenhaus Hohenzollern.* Lindenberg: Kunstverlag Josef Fink, 2013.

Krins, Hubert. *Kings and Queens of Württemberg.* Lindenberg: Kunstverlag Josef Fink, 2011.

Kroll, Maria (edited). *Letters from Liselotte: Elisabeth Charlotte, Princess Palatine and Duchess of Orléans, 'Madame' 1652-1722.* London: Victor Gollanz Ltd, 1970.

Langenburg Castle Administration. *Langenburg Castle: English Text.* Tübingen: Gebr. Metz.

Lorenz, Sönke and Dieter Mertens (edited by). *Das Haus Württemberg: Ein Biographisches Lexicon.* Stuttgart, Berlin, Köln: W. Kolhammer GmbH, 1997.

Louda, Jîrí and Michael Maclagan. *Lines of Succession: Heraldry of the Royal Families of Europe.* London: Orbis Publishing, 1981.

MacCulloch, Diarmid. *Reformation: Europe's House Divided, 1490-1700.* London: Penguin Books, 2004.

Marshall, Rosalind K. *The Winter Queen: The Life of Elizabeth of Bohemia 1596-1662.* Edinburgh: Scottish National Portrait Gallery, 1998.

McIntosh, David. 'The Fall of Thrones.' *Royalty Digest: A Journal of Record.* November 1998, 147.

Merten, Klaus. *German Castles and Palaces.* London: Thames and Hudson, 1999.

Merten, Klaus. *Weikersheim Castle.* Munich Berlin: Deutscher Kunstverlag, 1996.

Mueller, Carla and Katrin Rössler. *Barockschloss Mannheim.* München Berlin: Deutscher Kunstverlag GmbH, 2011.

Muller, Francis M. S. *A Short History of the Teutonic Order.* 1970.

Müller, Frank Lorenz. *Royal Heirs in Imperial Germany: The Future of Monarchy in Nineteenth-Century Bavaria, Saxony and Württemberg.* London: Palgrave Macmillan, 2017.

Munz, Peter. *Frederick Barbarossa: A Study in Medieval Politics.* London: Eyre and Spottiswoode, 1969.

Nash, Michael L. 'A Countess from Transylvania.' *Royalty Digest: A Journal of Record.* June 1998, 374.

Oman, Carola. *Napoleon's Viceroy: Eugène de Beauharnais.* London: Hodder and Stoughton, 1966.

Prince of Hohenlohe, Constantin. *The Hohenlohe Museum at Neuenstein Castle.* München Berlin: Deutscher Kunstverlag, 1992.

Prinz von Bayern, Luitpold. *Die Wittelsbacher: Ein Jahrtausend in Bildern.* München: Volk Verlag München, 2014.

Prinz von Hohenzollern, Johann Georg and others. *Hohenzollern, 950 Jahre: One Dynasty – Two Aristocratic Families.* Sigmaringen, Hechingen: Unternehmensgruppe Fürst von Hohenzollern.

Pursell, Brennan C. *The Winter King: Frederick V of the Palatinate and the Coming of the Thirty Years' War.* Aldershot: Ashgate, 2003.

*Queen Victoria's Journals:* www.queenvictoriasjournals.org. Windsor: The Royal Archives, 2012.

Reuss, Karl-Heinz and Anton Hegele. *The Staufen Dynasty: Companion Guide to the Exhibition in the Documentation Centre for Staufen History in Göppingen-Hohenstaufen.* Göppingen: Stadt Göppingen, 2016.

Röhl, John C. G. *Kaiser Wilhelm II 1859-1941: A Concise Life.* Cambridge: Cambridge University Press, 2014.

Ross, Josephine. *The Winter Queen: The Story of Elizabeth Stuart.* London: Weidenfeld and Nicolson, 1979.

Rothenhäusler, Gisela. *Reaching across the Barbed Wire: French PoWs, Internees from the Channel Islands and Jewish Prisoners from Bergen-Belsen in Schloss Wurzach, 1940-1945.* Lindenberg: Kunstverlag Josef Fink, Jersey: Channel Islands Publishing. 2012.

Sainz de Medrano, Ricardo Mateos. 'Karlsruhe: The Silesian Home of the Eugens of Württemberg.' *Royalty Digest: A Journal of Record.* October 1995, 115

Schmidt, Richard. *Schloss Monrepos Near Ludwigsburg.* Berlin München: Deutscher Kunstverlag, 1964.

Speth, Udo and Rebecca Simpfendörfer. *Bilder einer Ausstellung: 400 Jahre Schloss Öhringen, 300 Jahre Hofgarten.* Öhringen: Druckerei Speh Öhringen, 2012.

Stangl, Anja, Verena Helfert and Frank Thomas Lang (edited). *Sibylla Augusta; Ein Barockes Schicksal. Die Badische Markgräfin Zwischen Familie, Politik und Kunst 1675-1733.* Stuttgart: Staatsanzeiger, 2008.

Stephan, Regina and Patricia Peschel. *Grabkapelle auf den Württemberg.* Petersberg: Michael Imhof Verlag, 2017.

Symons, Susan. *Schloss Wurzach: A Jersey Child Interned by Hitler – Gloria's Story.* St Just-in-Roseland: Roseland Books, 2018.

Troll, Hartmut and Uta Schmitt. *Schwetzingen Palace Gardens.* Michael Imhof Verlag.

Urban, William. *The Teutonic Knights: A Military History.* Barnsley: Frontline Books, 2011.

Vallone, Lynne. *Becoming Victoria.* New Haven and London: Yale University Press, 2001.

Van Der Kiste, John. *Daughter of Prussia: Luise, Grand Duchess of Baden and Her Family.* South Brent: A & F Publications, 2017.

Vickers, Hugo (edited by). *The Quest for Queen Mary: James Pope-Hennessy.* London: Zuleika and Hodder & Stoughton, 2018.

Vögele, Konrad. *Grafen und Gräfinnen von Montfort im 17. und 18. Jahrhundert.* Tettnang: Lorenz Senn Verlag, 2010.

Wenger, Michael. *Ludwigsburg: The Entire Complex.* Berlin München: Deutscher Kunstverlag, 2004.

Wenger, Michael, Angelika Barth and Karin Stober. *Tettnang Neues Schloss und Stadt.* Berlin München: Deutscher Kunstverlag GmbH, 2004.

Wiese, Wolfgang and Karin Stober. *Heidelberg Castle.* Berlin München: Deutscher Kunstverlag GmbH, 2014.

Wilson, Peter H. *The Holy Roman Empire: A Thousand Years of Europe's History.* Allen Lane, 2016.

Wilson, Peter H. 'Women and Imperial Politics: the Württemberg Consorts 1674-1757.' *Queenship in Europe 1660-1815: The Role of the Consort.* Edited by Clarissa Campbell Orr. Cambridge: Cambridge University Press, 2004.

Wimbles, John. 'A Forgotten Princess: Alexandra of Hohenlohe-Langenburg.' *Royalty Digest: A Journal of Record.* March 2005, 265 (Part I: A Wedding), April 2005, 303 (Part II: Bored in Berlin).

Woodham-Smith, Cecil. *Queen Victoria, Her Life and Times: Volume I, 1819-1861.* London: Hamish Hamilton, 1972.

Zeepvat, Charlotte. 'Baden – A Family Album.' *Royalty Digest Quarterly.* 2 2007, 1.

Zeepvat, Charlotte. 'Württemberg – A Family Album.' *Royalty Digest Quarterly.* 4 2006, 11.

Zeepvat, Charlotte. 'The Bride Looked Lovely, but Deadly Pale ... ' *Royalty Digest: A Journal of Record.* July 2002, 2.

Zeune, Joachim. *Castles and Palaces: Germany.* Regensburg: Schmidt Verlag, 2004.

# THE SCHLOSS SERIES OF BOOKS

*Schloss* is the German word for castle or palace, and you are never far from one of these in Germany. For most of its history Germany was not a single country but a patchwork of royal states, held together under the banner of the Holy Roman Empire. The dukes and princes who ruled these states were passionate builders. Their beautiful castles and palaces, and their compelling personal stories, provide the material for the *Schloss* books.

*This book can be seen as an inspiration ... to get out there and find the lesser known palaces and learn more about their history.*
*Royalty Digest Quarterly Journal.*

Each of the *Schloss* books visits 25 beautiful castles and palaces in Germany and tells the colourful stories of the royal families that built and lived in them. Royalty have always been the celebrities of their day, and these stories from history can rival anything in modern-day television soap operas. The books are illustrated throughout and should appeal to anyone who likes history or sightseeing or is interested in people's personal stories.

*The second volume is as good as the first, maybe even better – a must...*
*Amazon review.*

# THE SCHLOSS SERIES OF BOOKS

The stories in the *Schloss* books include the mistress of the king who tried to blackmail him and was imprisoned for forty-nine years; the princess from a tiny German state who used her body and her brains to become the ruler of the vast Russian empire; the prince who defied his family to marry a pharmacist's daughter and then bought her the rank of royal princess; and the duke whose personal story is so colourful he has been called the Bavarian Henry VIII!

*Susan Symons has done another fantastic job, proving the point that history can also be fun...*
*The European Royal History Journal.*

The German princes abdicated in 1918, at the end of World War I, and Germany became a republic. As they lost their royal families, many of the castles and palaces went into decline and became prisons, workhouses, and other institutions. Some were behind the Iron Curtain for fifty years. The books chart these difficult years and their resurgence and use today as public buildings, museums, and hotels.

*The latest addition visits Bavaria – and what a treat it is. Fascinating reading!*
*The European Royal History Journal*

ALSO PUBLISHED BY ROSELAND BOOKS
www.susansymons.com

SCHLOSS WURZACH
A JERSEY CHILD INTERNED BY HITLER
– GLORIA'S STORY

Schloss Wurzach was a grand baroque palace built in the eighteenth century by one of Germany's noble families. But by World War II it had fallen on hard times and was used as a prison camp. The schloss was cold, damp, in poor condition, and very dirty, when ten-year-old Gloria Weber arrived with her family and hundreds of other civilian internees deported from Jersey on the orders of Hitler. They were horrified by what they found. Twelve of the islanders died in Wurzach during their detention and are buried in the town; others suffered fractured lives.

This short book by Susan Symons recalls Gloria's childhood experience and is illustrated with vivid pictures of camp life painted by her father during their confinement. It also describes how she and other internees returned to Germany in later life to celebrate their liberation with the people of Wurzach, showing there can be reconciliation and friendship between former enemies.

2019 is the 200 year anniversary of the birth of Queen Victoria. These three books focus on the Queen as a woman – her personal life, events that formed her resolute character, and relationships that were important to her. They use some of her own words from her journal, to help tell the story; and are illustrated with portraits and memorabilia from the author's own collection.

Victoria has a life story full of drama, intrigue and surprises. *Young Victoria* covers the bizarre events of her birth, with a scramble to produce the heir to the throne; her lonely childhood under a tough regime; and how she came to the throne at 18.

*Victoria & Albert* is the story of her marriage to Albert and how she balanced the roles of monarch and Victorian wife and mother. *The Widowed Queen* covers the long years of her life alone after Albert's early death, when she became an icon of the age; the longest serving European sovereign; and matriarch of a huge clan.

Made in the USA
Lexington, KY
17 December 2019

58691194R10133